COACH
YOURSELF
TO
SUCCESS

COACH
YOURSELF
TO
SUCCESS

101 Tips from a Personal Coach for Reaching
Your Goals at Work and in Life

TALANE MIEDANER

CONTEMPORARY BOOKS

Library of Congress Cataloging-in-Publication Data

Miedaner, Talane.
    Coach yourself to success : 101 tips from a personal coach for
reaching your goals at work and in life / Talane Miedaner ; foreword by
Sandy Vilas.
        p.   cm.
    Includes index.
    ISBN 0-8092-2536-0 (cloth). — ISBN 0-8092-2537-9 (pbk.)
    1. Success—Psychological aspects.   2. Self-management
(Psychology)   3. Self-actualization (Psychology)   I. Title.
BF637.S8M53   2000
158.1—dc21   99-31866
                                          CIP

The instructions and advice in this book are not intended as a substitute for
psychological counseling. The author and publisher disclaim any responsibility or
liability resulting from actions advocated or discussed in this book.
    In the interest of preserving client confidentiality, all client names and, in some
cases, identifying characteristics have been changed. The scenarios, situations, and
results are real.

Interior design by Scott Rattray

Published by Contemporary Books
A division of NTC/Contemporary Publishing Group, Inc.
4255 West Touhy Avenue, Lincolnwood (Chicago), Illinois 60712-1975 U.S.A.
Copyright © 2000 by Talane Miedaner
Printed in the United States of America
International Standard Book Number: 0-8092-2536-0
00 01 02 03 04 MV 18 17 16 15 14 13 12 11 10 9 8 7 6 5 4 3 2 1

I dedicate this book with love and gratitude to Penelope—the best mom I could ever imagine having.

Contents

Foreword

In the past five years, over two thousand coaches have completed the Coach Training Program at Coach University. As the president of Coach University and an experienced coach of ten years, I have had the privilege to work with many of them. In the process, I have found that the most successful coaches have a few key qualities.

The most successful coaches are demonstrably caring. Coaching is a people-development profession, not just an information-based one. Given that coaches spend much of their time developing, supporting, and training their clients, caring about their clients and their success and their values is the oil that keeps the coaching process working smoothly. Without true caring, the coach's effectiveness drops significantly.

The most successful coaches have the "spark." There is something visibly noticeable about them. They are upbeat, naturally positive, enjoy working with people, have a lot to give, have a sparkle in their eye, and naturally turn others on to life.

The most successful coaches are naturally perceptive. The coaching process requires that the coach be sensitive—able to feel the client's energy and mood, able to distinguish subtleties, able to feel the information rather than having to acquire it, able to sense the truth about what's being said, and able to intuit well. Part of the process of becoming a successful coach is sensitizing oneself and developing one's natural perceptive ability.

The most successful coaches dance well in a conversation. Given that coaching is conversation-based, the most successful coaches find that the give-and-take, back-and-forth flow of ideas, concepts, feelings, information, realities, wants, values, and priorities between themselves and the client occurs effortlessly. Clients need a coach who can catch on quickly and encourage them to say things they've never said before. Coaches who aren't able to "get" the information flow and who must fully understand everything the client is saying tend to hold the client back.

The most successful coaches have been formally trained as coaches. Good coaching requires several years of intense training among colleagues on a similar track. True, everyone in the world is a coach in a sense, and consultants and therapists and teachers and ministers certainly do some coaching. But to excel at this profession and offer the client all that is possible, formal training makes a world of difference.

The most successful coaches have coaches of their own. Every successful coach is on an accelerated growth track and wouldn't even think about not having a masterful coach in his or her corner, especially given how much is at stake for clients. Having your own coach is a matter of integrity. I have three who add value to every aspect of my life and business.

The most successful coaches continuously learn from their clients. Coaching technology, while proven effective, is still in its infancy. As such, the most successful coaches make it a practice to learn as much from each of their clients as they teach. This keeps coaches fresh, humble, open to input, and willing to adapt themselves and what they know to meet the needs of their current clients, not the clients they worked with last year. When coaches are open to learning from their clients, they are more effective because they are synthesizing versus lecturing.

The most successful coaches consider coaching to be an art, not just a technique. True, there are 200-plus coaching skills, 1,000-plus distinctions, 500-plus situational models, and hundreds of facts, techniques, and processes to learn on the path to becoming a Coach University Certified Coach. However, the best coaching is always performed as a work of art, not just a paint-by-numbers piece. The professional who approaches coaching as an art that requires specific tools and techniques is far more likely to be successful than someone who just "does" coaching.

The most successful coaches are inspiring models for their clients—a coach must walk his or her talk. In fact, coaches will likely fail to attract a full practice until they apply what they learn to their own lives and model the information, distinctions, well-being, standards, boundaries, and skill set that they ask their clients to. Their lives become the "message."

The most successful coaches attract their clients. This means that they don't try to pitch or sell their services. Instead they live "in the flow" and continuously add value to everyone around them.

Talane is one of these "most successful" coaches. She is a natural. As a treasured member of our teaching staff, she has added value to our program and to her students. Her enthusiasm for life communicates itself to everyone she comes in contact with.

Anyone unfamiliar with the remarkable results of coaching may be surprised at the wonderful transformations that have occurred in the lives of Talane's clients. Coaches are not surprised. It is what they have come to expect. One small change can have a tremendous impact on your life. This book is your blueprint for the life you've always dreamed about having. Work every tip and you will be amazed at the results—and have fun in the process.

Sandy Vilas
President, Coach University

Acknowledgments

MY DEEPEST GRATITUDE and thanks to:

Bonnie Solow, my fearless and fabulous agent. Thank you for being there for me every step of the way. I appreciate your integrity, persistence, and unflagging support. Judith McCarthy, my delightful and intelligent editor, for your attention to detail, insightful comments, and commitment. Kimberly Soenen, for your enthusiastic support in publicity—you are a gem. Erica Lieberman, Blythe Smith, and all the wonderful people at Contemporary who worked to make this book the best possible.

David Roth-Ey for your friendship and all your excellent advice in the publishing process. Scott Moyers for your enthusiastic response to my first draft. Beth Lieberman for your careful and thoughtful editing. John Gies, Joan Holmer, and Roland Flint for being extraordinary teachers. Julia Cameron and Elaine St. James for helping me find my muse. Victoria Moran for your generous referral to Patti Breitman and Patti for your enthusiastic referral to Bonnie. Thomas J. Leonard for founding Coach University and making coaching a true profession. Thanks for all your generosity and creativity. Many of the brilliant ideas in this book come from you. Sandy Vilas for your generous support and inspiring leadership. My first coach, Thom Politico, for seeing my potential. Without you, none of this would ever have happened. I am forever grateful.

All my wonderful coaching colleagues at Coach University for your support, encouragement, and great ideas, especially: Leona Nunn, Harriett Salinger, Byron Van Arsdale, Lee Weinstein, Cheryl Richardson, Karen Whitworth, Don Edburg, Mimi Ty, Marlene Elliott, Laura Berman Fortgang, Harry Small, David Goldsmith, Margaret Lichtenberg, Katherine Halpern, Paulette Playce, Sandra Bandler, Cynthia Stringer, Kelly Tyler, Madeleine Homan, Elizabeth Carrington, Val Williams, Stephen Cluney, Katherine Minton, Edie Periera, Pam Richarde, Jeff Raim, Bob Sher, Shirley Anderson, Terry O'Neill, and Bill Bennett. And thanks to the United Kingdom coaching community, especially Elizabeth Rowlands, Lesley McDonald, Bob Griffiths, and Sara Litvinoff for welcoming me into your country and being the most gracious and generous hosts. I am grateful for your love, support, and encouragement. I have learned so much from each one of you.

Tom Atkinson for your friendship and all those terrific dinners at Tre Promodori. Thanks for being there for me. Amir DePaz for your friendship and generous assistance. You are a wonderful human being. Mario de Grossi for the fabulous photograph. You are a master. Dan Sokol for your friendship and computer support. Raja Shaheen for all those great massages that kept body and soul together. Thanks for your love, faith, and encouragement. Sarkice Nedder, my mentor, for your love, sage counsel, and savvy business advice. Amy Gerdnic, for your friendship and enthusiastic marketing approach. My dearest friends in the world—Tracey, John, Allegra, Erik, Kate, Ralph, and Tom—for your love and encouragement.

All my family for their love and support, and with immense gratitude to: Grandma Margaret for your faith in me. My cousin, Ann, for never once complaining about the papers and books all over the sofa and for teaching me a thing or two about the value of space. My sister Keralee for clearing me of all imaginary blocks to success, and for your editing assistance and ideas. My sister Sarelyn for your amazing wit and generous help with research and editing. My dad, Terrel, for your confidence in my abilities and for inspiring me with your own book. My mom, Penelope, for your unceasing love, support, and encouragement from the first page to the last.

And most of all, thanks to all of my clients for sharing your hopes, dreams, and fears with me. Your stories bring this book to life.

Introduction

"There is only one success—to be able to spend your life in your own way."

CHRISTOPHER MORLEY

What Is Coaching?

Coaching closes the gap between where you are now and where you want to be. It is a professional relationship with someone who accepts nothing but your best and who will advise you, guide you, and encourage you to go beyond self-imposed limitations in order to realize your full potential. Think of Olympic athletes. These are the most successful and powerful athletes in the world—because of coaching. Their coaches give them the edge that allows them to go for the gold. They provide an outside perspective and keep the athletes focused on their goals.

A *life* coach points out things you can't see and gives you ideas on how to improve your performance while at the same time motivating you to be your absolute best. A life coach challenges you to go beyond where you normally stop. A life coach helps you tap into your greatness and enables you to share it with the world. Can you imagine how much more productive and successful you would be if you had your own coach? Well, you don't have to imagine anymore. This book contains the key elements of my coaching program and the latest formulas for achieving success and attracting everything you have always wanted. Coaching used to be reserved for CEOs and other top executives, and, of course, superb athletes, but now life coaching is available for anyone who wants to live his or her dreams. Today over 100,000 people use life coaches for advice and strategy on improving their personal and professional lives.

People often think that when they achieve success, they will be happy. This is not necessarily true. I myself was a very successful manager. In the eyes of the world, I had made it. I made more money than 90 percent of the population and my prospects for advancement were excellent. But, although I did very well at my job, I hated it. I used to have this absurd wish that I'd get hit by a bus while walking to work and then could go to the hospital instead. I knew I wasn't living up to my full potential.

I would like to be able to say that I hired a coach to help me figure out what to do with my life, but I hadn't even heard of coaching. My coach found me. He asked me if he could coach me and I told him, as politely as I could, to get lost. To this day I am extremely grateful that he was persistent because it changed my life completely. I am now doing exactly what I love to do. My work is incredibly fulfilling. I get tremendous satisfaction from leading seminars around the world and helping my clients achieve their goals and dreams. I now lead the finest team of coaches in the world. I have all the personal time I want, have found the man of my dreams, and have an amazing life that I thoroughly enjoy. Now *that* is success. And I'm no longer interested in getting hit by a bus!

You are the master and creator of your own destiny. You may already have a clear picture of what you want in life, or you may be clueless. It doesn't matter where you start. In fact, it is probably better if you are clueless so that you don't limit your options unnecessarily. You may be wondering if coaching will work for you. Try it and see. In one sense, nobody *needs* a coach; it is a fabulous luxury. But, like an Olympic athlete, if you seek to perform and be your absolute best, you'll want the edge coaching provides.

When clients first hire me, they are usually tired of struggling to achieve success in life and are looking for an easier way. Most of us live our lives backward. We spend a great deal of our time and energy working harder and harder to make more money to buy and do more things that will supposedly make us happy. This is the hard way to success. The easy way is to first *decide who you want to be, then act* on that decision. By doing so you will effortlessly attract the life you want. And a funny thing happens when you start living this way—you discover what you really want. You no longer waste precious time on goals, projects, or relationships that aren't fulfilling. This book will show you how to be your very best, most successful self. When you are happy, relaxed, having a good time, and doing what you love to do, you will naturally attract success. People can't help but be drawn to you, and opportunity lands in your lap.

Two Ways to Get What You Want

There are two basic approaches to getting what you want in life, whether you are after money, love, opportunities, or business: 1) set your goal and go after it; and 2) attract your goal to you. We've been trained to use the first method, but it often doesn't work. We end up trying to force or will our goals to fruition. This can be unnecessarily frustrating, stressful, and unhealthy.

People call attraction by many different names—serendipity, good luck, synchronicity, networking—and they would be right if this kind of thing was an occasional or random event. But amazingly lucky things happen to my clients and me all the time. One client, a regional marketing executive at a Fortune 500 company, was making a very nice income of $125,000 a year, but felt stuck and unsatisfied at work. We worked not on writing a résumé or job hunting, but on her life. She started getting rid of all the petty annoyances that were dragging her down. She began playing more golf on weekends to relax. I encouraged her to take better care of herself and get a weekly massage. She cleared out all the old files and papers cluttering her office and home. After nine months of working to get every aspect of her life in great shape, she received a call from a recruiter who arranged an interview with another company. Within the week she got the job, instantly doubled her salary, and now has a challenging career with people she enjoys working with. She didn't chase after this opportunity; it came to her. She *attracted* this result. My clients frequently experience this sort of success, and there is no reason why you can't too. You can systematically create a life that draws happiness and success to you. By removing the energy drains in your life and adding in pleasurable activities that increase your energy, you create the space for opportunities to come to you.

Most of us don't give ourselves credit for attracting success. Good things come to us and we chalk it up to luck or serendipity. What we don't know is that when we are at our best, doing fulfilling work and feeling happy and excited about life, it is natural to attract success. The problem is that lots of things prevent us from being our best. That's where some coaching tips can come in handy.

Using the practical wisdom drawn from my wealth of experience as a professional coach, as well as my years of corporate experience, I've collected 101 of the most powerful and effective coaching tips and presented them here in an easy-to-follow, ten-part program. Each part is filled with practical, proven tips and down-to-earth, real-life examples that will help you attract everything you have always wanted.

How Does Coaching Work?

After coaching hundreds of clients to attract what they want, I've found that the process is pretty simple. It all boils down to the raw basics: energy. Einstein figured out that all matter is energy. A solid mahogany desk is mostly empty space with a few little atoms whizzing around. We can do things that take away our energy or things that give us energy. Coaching will show you how to eliminate the things that drain your energy and bring in the things that give you energy. The more energy you have, the more attractive and powerful you will be. People who are energetic and full of life, people who are doing what they most love to do, are successful. Think of Gandhi, Eleanor Roosevelt, Oprah Winfrey. All epitomize the ability each of us has to attract what we want for ourselves and the world.

How to Use *Coach Yourself to Success*

This book is divided into ten parts that build on each other in natural progression. Each part contains ten tips that you don't necessarily have to do in order. In Part I you will learn to increase your natural power by getting rid of the major energy drains in your life and putting in some positive energy boosters. Once you've handled these basics, in Part II you will learn to make some space for the new things you want in your life. Excess "stuff" reduces your ability to attract success. Nature abhors a vacuum—back to the laws of physics again!—so if you want something new in your life, you have to create the space for it.

Part III addresses money. Why work for money when you can learn to make money work for you? This is where you will begin to tell the truth about money, plug the money drains in your life, and get on the path toward financial independence so that within ten to twenty years you won't have to work for a living. Most people get by on just enough money. If you want to be effortlessly successful you need more than enough money.

Once you have handled the money, the next step is to figure out how to make time when there isn't any. In Part IV, I share some secrets of creating time. You will learn to focus on what is truly important and eliminate the chronic time wasters that devour our lives before we know it. This creates a sense of balance and control in your life.

In Part V you will learn how to develop a supportive network of friends, colleagues, and mentors. It takes time to develop and maintain strong relationships, and many of us are so busy that we don't take the time to do so. Yet successful people readily acknowledge they couldn't have reached their goals without the help of their personal network. You will also identify and find ways to satisfy emotional needs that may have been unconsciously driving your behavior and choice of friends.

In Part VI you will discover what really turns you on in life and learn how to make the smooth transition to doing exactly that without financial risk. When you are doing work you love, you begin to attract powerful and interesting people who never would have looked twice at you when you were miserable and complaining about your job every day. People who are excited about their work are few and far between, so by that fact alone you will stand out from the crowd and attract even more opportunities.

In Part VII you will learn how to become exceptionally efficient, productive, and effective. You will learn how to get unstuck when you are in a rut and how to blast through your goals and achieve them in record time—and then eliminate goals altogether. You will learn to work smarter and to have more fun in the process, whether your goals are professional or personal.

In Part VIII you will learn the art of listening profoundly, so profoundly that you will actually bring things out of people that they themselves weren't aware of. Successful people usually have one key trait in common: they have learned how to communicate with power, grace, and style. Anyone can learn to do this. The simple tips here show you how to speak so that people not only listen to you, but are also motivated to take action. Here you learn the secrets of getting people to do what you want without manipulating them.

By Part IX you will be ready to start taking care of your number one asset: YOU. Here you will learn how to eliminate unnecessary stress, banish burnout, and surround yourself with luxury. Now is the time to pamper yourself and get your body in great shape. The payoff—a rejuvenated and energetic you! Good things will be landing in your lap on a fairly consistent basis. Now you need to learn how to have it this good. Most people think they don't deserve to have such an awesome life and end up sabotaging themselves in one way or another. But do not fear; this is curable. And one of the best ways to expand your willingness to have the good life is to start taking extremely good care of yourself.

In Part X you will strengthen the key characteristics of success. This part is not about doing things; it is about a way of being. It goes beyond having extra time and money or having a gorgeous house or body. We all know people who look successful on the outside but aren't much fun to be around. This is because success goes beyond the trappings. Part X is about being the kind of person who naturally attracts success. In one sense this is the most important step of all, but it is difficult to maintain your success if you don't have the other parts in place. At this point you will find that you may just have a notion, a thought about what you want and boom! It appears. I know this sounds like magic, but it isn't; you have laid the groundwork for this success. You will have so much energy and vitality that your thoughts will be more powerful. And why shouldn't they be? You have eliminated the distractions in your life and have set up your environment to give you energy. You will be incredibly magnetic at this point.

Let's look at the example of Frank, a computer programmer who was so bored with his job he was literally falling asleep at his desk. Frank had worked for the same bank for over seven years and all his efforts were getting him nowhere fast. He was being reprimanded for poor performance, but try as he might, he just couldn't muster up the motivation to improve. After three months of coaching, during which he cleaned out his entire house of clutter and furniture he no longer liked and got rid of everything that he had been tolerating, Frank landed a new job earning $20,000 more at a prestigious investment bank. More importantly, he had challenging work and a boss he admired and respected. Frank felt so much better about himself and his life that he effortlessly attracted a smart and professional woman who couldn't keep her hands off him! Needless to say, Frank was a happy camper.

Coaching works for anyone who is willing to take these actions. There is work to do, but the work isn't focused on striving to reach your goals. Rather, you will focus on being the best person you can possibly be today. This coaching program will help you realize your unique talents and gifts and then maximize them to achieve the success you want. Working on your own life is the most rewarding thing you can do. The good news is that the coaching process builds a natural momentum so you won't have to keep motivating yourself. Once you start in one area of your life, you will be drawn to work on another. Once you've experienced attracting what you want, you will never want to go back to your old ways of achieving success.

This is an action-oriented program, so you will want to find a special notebook or three-ring binder to keep your notes in. I also suggest that if you are not in the habit of keeping a journal or diary, you begin. Just write down a paragraph or two a day (or feel free to write more if you feel so inclined). The journal will show you how much you have accomplished and help you digest and adapt to the many changes you will make in your life during the coaching program. Finally, take the "How Coachable Are You?" test in Appendix A to see if you are ready to begin coaching.

A Final Word of Caution

Most of the ideas in this book are so simple that you may think you have done them just by reading them; this is a big mistake. Reading and taking action are two totally different things. If only it were true that reading an idea were sufficient—we would all be perfect by now. So pick a tip from Part I that appeals to you and then *do* it. Focus on one or two tips a week. Some can be done immediately while others may take quite a bit of time to complete. For example, while you may be able to sew on a button in two minutes, it might take you a year to save six months living expenses. Don't worry about how much time it will take to reach the end result. The important thing is to set up the structures for fulfillment of your goals and dreams.

If you can afford to hire a coach to support you in this process, great. I've listed resources to help you find one in Appendix B along with the questions you should ask when interviewing a coach. In Appendix D I've listed books and tapes that I frequently recommend to my coaching clients in addition to organizations and associations that will help you find the people you need to reach your goals. If you can't hire a coach, find a partner or buddy who will do it with you and call each other once a week to check in. Of course, you can do it by yourself, but it is much easier and more fun to do it with somebody else.

While it is perfectly okay to jump around the book and do whatever you most feel like, if you find you are struggling in one area or an idea seems impossible or far-fetched, it may be that you need to take care of something from an earlier part first. For example, it is hard to hire a personal trainer if you are still in debt. And it may seem ridiculous or impossible to go for financial independence when you are still figuring out how to pay the baby-sitter. However, financial independence will sound like a large but achievable project once you have paid off your debts and have six months living expenses socked away. It is easiest if you follow the process as outlined, but go ahead and do what you want. Above all, have fun and enjoy the process!

I.

∙∙∙

INCREASE YOUR NATURAL POWER

"There is a vitality, a life force, an energy, a quickening, that is translated through you into action, and because there is only one of you in all time, this expression is unique. And if you block it, it will never exist through any other medium and will be lost."

MARTHA GRAHAM

POWERFUL PEOPLE HAVE the ability to get what they want, to attract great opportunities and people and wealth, and to wield their influence to impact those around them. We are all powerful to varying degrees, but everyone can increase his or her own natural power and have more energy. The formula is a simple one: to increase your natural power, eliminate the things that drain your energy and add the things that give you energy. I said simple, not necessarily easy. The first place to start when you begin this coaching program is to dramatically reduce the number of things that are distracting you and draining your energy and replace them with some positive, nurturing energy boosters. This is where you get your life in good shape, get rid of the bad habits, and learn how to protect yourself from unpleasant people and remarks. This is the underlying foundation needed to increase your power naturally and attract the success you want. We often neglect to build a solid foundation for our lives because we are so busy going after our goals.

There are a couple of dangers in going after really big goals before you've taken the time to get your life in basic order. First, you may achieve your goal, but it may not last. Don't waste time building castles on sand; build your castle on bedrock. You've probably seen it happen to friends who sacrifice all to go for their goal, achieve it, and find the success short-lived. It is commonly believed that achieving great success can ruin you. That may simply be a case of not having laid the proper foundation, so when the first windstorm or calamity strikes, the whole thing crumbles to ruins. It may not be the success that ruins people, but rather the lack of a good foundation. Any work you do in this first section will strengthen you and make all the following steps of this book much easier to do. So while I know these may look simple, take the time to do them. It is critical to your long-term success.

The second danger is that you may reach your goals and then not feel fulfilled or satisfied. A reporter once asked me what was the number one reason why people don't reach their goals. I told her it is that they pick the wrong goals in the first place. Have you ever had your heart set on some objective and then, when you finally achieved it, found your victory was hollow? Either what you wanted wasn't as great as you had imagined, or you enjoyed it for a short time and then went all too quickly on to the next goal. This is extremely common. We are so heavily influenced by media and advertising that we often don't know what we *really* want as individuals, but instead adopt some media-inspired vision of what will make us happy. These aren't your true dreams or goals, but you may have been seduced into them with slick advertising. Obviously, reaching these goals will still leave you with those vague feelings of discontent. Before you can even figure out what makes you really happy, you need to handle the basics in life.

Start energizing your life by getting rid of everything you are putting up with. Cleaning out your closet and sewing on a button may not sound glamorous, but this is often the first step to getting what you really want. As Mom always said, "Eat your veggies, then you can have dessert."

1. Eliminate All Those Petty Annoyances

"To be really great in the little things, to be truly noble and heroic in the insipid details of everyday life, is a virtue so rare as to be worthy of canonization."

Harriet Beecher Stowe

If you are serious about being successful, start by eliminating everything you are putting up with, the things you are tolerating, enduring—those petty annoyances. You might be tolerating any number of small things, such as the overflowing in-box, the unpaid taxes you have to figure out, or even the tear in your bathrobe that nags at you every time you open your shower door and see it hanging there. Every time you see it, you think, "I've got to sew that up." That is an annoyance—something as small as a missing button, or scuffed shoes. It could be that you are also tolerating something bigger. Maybe you're tolerating your spouse's bad breath, or your best friend's habit of always showing up late, or you're tolerating something about your work, perhaps a boss who micromanages you. Or you could be tolerating your own bad habits—that you bite your nails or can't find important papers because your files are disorganized. You could be annoyed by the pollution in your city, the fact that your car is messy, or that you have a long commute to work.

Everything you are tolerating drains your energy, makes you irritable, and wears you down. It is very difficult to be successful if you are putting up with a lot. From my coaching experience, I've found that most people tolerate anywhere from 60 to 100 different things. To eliminate what you are putting up with, simply write down the 60 to 100 things that you are tolerating. Make the list. It doesn't do any good to just keep a mental list in your head; you must write them down to get them out of your head and onto paper. Then call a friend and buddy-up with someone else who wants to get rid of the things they are putting up with too. Set aside a whole Saturday or Sunday as a blitz day and start working down your list on anything that can be done in one day. If you start to lose steam, call your buddy to check in for a pep talk and report your progress. And set a deadline. After the blitz day treat yourself to dinner and the movies.

Some of the things you won't be able to handle in one day, so give yourself one to three months and whoever gets the most items eliminated gets taken out to dinner or wins some special treat. Petty annoyances drain your energy, reducing your natural ability to attract success. Don't sweat the small things. Just get them out of your life. As for the things that seem impossible to handle—like your boss, the long commute to work, or your spouse's bad breath—just write them on the list and don't worry about them. The solutions will come to you in time.

Take the example of Jason, a successful portfolio manager on Wall Street. Jason loved the financial world, but was extremely frustrated in his work, where he seemed to be putting in long hours day after day. He had been in the same position for over seven years and felt he wasn't getting the recognition or salary he deserved. Jason told me, "I feel like a rat on a treadmill. I keep running faster and faster and working harder and harder and it is getting me absolutely nowhere. What do I do?" I asked Jason to list all the things he was currently tolerating about his life, both personally and professionally. He came back with a fairly long list, which included items such as: no social life, eating alone, no recognition at work, a tear in his favorite leather jacket, ironing his shirts, the stack of papers piled high in his in-box, a poorly trained assistant who chewed gum all the time at work, paying bills, and the bathtub needing caulking, to name a few. The list of his problems seemed endless. Like many unhappy people, he was stuck. I said, "Jason, it's time to start taking excellent care of yourself." I suggested that he begin rewarding himself, doing some things he especially liked even when all the paperwork wasn't finished. He needed to stop pushing so hard for a few minutes and rest. The result was gratifying. One day he went for a walk in Central Park and watched the sunset—a simple thing that he really enjoyed but hadn't taken the time to do in years. He started taking a martial arts class—something he had always wanted to do but just couldn't seem to justify the time for. Now Jason had something to look forward to after work and he found himself getting his work done more efficiently so he could go to his classes. He cleaned up all the papers on his desk and caulked the tub, then things began to turn around. Jason talked to a recruiter about job prospects, and within two months he had a new job at another invest-ment bank where he felt more valued and received a $30,000 increase in salary. Not to mention the fact that he started dating again.

Lori made her list and realized that, among a whole host of smaller things, she was putting up with a boyfriend she didn't like that much any-more and living in a city she hated. She promptly broke up with the guy and moved to another city two weeks later. Not everyone can take such rapid action, but if you can, why not? Once she realized how much it was costing her, she wasn't willing to put up with anything less than she deserved. Now she is living in a comfortable home in Chicago and dat-ing until she finds just the right guy.

Robert made his list of annoyances and called me back the next week to say he couldn't believe what a difference it made to get rid of all the little pesky stuff in his life. He replaced the lightbulb for the fridge, which had been burned out for over a year. He threw out a very moldy shower curtain and bought a new one. He sewed on missing buttons and threw out clothes that were stained or torn. He had his shoes resoled. Robert confessed that he thought these little things weren't that important and that he would casually dismiss them, thinking he would be better off spending his time focusing on the bigger goals. After getting rid of twenty-three things that he had been tolerating, he got a tremendous burst of energy and began building a deck off the back porch—a pro-ject he had been saying he was going to do for the past three years. His wife was thrilled.

Once when I was leading a telephone seminar, I challenged the par-ticipants to come back the next week with their list of everything they were tolerating and to eliminate the biggest one on the list. One guy came back and he was practically bouncing off the walls with energy. In writ-ing down his list, the first thing he realized was that he wasn't happy with the therapist he had been using. He stopped seeing that one and hired a different therapist with whom he really felt comfortable. He had been tol-erating this ineffective relationship for nine months.

Some people sit down to write their list and have great trouble get-ting started. In 99 percent of the cases, this isn't because they don't have any pesky annoyances in their lives, but rather that they are so numb to them that they can't even think of them. Once you eliminate one item, another petty annoyance that you hadn't even realized you were putting up with comes to mind. Sometimes it helps to think of the different categories of things you tolerate—what are you tolerating about work, home, your friends and family, your pets, your body, your own habits?

The next trick is to lump the things you are tolerating together and see how you could eliminate a whole bunch of them at once. For example, John was tolerating not making enough money, a messy desk at work, his boss, not having enough responsibility, and not getting enough acknowledgment, among other things. He realized that if he got a different job, he would wipe out a whole pack of annoyances at once. He cleaned off his desk, then talked to his boss about the possibilities of working in another department where he would have more responsibilities. He got the transfer and a few months later a salary increase to match his increased responsibilities.

You may find that you are putting up with something for a very good reason. Jessica worked like a demon to eliminate her entire list of eighty-nine annoyances. She was very proud of her accomplishment but was a bit discouraged on our next call. Now that she had eliminated all the piddling stuff that had been bothering her, she realized the big one that was staring her in the face—she was having trouble in her marriage of twenty-seven years. She had been hiding from the fact that the relationship wasn't working even though she knew she'd have to deal with it if she was to be successful in her business and happy in her life. All the little things she had been tolerating distracted her from the big issues in her life.

When you finish your list, you will find that a number of things seem beyond your control and you don't know how to fix them. Not to worry, just leave them on the list and work on the ones you can do something about. I gave this assignment to my sister before I realized it wasn't a good idea to coach one's own family. She made her list and showed it to me, and when I told her I was sorry, I shouldn't coach her, she never pursued it. One of the items on her list was her cubicle mate at work. Without doing anything, she was given a different partner a month later. You will find that if you write your list, stuff it in a drawer, and come back to it a month later, you'll be able to cross some stuff off even though you weren't working on it. So whatever you do, at least write the darn list!

2. Plug the Energy Drains

"Cocaine habit-forming? Of course not. I ought to know. I've been using it for years."

Tallulah Bankhead

Once you start eliminating what you are putting up with (Tip 1), you will see just how much energy those petty annoyances were taking from you. Just like the hum of an air conditioner: you don't realize how loud it really is until you turn it off. Lots of things drain our precious energy, and we aren't even aware of it. Take TV, for example. When was the last time you felt zippy and alive after watching TV? Tabloid papers have a lot of negative, gossipy news that can drain your energy. Needy relationships will take up inordinate amounts of your time and energy. As will any and all addictions, including alcohol, sugar, shopping, computer games, caffeine, gambling, smoking, chocolate, TV, sex—you know which ones are yours. I'm not saying you can't have a cup of coffee once in a while, but more than three cups a week and it's an addiction.

I didn't think I was addicted to coffee. I didn't even like it that much and only had one cup a day, in the morning. When I decided to give it up, I thought it would be easy. After three days of skull-splitting, mind-numbing headaches (and I don't usually get headaches), I realized this was a powerful drug, not just a nice cup of coffee. Try it yourself and see. Plus, if you are interested in losing weight, studies show that caffeine causes insulin production to go up, which increases fat storage. Now that I've given up caffeine, my energy is more even and balanced throughout the day, and I don't buzz around in the morning thinking I'm accomplishing a lot when I'm really not. Feeling stressed, under the gun? Definitely not the time for coffee. It will make things worse, exacerbating the stress you already feel. When you give up caffeine, plan on getting headaches. One client, formerly a coffee aficionado, swears by this technique: stop coffee, but drink as much tea as you want for one month and then switch to herbal tea. He finds he now has more energy and feels much more relaxed.

Another client, a senior editor at a publishing house, was addicted to sugar and found herself headed for the vending machines a couple times a day. She decided to quit cold turkey. Anytime she felt inclined to head to the vending machines for a candy bar and a coke, she just told herself, "Sugar isn't going to help. In fact, it will just makes things worse." This mantra worked for her. Sugar was a way for her to get a quick energy burst, and it was also a way to put off work on a difficult project. Instead she focused on the task at hand or addressed the project head-on. Not only did she lose weight, but she discovered she was even more productive at work.

What are the seductive energy drains in your life? Don't be shy about getting support. There are all sorts of excellent 12-step programs that help people get over their addictions—CODA for codependency issues, AA for alcohol, AlAnon for family members of alcoholics, OA for overeaters. There is something for everyone. Get the support you need to eliminate this energy drain once and for all. If you think you can manage your addictions on your own, make a list and eliminate one each month until you are free.

Addictions take over your life and are extremely difficult to stop on your own. If you try doing it on your own and fail, do not despair. This does not mean that you have no willpower or are a weak and terrible person. Stop beating yourself up about it. All it means is that you really *are* addicted and the only thing missing is a really powerful support system to help you break it. A hint from an herbalist friend: most addictions are associated with rituals. Part of the pleasure of smoking marijuana is getting out the paper and rolling the joint. If you want to quit smoking pot, it helps to create a new, healthy ritual to replace the old one. I don't know, perhaps you could make origami designs out of the paper? Take some time to create a new ritual that you will enjoy instead. If you do have an addiction that starts to consume your life, coaching won't work because the addiction will be running your life, not you.

3. INSTALL TEN DAILY HABITS

"Good habits, which bring our lower passions and appetites under automatic control, leave our natures free to explore the larger experiences of life. Too many of us divide and dissipate our energies in debating actions which should be taken for granted."

RALPH W. SOCKMAN

Most of us have a few bad habits that really don't nurture and support us. They might even have evolved from a habit to an addiction, as my daily cup of coffee did before I even realized it. Experts say that to break a habit you need to replace it with a different habit, or you might go right back to the old habit. Ideally you want to replace a bad habit with a good habit—"good" meaning that it gives you energy rather than drains your energy. What are ten pleasures that you could put in place on a daily basis that you'd look forward to doing? Perhaps you'd like to spend fifteen minutes of quiet time to plan your day, or on creative thought? How about a stretch for ten minutes after you get home from work to get the kinks out? Or you may want to walk or bike to work instead of driving. Try eating lunch outside under a tree instead of at the cafeteria. Or packing your own lunch instead of buying it or eating at a fast-food place. Experiment with going to bed a half hour earlier and getting up a half hour earlier. The idea here is not to put in place a "should" habit—something you think you should do—but rather a habit you'd *love* to do, something that would be a treat for you. This will be different for each person. Most people are so stressed out when they begin this assignment that they can't even think of ten pleasurable habits. This was true for me. I had completely lost touch with what I enjoyed doing. (This was around the time when I was hoping I'd get hit by a bus on the way to work so I could lie in traction in the hospital for a while.) I couldn't think of anything except "shoulds" like "I should exercise daily," or "I should eat more veggies." This didn't light me up or turn me on so I had to think back to what I used to do for fun. My list of ten daily habits ended up as a combination of some fun things and some things I knew I needed to implement on a regular basis:

1. Walk to work instead of taking the subway. (I timed it and found that the subway took forty minutes, and I could walk door to door in one hour. I figured for an extra twenty minutes, I'd gain an hour of exercise and save a buck-fifty. This ended up becoming a sort of walking meditation for me.)
2. Floss daily (sort of a "should," but I don't mind flossing and it definitely makes my teeth happy).
3. Call a friend or send a note of thanks daily.

4. Eat an exotic fresh fruit (raspberries, strawberries, a mango, a papaya, a juicy pear).
5. Do one "pamper me" thing daily (a bubble bath, a manicure, a new magazine, a walk in the park, fresh flowers for the office).
6. Take a vitamin C and a multivitamin (a pretty easy one).
7. Do daily back exercises (I had lower back pain and these kept me mobile).
8. Tell someone "I love you" every day.
9. Spend fifteen minutes to plan my day every morning.
10. Clean my desk off before leaving the office every evening.

If you are having trouble breaking a bad habit or starting a good habit, you may want to create a visual display to chart your progress. It doesn't really matter what you use as a visual display, but you need some daily visual reminder to keep you on target. For example, in her book *Inner Simplicity*, Elaine St. James suggests using the gold star method. If you liked getting a gold star when you were in kindergarten, you can still employ this technique or create any other visual display. Here's what you do: give yourself a gold star for every day that you successfully did something. Suppose you want to stop watching TV (Tip 32). Every day that you don't watch TV, give yourself a gold star. Put it on a wall calendar that is clearly visible. You don't have to tell anyone else what you are working on; in fact it is better not to tell anyone—keep it to yourself so you won't have someone nagging at you. Once you have a whole month of gold stars, give yourself a special reward—just make sure it is not the habit you just broke. Or maybe you'd like to design a bar graph to record your results. Some clients cut out pictures from magazines and create a collage that inspires them to stick to their new habits. One of my clients sent himself an automatic E-mail reminder to send out a thank-you every day until it became a habit. Our lives are usually so full of things that it is helpful to have a daily reminder until your new habit becomes as natural as brushing your teeth. It may be easiest to work on installing one new habit at a time if ten seems overwhelming.

This may sound silly, but it really helps to have some sort of visual display or to make a minicontest or game out of it. Kendall, an athletic client, was addicted to sugar and did the gold star technique for every day without sugar. He didn't want to see a blank day on the calendar. The visual display not only shows you in black and white just how well you've really done, but it motivates you to keep on going. He used to keep track in his head and was sure that he gave himself a better score than he really achieved. It is easy to forget the French toast with maple syrup or the handful of mints if you aren't keeping track. The longer you go, the more powerful it becomes. After two weeks without sugar, he didn't want to ruin a perfect run of gold stars. This technique also works for installing a good habit, like walking the dog or eating three fresh vegetables a day. Write down a list of ten daily pleasures and start enjoying yourself every day.

4. ELIMINATE THE "SHOULDS"

"To be good, according to the vulgar standard of goodness, is obviously quite easy. It merely requires a certain amount of sordid terror, a certain lack of imaginative thought, and a certain low passion for middle-class respectability."

OSCAR WILDE

The "shoulds" are those things we think we have to do, gotta do, but don't really want to do. For example, I *should* lose weight. I *should* exercise. I *should* network more. I *should* wear a size 6 dress. I *should* be making more money. I *should* learn to speak a foreign language. I *should* do this, that, or the other thing. All these "*shoulds*" are killing you, weighing you down and keeping you from getting on with the really interesting stuff in your life. I'm sure you could make up a nice little list right now and I recommend that you do. And then crumple it up, wad it into a ball, and burn it. Yes, you got it. You must get rid of the "shoulds." They are weighing you down, getting you nowhere, and sapping your precious life energy. Far better to think up a whole list of new goals that really turn you on and ditch the "shoulds."

How can you tell if it is a real goal or a "should" goal? Well, one surefire way is to ask yourself, "How old is this goal?" If you've had it for a year or more, then it is a "should" goal that is completely lifeless. You don't want that dead goal hanging around one minute longer. Get rid of it! And I mean now! Ah, but you protest, if I give up my goal to lose weight then

I'll never lose weight. Well, that may be true, but you've been saying you need to lose weight for how many years now? I don't think this is ever going to happen so you might as well give it up and replace it with something that you are *really* interested in creating. At this suggestion, a few of my clients gleefully get rid of the old goal, but most want to keep it. It's amazing how attached we get to these "shoulds." If you've gotten along this far in life as a size 12, who cares if you are a size 6? If you have gotten along fine without speaking French, then perhaps you don't need to keep this goal around any longer. If they still hang on, then I say it is time to expand the goal into one that will turn you on. For example, instead of focusing on losing weight, how about making a goal to take extremely good care of yourself? This means the whole package: see a nutritionist for a food plan that will work for you; get a personal trainer to get your butt off the sofa; see a massage therapist bimonthly or weekly; get a regular facial; sign up for the jazz dance class you've always wanted; hang around with people who eat the way you'd like to eat and have healthy habits, and start spending less time with friends whose habits don't support the new ones you'd like to incorporate. This goal is suddenly a whole lot more fun, full of life, than "I really should lose weight."

So go down your list of "shoulds" and throw out as many as you can. If you really feel you can't, see how you can delegate it. Suppose you really should exercise, and you feel that you can't in good conscience cross it off. Well, hire a personal trainer, join a walking club—DO something, but don't let it sit there weighing you down as a "should." Or suppose you think you should get a better job, but just haven't gotten motivated yet. Update your résumé (you can even hire an expert to do this for you), get it to a headhunter, and let him or her find you a new job. If you aren't ready to update your résumé, network, contact a recruiter, or go on interviews, then you may as well forget this goal too. Far better to delete and move on. You'll feel much lighter immediately.

Sandy, a forty-five-year-old social worker, hired me because she had recently divorced and wanted to find a new man. She wanted to start working out and to lose weight but just couldn't seem to get started. She would go to the gym sporadically, but it wasn't enough. Sandy blamed herself for a lack of discipline and willpower. I suggested that willpower was entirely unnecessary if she had an effective structure for support. I encouraged her to set up a support system that would make it easy for her to work out.

She was a very conscientious person, and I knew that if she had an appointment to meet a friend at the gym, she wouldn't miss it. She put her gym bag in the car so she'd be able to go directly after work, because she knew herself well enough to know that if she went home first, she'd never make it back out again. Sandy made an appointment with a girlfriend who was also committed to getting back in shape. They met at the gym and ended up doing thirty-five minutes of exercise. Sandy felt terrific. Her colleagues at work noticed her enthusiasm and one particularly handsome man asked her if she'd like to go running together. One thing led to another and soon Sandy not only lost eight pounds, but she was exercising regularly and had a great-looking exercise buddy.

What are your tired old goals? If you haven't done anything about them in the past year, get rid of them or reinvent them. I highly recommend that if you have had weight loss as a goal for years that you just get rid of it. Remember, you can always pick it up again later, but give yourself a break and let go of that burden for awhile. Another client, Howard, gave up his weight loss goals and took up tai chi instead. I met him for lunch a few months later and even though he wasn't any thinner, he looked more relaxed, confident, and attractive. Why struggle if it isn't making a difference anyway?

Another client, Jim, was a dynamic mortgage broker and a great list-maker. Every year he would make an astonishing number of New Year's resolutions. This year, he showed me his list of twenty-five goals, and I asked him to review it for any goals over a year old and, in addition, to delete any "shoulds." He pared the list down to four key goals that he was really excited about working on, and he felt a surprising relief. Get rid of the dead goals now, as they will only slow you down the rest of the year.

5. Establish Big Boundaries

"The way in which a person loses their true goodness is
just like the way that trees are destroyed by the ax. Cut
down day after day, how can the mind, anymore than the
tree, retain its beauty or continue to live."

Mencius, fourth century b.c.

It is almost impossible to be successful without firm and clear boundaries. We naturally respect people who have strong boundaries. Boundaries are simply the things people can't do to you, lines that will protect you and allow you to be your best. For example, most people have in place the boundary that it is not okay for anyone to hit them. Now we know that some folks don't even have this boundary in place—we've heard about or know people who stay in abusive relationships for whatever reason. These people are missing the basic boundary, "You can't hit me." Okay, let's assume you have this boundary in place and people don't hit you. Do people yell at you? Well, that is only one level out from hitting—not a whole lot of protection. You need to expand your boundary from people can't hit me to people can't yell at me. Not even your boss, certainly not your lover or spouse.

Susan, a sales assistant at a retail shop, was having a tough time with an extremely demanding boss who thought nothing of blowing off steam by ranting and raving at her subordinates. She would yell at Susan for making even the smallest error. Susan also allowed her colleagues to tease her about her midwestern expressions and accent. A friend of hers would take advantage of her and crash at her house whenever he didn't feel like going home. All of this is a simple case of missing boundaries. Once Susan decided it was no longer acceptable that people yell at her, make her the butt end of a joke, or take advantage of her, everything began to turn around. Her colleagues stopped teasing her and her friends stopped taking advantage of her. As a side bonus, she got a big promotion at work to sales executive because now her boss, her colleagues, and even her clients had more respect for her. How did she do this? She simply informed them, using the four-step communication model in Tip 6.

Boundaries work equally well at home. A client's boyfriend had a hot temper and he would get angry on occasion and yell at her. She thought this was normal and something that had to be tolerated. I asked her to expand her boundary. It was not okay for him to yell at her for any reason. She explained to him that she loved him and would never intentionally harm him or hurt him in any way. The only reason he should be angry with her was if she intentionally tried to hurt him. So if she was ten minutes late for a date, he could let her know it bothered him without being angry or yelling. At first he was still used to his old ways and so of course he started to yell when he was upset with her. She calmly informed him that he was yelling at her and asked him how much longer he needed to be angry. Five minutes? Thirty minutes? She'd be back when he calmed down. He realized how silly it was and started to laugh.

Once you have this boundary in place and you find that people don't yell at you, try expanding it even further so that people can't give you unsolicited criticism, or make derogatory remarks or jokes at your expense. Even if these remarks are meant in fun, they aren't funny. This type of comment hurts and it just isn't acceptable. Derogatory jokes and comments diminish you, taking away your energy and reducing your ability to attract the things you want in life. Do not allow this!

Now you are probably thinking, "This sounds great, but what do you do when someone yells at you or shows up late or takes advantage of you?" You know this is your new boundary, but how do they know? It's simple, you just need to learn how to protect yourself gracefully. So read on.

6. Protect Yourself Gracefully

"No one can make you feel inferior without your consent."

Eleanor Roosevelt

A simple four-step communication model that I learned at Coach University will help you protect yourself from unpleasant comments. Whenever someone does something that hurts you or bothers you, you are allowing that. Here is how to stop this behavior in a graceful and effective manner. (Ladies, pay attention; we tend to be particularly weak in this department.)

1. Inform. "Do you realize that you are yelling?" or, "Do you realize that comment hurt me?" or, "I didn't ask for your feedback." If they continue with the unwanted behavior, then take it up to step 2, but only after you've tried step 1.
2. Request. Ask them to stop. "I ask that you stop yelling at me now," or, "I ask that you only give me constructive feedback." If they still don't get it and the behavior continues, try step 3.
3. Demand or insist. "I insist that you stop yelling at me now." If they still persist, you take it to the next level.

4. Leave (without any snappy comebacks or remarks). "I can't continue this conversation while you are yelling at me. I am going to leave the room." If you are in a relationship and the other person doesn't change his or her behavior after you've tried this model numerous times, you may need to leave the relationship and/or get a therapist. The people who really love you will respect your boundaries.

The key to success with these four steps is to say them in a neutral tone of voice. Do not raise your voice up or down. Keep it calm and flat. You know when you've got a little charge or fire or judgment or anger in your tone. Remember, you are *informing* the other person. Think of going through the four steps in the same way you'd say, "The sky is blue." No emotion, no excitement, just a neutral tone of voice. You can say just about anything to anybody if you say it in a neutral manner.

Now Susan (from Tip 5) had some ammunition ready for the next time her boss yelled at her. She used this four-step model to inform her boss in a neutral tone of voice. Be careful here. You could risk your job if you don't have this tone of voice down pat so practice on friends and family until you are sure you can do it. Susan made a small mistake at the office the next day, and as usual, her boss began to rant and rave. Susan very calmly, without the slightest hint of sarcasm or judgment in her voice, replied, "Do you realize that you are yelling at me?" This stopped her boss right in her tracks. Then Susan said, "I really want to do my very best work for you, and find that I work best when you point out my errors in a calm voice." Susan's boss immediately calmed down, apologized, and later took her out to lunch. This is a very powerful and attractive way to communicate.

At this point, you are probably thinking, "Well, that is fine for Susan, but I could never speak to my boss that way." Quite frankly, that is what *all* my clients say when I tell them that they need to inform their bosses they have just crossed a boundary. The key to dealing with your boss is to use a completely neutral tone of voice and to be extremely tactful. *Never* correct your boss, or anyone for that matter, in front of another person and especially not in a meeting. Being casual and subtle is also good. You don't want to make a big deal out of your boss's behavior. For example, one client, Lee, a branch manager, felt that his boss, the division executive, was always micromanaging him and had stepped over the bounds by scheduling a meeting with one of his employees without checking with him first. He obviously didn't want to offend the division executive who would be determining the size of his bonus later on. At the same time, he was frustrated by his manager's seeming disregard for his need to manage his own branch. The next day his manager called him about some reports and Lee casually mentioned, "John, my teller, said that you had scheduled a meeting with him. It would make job scheduling easier if, in the future, you'd let me know of such meetings." That was it. Lee used a straightforward informing tone that very subtly let his boss know she had just crossed a boundary. And believe me, he was scared to death to do it, but it did the trick. The next time the division executive wanted a meeting, she called Lee first and set it up through him.

As for the micromanaging, I told Lee to find out what reports his boss wanted and, even if she didn't want them, to type up a brief memo of the results and sales activities of the week so she would be informed of everything that was going on. I also asked Lee to set up weekly meetings with his manager either by phone or in person to give regular updates of what was happening. After one month of this, his division executive said that monthly meetings would be sufficient and that he could discontinue his weekly reports. Lee had won the confidence and trust of his manager and now had the independence to do his job.

Another client, Marcia, had recently made a huge transition from being a full-time engineer and the primary breadwinner of the family to being a full-time mother of three children. She had decided at the birth of her third child to quit her job and take a few months off to enjoy motherhood and get started on her home-based business. The sudden and dramatic reduction of income was stressful, and Marcia felt guilty that she was spending but not earning money for the family. To compound matters, she discovered that people would make little comments all the time about her that made her feel bad, such as, "Well, you're not working now so you should have plenty of time to bring in clients for your business." Or comments that diminished her sense of accomplishment, such as, "It must be nice to hang around the house with the kids all day and have your husband support you now." I pointed out that she was missing the boundary that people can't disparage her work. This was a revelation and she immediately put it in place. The next day her husband had to take her to the hospital, and when the nurse asked what Marcia did her husband said,

"She stays at home." Marcia felt diminished by this comment but realized the boundary had been crossed. Later, she informed her husband about the comment he had made at the hospital. He didn't mean it in a negative way at all, but just thought it was the easiest response. Marcia asked him in the future to say that she was a business consultant and to give out her office number. He was glad to do this.

Which brings up another point. When you inform people, the whole point is to give them a graceful exit. However, oftentimes we don't let them take it. This defeats the whole purpose. Let me demonstrate. Take the example with Marcia. When Marcia's husband replied, "I'm sorry, I didn't mean it to sound that way," Marcia might have said, "Yes, you did! You rat fink #@$%%!" Don't laugh—we've all been guilty of this. Let them off the hook. If they don't apologize, it is okay to ask for one. "I'd like an apology for that." Sometimes an apology isn't enough, and you may need to ask them to make amends. "I appreciate your apology for spilling red wine on my linen suit, but I'd also like you to pay the dry-cleaning bill."

Our natural tendency is to skip steps 1 and 2 and go right to 3 or 4— usually not in a neutral tone of voice, either. The trick to staying neutral is to address things on the spot (Tip 7).

The good news is that eventually you won't even need these boundaries—people wouldn't think of making an unkind remark to you. There is another interesting side effect to enforcing your boundaries. We assume that enforcing a boundary will make people dislike us or think we are pushy or aggressive or perhaps demanding. However, it is the exact opposite. When you have strong boundaries in place, people will stop treating you like a doormat and start respecting you. You'll be the kind of person people naturally respect and treat courteously. When I was a little girl in the first grade, a big bully of a fifth-grader (and you know how big fifth-graders look when you are in first grade) was always picking on me and threatening me. I told my dad, and he taught me how to throw a punch. One day on the playground Mark was with a bunch of his friends and started to taunt me. I spun around and punched him right in the nose. To my own shock and amazement, he fell flat on his back and had a bloody nose. His friends stood around him, jaws agape, as shocked as I was. I was terrified that they would tear me from limb to limb and decided to get out of Dodge and literally skipped off. The next day at school I was wary, but to my complete amazement, Mark came up to me and treated me with great respect. He stopped bullying me, and we actually became friends and went frog catching together. Once he went to buy my next-door neighbor friend, Jamie, and me a soda and he dropped one of them on the way back. He gave the dropped one to her, not to me. I had won his respect. This kindergarten story is a great example of how effective and powerful boundaries are. Now of course I'm not suggesting that you go around punching people in the nose—but do start informing and requesting.

At some level people know when they are doing a number on you and they don't really want to get away with it. If you let them get away it, not only do you diminish yourself, but you also diminish them. What boundaries would you like to put in place now that you know how to protect yourself gracefully? See if you can come up with at least five and write them down.

7. Don't Be a Duck

"Self-confidence is the first requisite to great undertakings."

Samuel Johnson

This tip will do wonders for building your self-confidence. Power, confidence, and success all seem to go hand in hand. The trick is to step over nothing. Get in the habit of addressing everything that bothers you on the spot or as soon as is possible and appropriate afterward. It seems easier to let those little negative comments and subtle digs roll off like water off a duck's back. So many of us erroneously assume that it's better to let the little stuff go by and save our breath for the big ones. The problem with this approach to life is that it costs you too much. All those little comments add up and can undermine your self-esteem. Don't ignore the little stuff. If you do, it will build up and you'll blow up. The time to inform is right away: "Do you realize that you left the dirty dishes on the table?" Don't do what I used to do: clean them up and say to myself, "Oh, it's just a little thing," and then chalk it up as one point for the good guys—me! Give up being the saint and start letting people know what bugs you.

The really "big" person doesn't tolerate unpleasant behavior from others. So for example, if your colleague makes some negative remark like, "What an idiot you are . . . ," instead of letting it slide by, simply inform: "Did you realize that comment hurt me?" Or, "Ouch! That hurts." Or the all-purpose, "That remark was inappropriate." It doesn't take much to put an end to these destructive comments whether they come from friends, family, colleagues, or strangers. It takes a little practice, but if you follow the four-step communication model (Tip 6) and keep your tone of voice neutral, you will soon find that people won't be making these sorts of comments about you. You won't be able to chalk up any points for being the "good guy" anymore either, but you will keep your relationships clean and your confidence up.

As you start to put in place your boundaries, you will begin to realize just how much you have been putting up with in the way of unkind comments and remarks from others. Most of us have been taught that ignoring rude remarks is "nice." We aren't accustomed to addressing things on the spot. So at first you will probably miss the opportunity in the moment. One client, June, was learning how to dance the West Coast swing. Her friend took her around the dance floor, and because he was a very strong lead, she actually appeared to know what she was doing. A fellow came up and asked her to dance, and she couldn't seem to follow him. He was clearly frustrated with her inexperience and said, "You have nothing but two left feet." June was so stunned by the comment that she didn't respond at all. Later she realized she could have informed him in a perfectly neutral tone, "That comment was rude." Now she is much better at catching things immediately. Just the other day, she gleefully reported that she enforced a boundary at work. Her boss went on vacation and left his college-age son to run the shop. Filled with a sense of power, the son started to pick on the employees and drop little snide comments. My client felt annoyed, realized this was not acceptable, and firmly and calmly informed him that she did not appreciate the insinuation that she was stealing sales from the other salespeople. She told him she would never do such a thing and asked him to explain why he said this. He was taken aback, said he was just joking, and that was the end of it. June was pleased to have caught this one on the spot.

You won't always catch things in the moment, but as soon as you realize a comment is hurtful or inappropriate, call the person up and inform him or her. For example, "Bob, did you realize that comment you made at lunch yesterday was rude? It's still on my mind. I ask that you apologize." Many people think it is too late and decide not to address it. This is fine if you can really let it go, but don't kid yourself. Most people are still harboring a grudge years later. The fact that June still remembered the dancing incident is a good indication that it hurt. If she had addressed it on the spot, I doubt she would even remember it. What a waste of energy. Better to be on the safe side and inform the other person as soon as you realize the offense.

If you are still thinking about some comment your cousin made fifteen years ago, better to address it now than to let it stew for another fifteen years. I'm serious about this. If you are still thinking about a comment or insult then you haven't forgiven the person. Here is how you resolve this once and for all. Call the person, tell him or her that something has been bothering you for a long time that you want to clear up, and then state in a calm tone the facts as you remember them. Just stick to the facts and don't add any emotion. The person may share with you his or her side of the story, or may not even remember the incident. Many people will graciously apologize. Some people might get defensive, in which case you probably weren't using a neutral tone of voice. It really doesn't matter how they respond. The point is for you to say what you haven't been saying all these years and ask for an apology or amends if appropriate. Then you can tell them that you forgive them.

For example, James was angry that his boss and colleagues hadn't allowed him to take a special vacation trip that his fiancée had given him as a present. She had booked a two-week trip to Israel over his birthday in order to introduce him to her family. Unfortunately, she had neglected to check the vacation dates with James's manager, and the dates were already taken by one of his colleagues. James explained the situation, but his colleague apologized and said her plans were already fixed. He asked all of his colleagues if they would be willing to switch their vacation dates, and all of them had similar stories. In the end James had to cancel the trip altogether. For three years he resented his colleagues although he had long since been promoted to a different department. I asked him to call these people up, state the facts, and ask them why they weren't willing to switch dates. He didn't want to do this assignment because he didn't think it would serve any purpose. I insisted he give it a try. He called up one colleague, said there was something he wanted to clear up, stated the facts of the situation, and asked why she hadn't been willing to change dates. She simply said that she had no idea it was so important to him and that, at the time, she really did think her plans were fixed, although they changed later. Suddenly James realized he was being resentful for nothing and wasting a whole lot of precious energy. He didn't even bother to call the other colleagues because the incident was cleared up in a single conversation. He realized he had been taking the incident personally when it wasn't personal at all.

At this point people usually ask, "Won't people just think that you are too sensitive?" They might. Tell them it is true, you *are* sensitive and would appreciate being treated with respect. There is absolutely nothing wrong with being sensitive. It enables you to feel and sense the subtler emotions and thoughts of others before they even do. The more sensitive you are, the bigger the boundaries you need, so make sure you establish some really big ones (Tip 5).

Sometimes my clients confuse boundaries with walls. A boundary simply defines what people can and can't do to you and actually enables people to get close to you. It's the people who *don't* have boundaries who get hurt by others and decide to protect themselves by putting up walls and barriers to keep people at arm's length. When you have strong boundaries in place, you automatically feel safer, which enables you to open up to the people who respect and honor your boundaries. A word of warning: some people won't be able to respect or honor your boundaries, and you may need to leave their presence, end the relationship, or even quit your job to work with people who respect you.

Other clients worry that they will be perceived as nitpickers or prima donnas who fuss over every little thing. Actually, it works in reverse. The more clearly, firmly, and immediately you address things, the less likely you will ever end up whining and complaining. After a while, you won't have to say anything at all because people will unconsciously sense that you have these boundaries and won't even think of crossing them. Think of people whose mere presence inspires you to automatically speak in a respectful manner. Then there are those people whom you are always poking fun at. The difference is strong boundaries. Remember, it is only when we allow a history of little abuses to occur that we lose our cool and come across as unprofessional. Politely nail them on the spot, and people won't mess with you—they will respect you.

Let me share with you an example from my experience in banking. I used to be the sales manager at one of the most notoriously difficult branches of my bank, which had some of the crankiest customers in the region. In the management training program I was taught that part of giving good customer service was letting customers vent their frustrations and then trying to help them. As the manager, I got the worst customers of all, the ones my customer service staff couldn't handle and sent up to me. I would spend a good part of every day listening to these customers yell and rant and rave about whatever was bothering them. I decided that I'd see if this boundaries stuff would work at the bank. Sure enough, the next morning in walked a slightly drunk, forty-five-year-old man who started by yelling at the customer service staff. I could hear him all the way from my office and decided to walk right out there and try my new skills. I came around and he started to yell at me about some problem with his account. I told him, in a perfectly neutral tone of voice, "Do you realize that you are yelling at me?" He said, still yelling, "I'm not mad at you, I'm mad at the bank!" I replied, "You are still yelling at me. I ask that you stop yelling immediately." (I moved it up to step 2— request.) He was completely taken aback, muttered something under his breath, and went to cash his check at the teller window. He then went over to the customer service desk and actually apologized to the customer service reps. Then he came back and apologized to me. I was stunned. The boundary stuff worked, and not only that, it was incredibly powerful. We resolved the initial problem and this customer left happy. It was unlikely that he would ever yell in our branch again. If I had let him rant and rave, as I was accustomed to before, he would not have left happy and would have repeated the behavior. This was very interesting indeed. I immediately taught my staff how to handle angry customers using this four-step model and the neutral tone of voice. Within weeks we had transformed the entire ambience of the branch. People just didn't yell anymore. In fact, it was more like a library where people walked around in hushed and respectful silence. Staff morale soared because they now had the tools to handle customers in a way that was professional and respectful. They had more energy to do the work and weren't dreading coming in every day to face an onslaught of tirades. This is so simple and yet incredibly effective. I've used this communication tool to help numerous organizations, from hospitals dealing with unhappy patients to law schools that needed help with disgruntled students expecting a job on graduation. Try it yourself and see.

8. RAISE YOUR STANDARDS

"Life is a process of becoming, a combination of states we have to go through. Where people fail is that they wish to elect a state and remain in it. This is a kind of death."

ANAÏS NIN

The flip side of boundaries is standards—the conduct you hold yourself to. It doesn't make much sense for you to have a boundary that people can't make derogatory remarks about you if you do this to others. The neat thing is that by extending your boundaries, you'll be raising your standards and vice versa. They go hand in hand. You can choose your standards. For example, I always tell the truth. I only give constructive feedback. I eat food that nourishes me. I never raise my voice. I always show up on time. I don't give advice unless asked. Choose the standards you are ready for, not the ones you think you "should" have. Make a list of people you admire. Write down their top qualities, and think about the standards of behavior they hold themselves to. Now write down the standards you'd like to adopt for yourself.

Paul, a busy publishing executive, used to always run late. He didn't even show up on time for his own staff meetings. Even his friends expected that he would be late. People often make the mistake of thinking that if they are always running late, people will assume they are busy and important. If people are waiting for you, then you are in some way controlling them. This was precisely what Paul was doing, unconsciously, in order to feel in control. A very annoying habit. I asked Paul to raise his standards to always be early to appointments and meetings. For the first time, he actually showed up early for his own meeting, and sure enough all of his staff arrived late and were really surprised to see him sitting there waiting for them. A few people even made a comment or two to that effect. It will take a few times before people realize that he is now punctual, but they are already taking him more seriously.

Standards are equally important in your personal life. Margo, an extremely attractive client in the fashion business, consistently complained that she seemed to attract guys who didn't treat her well. One fellow in particular, an ex-boyfriend, would call her up and invite her over for pizza and a video at his place. The unstated invitation was also for sex. Not having anything else planned, she would go and invariably feel terrible about herself afterward—used, cheap, worthless. I told her this wasn't the case. She was a stunning blonde, fun to be with, and there was nothing wrong with her. Margo's problem was simply a matter of low standards. The next week she couldn't get this thought out of her mind. Low standards! When the ex-boyfriend called again, she declined the invitation and jokingly said, not believing it herself, "No thanks. I've got standards." In the next few weeks she started to attract nice guys who wanted to take her out to dinner and who treated her with respect and courtesy. She had raised her standard to "I only go out with people who treat me extremely well." Often having standards is simply a matter of saying so.

9. It's All Good, Even the Bad Stuff

"I don't have a warm personal enemy left. They've all died off. I miss them terribly because they helped define me."

Clare Boothe Luce

"What seems nasty, painful, evil, can become a source of beauty, joy and strength, if faced with an open mind. Every moment is a golden one for him who has the vision to recognize it as such."

Henry Miller

It is easier to have a positive attitude if you realize that everything is good, even the bad stuff. In order to fully appreciate the good things in life, we almost have to experience their opposites. Take happiness, for example. If you were never sad, would happiness be so rich? You couldn't choose goodness, if it weren't for evil. As a colleague of mine always said, "Bad things don't happen to us; we attract them to us so we can learn a lesson."

When I was five, I had terribly painful earaches and was often confined to bed. Being a very active tomboy, I hated having to lie in bed, and the pain was terrible. I remember lying in bed, wishing I could go outside and play. Then one day I realized that being sick had one redeeming feature: if I had never gotten sick, I wouldn't have appreciated how marvelous it was to be well. This applies to everything in life. If it were always sunny outside, you would take the fine weather for granted. When it rains, you really learn to appreciate those lovely sunny days. In a sense then, all things become good. You need sickness to know health. You need rain to know sun. You need evil to know good. You need anger to fully know joy. Since I realized this when I was five, I naturally assumed that everyone saw things the same way I did. Now I see that very few people do. A positive outlook has numerous advantages:

- Instead of complaining, you make the most of your current situation.
- You won't get stuck in bad situations for long because you aren't resisting them. What you resist persists. Instead you will simply take action.
- You will be more accepting of the emotions you experience. When you are sad, you will fully experience the sadness. When you are angry, you will be angry. When you are happy, you will enjoy the happiness.
- You won't be so judgmental about events. Life is life. It is just what's happening. Everything that happens is instructive in one way or another. It is all part of the grand experience. In a world where no one ever got sick, no one would appreciate health. Everyone would take it for granted. Maybe the "bad" things happen so you will be grateful for the good things. Just an idea.

In any case, optimistic people tend to be happier and more successful in life, so why not give optimism a try? Start looking for the good in all the bad. Consider it a challenge.

I read an interesting story in the *Wall Street Journal* about the flooding that ravaged Missouri in 1993. The headline was "Watershed Event:

Business Revitalization in One Missouri Town Has Flood as Its Source. Chesterfield Employers Use a Deluge as Opportunity to Rebuild Companies." The town of Chesterfield was devastated when the Missouri River overfilled the levee and flooded everything, forcing 2,500 people to leave. A few people tried to save their businesses, including a Mr. Hoffman, who desperately tried to shore up his auto parts business to no avail. By morning, his plant was submerged, and he had to escape through a second-story window. The company sustained $33 million in damages and only a third of the loss was covered by insurance. The Chesterfield disaster was part of the massive flooding that hit the Midwest in 1993 and was so destructive that one-third of business owners abandoned their ruined firms and left for good. Three years later, those who stuck it out said business was booming *because* of the flood! "Most positive thing that ever happened," said Mr. Hoffman, whose company's payroll increased from 125 to 350. A landscape equipment distributor who had suffered $500,000 in uninsured damages said, "The flood was a good thing."

Although natural disasters take an enormous toll emotionally and physically on the community, the article said, the Chesterfield experience showed that when "business owners treat a natural disaster as an obstacle to overcome instead of the tragic end to their firms, the results can be surprising. . . . At some companies, the physical strain of the cleanup chased off lazy employees but created an intense bond among workers who remained. At others, surviving the crisis either instilled new self confidence to expand operations or deeply impressed customers, who then decided to place larger orders. Faced with rebuilding, some owners restructured operations, bought better equipment, or made investments they had been postponing." So you see, it's all good, even the bad stuff. It just depends how you look at it.

10. Have Something to Look Forward to Every Day

"Life isn't all beer and skittles, but beer and skittles, or something better of the same sort, must form a good part of every Englishman's education."

Thomas Hughes, *Tom Brown's School Days*

It is amazing how quickly our lives can become drab and colorless if we do not have something to look forward to. We wait far too long for that once-a-year vacation or that special event. That just isn't enough. Or it might be enough, but being successful is not about having just enough— it's about abundance. You need an abundance of good things to look forward to—as a bare minimum at least one thing every day. And don't overlook the simple things, which are often the most rewarding.

To get you thinking, here are some things you could look forward to: a half hour alone, a walk in the woods with your significant other, a bike ride through the park, bringing a beautiful bouquet of fresh flowers home to your husband or wife, renting an old movie and eating popcorn with your buddies, taking a bubble bath with your rubber ducky or, better yet, your honey bunny. Crack open a bottle of champagne and celebrate the sunset. Tinker with the car in the garage. Buy flowers for your office to brighten up your day. Write in your journal or diary. Bring in chocolate kisses and pass them around to everyone at the office. Play a round of golf. Call a friend you haven't heard from in a while. Take your assistant out for lunch. Take your boss out to lunch or for a drink after work. Ride your Harley. Buy a magazine you've never read before. Eat your favorite fried chicken dinner with mashed potatoes. Enjoy lunch with a friend from work. See a play, an opera, or a jazz band. Get a manicure on your lunch break. Hire a housekeeper so that you have a clean house when you open your door after a long day at work. Try out a new restaurant. Every day you need something to look forward to. Put it in your calendar if you have to, but make sure you have something special to look forward to every day. This will make even the drabbest of days more fun and keep you from slipping into the doldrums or from losing your appreciation for life. There are so many wonderful things to enjoy about life.

Sometimes, instead of lots of little things, one big thing to look forward to can make all the difference. Byron, a fifty-six-year-old business owner, found his days so busy and so full of work that he felt he had no time for play or fun stuff. He was depressed and seeing a psychiatrist. I suggested that he create something to look forward to that would make life worth living. He was not terribly optimistic. But then, almost miraculously, he found a house in the mountains that he loved. It inspired him. Byron thought he'd be able to write a book in this house, it was in such a beautiful part of the country. He bought the house and his whole attitude shifted. He had something to look forward to, a goal that made life worth living. Now even though he is still facing some difficult challenges ahead, Byron feels that even in the worst case, he could make it through the experience because he has this house in the mountains to move into. While this is an extreme case, it shows the importance of having something to look forward to every day of your life.

Marjorie had a great life. She shared a beautiful home with a loving and supportive boyfriend. She was starting an exciting new business that she loved, and she was taking courses that interested her. But she discovered that she didn't want to get out of bed in the morning. I suggested she design an ideal morning. Next week she shared it with me: She would get up at 8:00 A.M. and do a twenty-minute meditation. Then she would go for a half-hour walk in the woods around her house. After that she would shower and have fresh-baked muffins and hot tea out on the veranda while she wrote in her journal. She realized that she needed quiet time alone in the morning to collect her thoughts and make her plans for the day. Marjorie also realized that all of the elements of her ideal morning were possible to do every day. Now Marjorie is glad to get up and start the day because she gives herself the time to enjoy it.

What is your ideal morning? What about your ideal evening? What would your life be like if every day you started with an ideal morning and ended with an ideal evening? Treat yourself with as many elements of your ideal day as possible, **and you will be happier and more energized** throughout the day. Take a few minutes right now to write down in vivid detail your ideal day from the moment you wake up in the morning until you fall asleep at night. Remember, this is your *ideal*, so don't limit yourself in any way. (My ideal morning has a maid knocking on my door and bringing in fresh croissants, fruit, and a pot of hot tea. This hasn't happened—yet!)

II.

··

CLEAN UP YOUR ACT

*"Space is almost infinite. As a matter of fact, we
think it is infinite."*

DAN QUAYLE

IN PART I you increased your natural power by eliminating the energy
drains and adding energy boosters. Now it is time to create the space for
what you want. The more successful you become, the more you will
attract, so you had better make some room. Otherwise, where on earth
are you going to put it? One super-busy executive said he wanted a woman
in his life. I asked him when he would have time to see a woman—his
schedule was already overbooked.

If you want a new relationship, you may need to let go of an old one
first. If you want a new client, it may be time to clean out your files at
work. If you'd like some new clothes, go clean out that closet. Anytime
you want something new to come into your life, create some space for it.
In fact, it really doesn't even matter what you get rid of. After all, matter at its essence is simply energy so *anything* you throw out will give you
more space. You can clean out the garage and get a new business client.
Ever notice how great you feel after you clean out the closet? This is not
hocus-pocus, mumbo jumbo. This principle is based on a law of physics:

nature abhors a vacuum. Create a vacuum and the universe will quickly send new things to fill your empty space.

11. UNCLUTTER YOUR LIFE

"The pleasure of possession whether we possess trinkets or off-spring—or possibly books or chessmen, or postage stamps—lies in showing these things to friends who are experiencing no immediate urge to look at them."

AGNES REPPLIER

Would you like something new and wonderful to come into your life? A new job, a new friend, an opportunity? A relationship? One of the easiest, most effective ways to attract something new into your life is to create the space. If you feel stuck, start clearing the decks. Go through your files at the office and toss out all those old memos, reports, and articles you've been saving in case you need them someday. The easiest way to get ruthless is to imagine that you are being promoted and are relocating to another office. I was amazed at one of the sales managers at my bank. She was given a job managing a different team of people, and when she cleaned out her desk, all she had to take with her was one small manila folder. I asked how she managed that, and she said the new department would have all the information she needed there. She was right of course, but I was very impressed—most people end up packing two to six boxes of binders, reports, files, memos, and personal objects they will probably never use. Spend a half hour to an hour a day for a week just clearing out junk, and you'll be amazed at how much useless paper you've accumulated. When you do get promoted, you'll be ready to go.

Once you've tackled the office, start clearing the decks at home. Your home is a sacred space where you need to relax and recharge so you have the energy to tackle your work. If you come home to a cluttered and uncomfortable space, you aren't giving yourself a chance to fully recharge your batteries. If you are like me and have the instincts of a pack rat, you may need some help in this process. Start with the inspiring book *Clutter Control*, by Jeff Campbell. Then enlist the help of a friend or hire a professional organizer. The best thing to ask yourself is, "Have I used this in the past six months?" If the answer is no and it isn't a seasonal thing like Christmas ornaments, then out it goes. This isn't easy, but you'll get better with practice. It is easier to start with a trusted and ruthless friend who will say supportive things like, "That handbag does not live up to your great new look," or, "Just how many makeup cases do you think you need?" or, "Hmm . . . I didn't know you played tennis. Just how many years has it been since you've picked up that racket?" Before you have a chance to change your mind, cart everything off to a local charity and get a tax receipt. If you put it in the garage, you will be tempted to go back in there in the middle of the night and start pulling things out of the bag. I threw out a pile of old love letters and then slipped down late in the night to rescue them from the trash. Okay, so I'm a bit sentimental. If you can't bear parting with some sentimental items try this idea from one of my seminar participants: create a "Band-Aid Box" full of special things that make you feel good. Whenever you feel bummed out or discouraged, look through your box and get an instant boost. (Old love letters can remind you that you are lovable and loved.) If you don't know where to begin the uncluttering process, start in the left-hand corner of your bedroom and do one room at a time. Getting rid of clutter is incredibly therapeutic and will give you a huge burst of energy. That is why we start the coaching program here—so you have the newfound energy to tackle your really big goals.

Many clients who come to me feeling stuck are almost too tired to get out of the rut. They don't realize that the clutter is sapping their energy. Ninety percent of the time they have clutter in their lives, even if it isn't visible. When I was doing a seminar abroad, I was invited to stay with one of my clients in her home. She had an immaculate, white, spacious, modern home that was lovely to look at. I didn't think she had much clutter to clear out judging from the surface of things. But when I commented that she had done a great job, she admitted she had tons of papers, books, and magazines neatly stashed away in her closets behind closed doors. She spent the next few weeks tossing out old magazines, donating books she would never read again to friends and the local library, and cleaning out papers from her files. Within one month she was offered two different jobs, and the opportunity to go into business with a friend. Suddenly she was unstuck. The most amazing thing to me was that she decided to sell her beautiful home in London and move to the shore. Freeing the house of clutter gave her the energy to attract and respond to new and better career opportunities and even freed her of the house itself, which, though lovely, was keeping her tied to a job she didn't like due to the hefty mortgage payments.

Once you create some space, the universe will try to fill it, so be careful to say "No, thank you" if what comes along isn't what you really want. For instance, be very careful before you agree to store things for friends and family. If you do agree to store things, make sure you set a specific time limit and decide what will happen to the items if the time limit is exceeded.

As you create an abundance of space, there is more room for good things to come into your life. Make this a formal ritual. Load up a bag of clothes that don't fit or are out of style or that aren't flattering and take them to charity. Drop off the bag and silently say, "I am getting rid of the old to make way for something new and better to come into my life." It sounds corny, but every time I do a thorough cleaning, I get a new client. It all goes back to energy—you are freeing up the energy attached to your belongings, allowing room for the new.

12. KEEP ON UNCLUTTERING

"Never underestimate the effect of clutter on your life."

KAREN KINGSTON, *CREATING*
SACRED SPACE WITH FENG SHUI

If you come from a long line of pack rats, you won't be able to unclutter your office or home in just one or two days. Keep asking yourself, "Is there anything in my house or storage that I do not need?" That is the acid test. It is amazing how much a body can accumulate over the years. Just like losing weight, it isn't rational to expect it all to come off overnight. I was much encouraged when I read that Alexandra Stoddard, the author of *Living a Beautiful Life*, unclutters on a monthly basis. This is an ongoing process. Like anything else, it gets easier with practice. Soon you will recognize the red flags and catch yourself saying, "Hmm . . .

this might be useful one day . . ." or, "This reminds me of someone I love," and you will automatically know it should *definitely* go into the garbage.

The cleaning process seems to perpetuate itself. Once you realize you can live without stuff, it is easier to make a second and third pass and reevaluate objects you wouldn't have thought of tossing earlier. My client Ed, on his first pass, threw out stuff he hadn't used in one year. Now he is looking at stuff he hasn't used in six months. He ended up giving the slow cooker to one sister and the food processor to the other. Ed had all these kitchen appliances in his coat closet because his kitchen is the size of a peanut. This led to an interesting phenomenon: he began to value the space more than the stuff. In fact, he started to feel that things were invading his space.

This was a major turnaround for a die-hard pack rat who kept things worth ten cents at a garage sale. More benefits started to accrue. His file drawer at work actually had room for new documents. When he was looking for something, he could find it within minutes instead of wasting countless hours digging through stacks of papers on his desk. At home, Ed could open the closet door without anything falling down and hitting him on the head. His thinking got clearer, and he started noticing things around him that he hadn't noticed before. Then he met a woman he liked and, for a change, wasn't ashamed to invite her to his home after a romantic night out. He kept reminding himself that stuff is just stuff. This Chinese proverb keeps things in perspective: "To pretend to satisfy one's desires by possession is like using straw to put out a fire."

One simple trick that helped me get rid of unnecessary stuff was to keep only two extras. What a revelation! It takes all the guesswork out of getting rid of the clutter. Even after eliminating the obvious clutter, I felt claustrophobic in my own home, weighed down by all the stuff. Even though it was pretty nice stuff it was suffocating. Having too much of everything can be just as bad as too little. I felt ready for another pass. I had six pillows on my full-size bed, plus three decorative throw pillows. According to the "Only Two Extras" formula, I needed two pillows for myself and two extras for guests. That equals four pillows. I immediately gave two pillows to a friend who only had two. I applied the same principle to my linens. I have one bed and therefore need only three sheet sets. I immediately got rid of all the incomplete sets, picked my favorite three, and gave the rest to charity. Suddenly I had a very spacious linen chest. It is so simple and easy. You'll streamline your house in a flash using this "Two Extras" formula. Try it in the kitchen—I got rid of a pile of coffee mugs with silly slogans on them. It is a quick way to create an instant reserve of space. Don't forget the office. Give one of your colleagues that automatic pencil sharpener you never use. Instead of a drawer full of cheap pens, keep three that you really like. You will feel lighter immediately.

This explains the cliché "less is more." Less stuff equals more energy for you. This might also explain the tendency of spiritual types to go about in loincloths. They understand this principle. Being one who rather likes stuff, I'm not suggesting that you go to this extreme, but that you keep only those things you really enjoy. Just make sure you get rid of the belongings that no longer represent you or enhance your life. It might be a useful vase, but do you really *love* it? Often one lovely vase on a shelf is more stunning than five vases jammed together. Pass things on to someone who will use and appreciate them. Start getting rid of little things—clothes, furniture, books—and it will be easier to get rid of the big things—an unfulfilling job or a relationship that isn't right for you.

13. SIMPLIFY! SIMPLIFY! SIMPLIFY!

"Simplicity! Simplicity! Simplicity! I say, let your affairs be as two or three, and not a hundred or a thousand; instead of a million count half a dozen, and keep your accounts on your thumb-nail."

HENRY DAVID THOREAU

Now that you've lightened your material load, you might want to take a look at some other ways to simplify your life. If you feel your schedule is too busy, overcrowded with stuff to do and people to meet, it is time to simplify. Everything in your life takes up a certain amount of your energy, whether it is actual physical stuff or work, social obligations, and family commitments. The more energy you have available, the more successful and attractive you'll become. Most people think that being super busy and having an overbooked schedule is a sign of success. What they don't realize is that they are too busy to notice what is happening around them and may miss key opportunities. This is a powerful incentive to be extremely selective about how you use your time and energy. Successful people book a reserve of time in their schedules so that they have a buffer zone when things don't go according to plan (which is the way most things go, so you might as well account for it from the start).

The best little book I've seen on the subject is *Simplify Your Life*, by Elaine St. James. She suggests such things as consolidating your checking accounts, moving to a smaller house, getting rid of the lawn and putting in ground cover, buying in bulk, dropping call-waiting, getting rid of your nail polish, building a simple wardrobe, getting up an hour earlier, and a whole host of other practical pointers to help you simplify every area of your life.

You can also take advantage of technology to simplify your life—but make sure it actually saves you time. One client, Donald, a busy real estate broker, was always on the road and was continually stopping to check his voice mail at the office. He invested in a cellular phone and now receives all his calls immediately. This simplified his life immensely, and he feels much calmer knowing he won't miss an important call. However, another client who also had a cell phone felt she never had a moment of privacy and that people could get her anywhere. She simplified her life by getting rid of her phone and using a regular answering machine instead. Make sure the latest advances in technology *improve* the quality of your life. It is easy to get caught up in the latest trend without evaluating whether a product or service fits your unique needs and lifestyle.

Another client, a recruiter on the road three to four days out of the week, discovered that on-line banking was a great way to simplify her life. She can pay her bills and check her account from her portable computer while she is on the road. She used to come home and spend her weekends updating her accounts; now she does this in the hotel so her weekends are free for fun stuff. Thomas ran a small consulting business from his home office and was still doing all his bookkeeping manually. Every quarter it would take him a good day to figure out his sales tax, and he was annoyed that he had to waste his time doing such tedious work. I suggested he buy some good accounting software and invest in a few hours for a computer specialist to come over, set up the program for him, and show him how to use it. There is no point in struggling through the manuals for hours by yourself when you can have an expert show you how to do it. Thomas was thrilled with the results. Now with a few keystrokes he knows exactly what sales tax is due, and he can fill out the tax form in five minutes. In addition, he can immediately create a balance sheet, a profit and loss sheet, and any number of reports to track his business growth. Thomas also saves money on his accountant because his records are in such good order.

What are some ways you could simplify your life? Think of ways you can automate and leverage the latest advances in technology to streamline your life. Now list ten ways you could start to simplify your life today.

14. HIRE A HOUSEKEEPER

"Invisible, repetitive, exhausting, unproductive, uncreative— these are the adjectives which most perfectly capture the nature of housework."

ANGELA DAVIS

One quick and easy way to clean up your act is to get someone else to do it. If you love cleaning the house, this suggestion is not for you. However, if you are like me and don't particularly enjoy scrubbing the toilet, even if you could find the time for it, then hire a housekeeper. I didn't think I could afford to hire a housekeeper at $40 a visit. After graduation, I was paying off credit card debts and student loans, living in a small one-bedroom apartment in Manhattan. I was brought up to do chores, and my mom never had a housekeeper. I resisted this idea and kept thinking I should be able to do it myself. One Saturday I realized that my weekends were precious, and I deserved to relax and play all weekend. I also realized that I was never going to find the time to clean the place myself. I broke down and hired a housekeeper to clean once a month. This was one of the best things I ever did for myself. I would come home from work and everything was sparkling. I didn't have to clean! Then I found myself doing a little straightening before she came, and I realized that I had too many knickknacks around. I put them in a box in the closet. This spawned an uncluttering process that lasted a year (Tip 11). A few months later I hired her to come in twice a month. Now my home is always clean, and I never have to worry about inviting guests over. This is a gift to myself, a way that I take extremely good care of myself. I decided I couldn't afford *not* to hire a housekeeper. Even if you think you can't afford it, it will free you up to find a higher-paying job or get the training and education you need to earn a better salary.

I am always astounded at the number of successful, well-educated, dual-income families with kids that are still doing the housework themselves. And then they come to me complaining that they don't have time. What a ridiculous waste of time and energy. I know of a single waiter in Manhattan who hired a housekeeper even though he was only making a few dollars more per hour than his housekeeper. He knew it was worth it to him. Another client, a professional speaker, decided that during the three hours he had the housekeeper over he would make outgoing sales calls and follow up with prospective clients. He felt this was the only way he could justify the housekeeping expense. The next day, he received a callback and booked a speaking gig for $1,200—not a bad return for a $50 investment in a housekeeper.

Stop trying to do everything and start delegating everything you possibly can. The peace of mind and the sense of being taken care of is well worth the money spent. Now, some people say they enjoy cleaning the house. The danger of cleaning your own house is that it may give you the illusion that you are accomplishing something when in reality your time would be better spent working on your big goals and dreams. You could spend your whole life just cleaning house and never get around to writing that screenplay, taking sailing lessons, or staying connected with friends and family.

15. Don't Be Afraid to Hire Help

"The difference between the rich and poor is that the poor do everything with their own hands and the rich hire hands to do things."

BETTY SMITH

Don't be afraid to hire help. This may also mean that you need to delegate some tasks. Men tend to be better at delegating than women; they don't usually feel guilty about hiring a housekeeper, a personal trainer, or an administrative assistant. In contrast, women tend to think they have to do it all. One of my clients was in a complete dither because she had to give a ten-minute presentation on her lunch hour, attend a sales presentation of new computer software, and take the cat to the vet. She had scheduled all this on her lunch hour! This is the wonder woman mentality at work. I asked her why she was taking the cat to the vet—was it dreadfully ill? No, her husband couldn't and the cat needed its annual shots. Mind you, this client is an extremely bright woman with an income in the top 10 percent of the country. She works full time and is starting a business on the side, and has a husband and two small children. She feels like she has to do it all—star employee, wife, mom, housekeeper, businesswoman, and gourmet chef. She's been doing it all, but at the tremendous cost to herself of added stress, frequent colds, exhaustion, and frustration.

I asked her to arrange her schedule to work *for* her and eliminate ten things she thought she had to do that week. She rescheduled the vet appointment, moved the sales presentation to another day, and suddenly her life was a whole lot easier. In order to do something well, you need the time and the space to do it. Hire the housekeeper, hire the babysitter, send out the laundry. Get the support systems in place that will free you up to do what you really love. Hire a tutor instead of trying to learn a new software program on your own. Yes, there is an initial expense, but in the long run, the time and frustration saved will be well worth it.

Anytime you catch yourself struggling and frustrated, ask yourself how you could delegate the task or get the training to make it effortless. When I was pulling my hair out trying to do my taxes, I realized that it might be worth it to delegate this unpleasant task to someone who actually likes to do it. (Hard to believe, but yes, some people actually enjoy doing taxes.) I hired a bookkeeper and an accountant. What a relief! For every job you don't like or aren't very good at, there is an expert who loves to do it and does it well. My bookkeeper loves to balance the accounts, and she does it with a certain zeal. I can't say I feel the same way about it. It makes sense to let the person who loves to do taxes do *your* taxes. This in turn gives you the time and energy to do what *you* love to do.

16. Perfect the Present

"Paradise is where I am."

Voltaire

"Time past and time future
What might have been and what has been
Point to one end, which is always present."

T. S. Eliot

If you have the "not enough" conversation—not enough money, not enough time, not enough space—there is something you need to learn. Life is a master teacher. If you catch yourself saying, "I don't have enough (fill in the blank)," there is something imperfect about your present situation. Yet one of the principles we use in coaching is that the present is perfect. Something has to give, and it isn't going to be the principle. For example, when I was up to my eyeballs in debt, I thought I didn't have enough money. If not enough money is the problem, then the solution seems to be to make more money. This wasn't happening as fast as I was spending. Then one day I realized that the debt was a good thing—getting out of debt would require that I change the way I handled money. I was supposed to *learn* something here. The challenge was to learn how to save and to stop spending like a banshee. I realized that when I did come into big money, I would know how to handle it responsibly instead of frittering it away on meaningless things. In three years I went from being in debt to having a year's worth of living expenses in savings (Tip 24). I had learned the money lesson.

Then I was sitting in my lovely New York apartment where I had all my worldly possessions in three rooms and guess what the conversation was? Not enough space. A pattern emerges. Since the present is perfect, how could this be? Clearly I needed to learn how to live with less stuff. What about my office with those piles of papers? The problem wasn't the lack of space, but rather that I needed to learn how to handle paper only once. The problem becomes a challenge and a game. The interesting thing is that once you master the game, you usually get rewarded. When I learned how to live with less stuff, I ended up living in a spacious place.

Why I needed to learn to handle this I don't know, but instead of moaning about the lack of storage space, I made the present perfect and tossed like crazy. What is your "not enough" conversation? What new skills and habits do you need to learn? Start perfecting your present situation now.

17. STOP SHUFFLING AND START ORGANIZING

"One must live the way one thinks or end up thinking the way one has lived."

PAUL BOURGET

Take the time to invest in setting up systems to make your life even easier. Many of my corporate and professional clients feel they don't have time to organize; they are too busy. As a result, they work in cluttered, crazy, paper-piled environments. Big mistake. What they don't realize is that they will be twice as productive when they get organized. Today's workers report that they spend almost half their working day shuffling papers around. One survey of fourteen companies in seven different industries revealed that senior executives spend 46 percent of their time on unnecessary paperwork, middle managers 45 percent, professionals 40 percent, and clerical support staff 51 percent. What an appalling waste of time! It is time to stop shuffling and start organizing.

Start by blocking off one hour a week strictly for organizing, systematizing, or automating, *not* for doing the actual work. You might spend this hour setting up a system to handle a manual procedure. For example, you might spend an hour training your assistant how to do a task that you have been doing or designing a computer spreadsheet that will automatically calculate what you've been doing by hand. Set up direct debit for your bills instead of writing checks month after month. The time you invest up front to set up a system will pay back big dividends in future time saved. Spend fifteen minutes filing papers, tossing out old papers, or just clearing off your desk. The more you automate, systematize, and organize, the more time you'll have for the interesting projects.

Here is a trick I learned from one of my coaching colleagues. She couldn't tame the paper tiger until she tossed out her in-box. What a radical concept! She discovered that not having a box to stuff papers into forced her to deal with each piece of paper on the spot. She used the TRAF method—Toss it, Refer it to someone else (delegate it if possible), Act on it, or File it. Things that couldn't be handled the same day were put in a pending file or in a file for that particular project. As a side benefit, she was able to find what she needed in a fraction of the time now that she didn't have to sort through stacks of papers in her box. She made a policy of clearing everything off her desk every day. It gave her a sense of completion and accomplishment for the day, and the next morning she didn't feel weighed down by the piles of paper. The average office worker has a backlog of about forty hours of paperwork and typically spends twenty minutes every day looking for something in that pile. Use that twenty minutes filing and organizing instead and you'll gain ten full days of work in a year.

One client spends an hour every morning with his assistant going over everything that might come up during the day. Then the rest of the day goes by like a dream without problems or interruptions. Spend one hour a day organizing your work. You will be thrilled at how much time this frees up. Not only will you feel happier, but you will be twice as productive the rest of the day or week. Setting aside time to organize is essential to success.

18. Just Say No, and Say It Often

"A peacefulness follows any decision, even the wrong one."

Rita Mae Brown

Now that you've created a vacuum by uncluttering your life (Tip 11) and have extra time, watch out. All sorts of people, invitations, and opportunities will come into your life. This doesn't mean you have to say yes to any or all of them. Be picky. Some people worry that if they say "No, thank you" it will end the flow of new opportunities. Actually, it is the reverse. You will be maintaining the space for the right opportunities and relationships.

Many of my clients constantly get themselves overcommitted with work and social obligations because they say yes instead of no. Women in particular tend to have a need to please and to be liked. This is a cultural phenomenon—women are raised to be good while men are raised to be right. As a result, it is usually harder for women to say no, and it handily explains why men don't like to ask for directions (they are supposed to know already). The assignment I give my chronic "yes" clients is to go to the opposite extreme for one week and say no to every offer or request. If they change their minds later, they can go back and say yes, but the first response is no. "No." "No, but thanks for asking." Even extremely successful women have difficulty with this assignment, but it breaks the "yes" habit. They begin to see that the earth won't crumble around their feet if they say no. Their friends won't leave them, and their dog will still love them.

If you just can't seem to say no, try buying some time and say, "Thank you for the invitation; may I think about it and let you know tomorrow?" Often it is difficult to determine on the spot whether you really want to do something, and our initial response is usually to please the other person, which produces a "yes" when you really mean "no." If you give yourself some time to think about it, you can call back the next day and accept, decline, or counteroffer. If you receive a wedding invitation or an invitation to a special event, you don't automatically have to go. Think about it a day or two and if you really would enjoy it, then go. Of course, if you are dying to do it, just say yes!

Janet was a chronic "yes" case. She felt that if her boss asked her to do something she had to say yes, or she would be seen as a poor employee. As a result, she had taken on too many projects and was inundated with work. When she hired me, she was worried that she might even lose her job because she had just turned in an important project a few days late. Her boss was extremely displeased and told her she would have to do better at meeting her deadlines. Janet explained to him that she was busy working on another project that she thought was more important and hadn't had time to get to this assignment. He said she would have to stop making excuses and get down to business. Naturally, Janet was upset. I suggested she go back to her boss with a list of all the projects she was currently working on and ask him to help her prioritize her work. Then, whenever anyone asked her to work on another project, she could simply say, "No, I can't take that on right now, as I'm working on XYZ project." If her boss came up to her with another assignment, she could simply ask, "Does this take priority over XYZ project? If I take this on, I will need an extension on XYZ." Your boss may not be aware of all the different things you are working on at any one time, and it is very helpful to point these facts out and ask him or her to determine the priority for you. You want to appear to be a team player eager to take on new projects, but you also want to make sure you don't overextend yourself and get into hot water by doing poor work.

Clients who have trouble saying no at work usually have trouble saying no in their personal lives too. Jean complained that, except for a handful of old friends, she didn't have much of a social life. I asked if she had time for a social life. She realized that she didn't and started saying no to requests to volunteer in order to keep her evenings free for socializing. Jean had always felt that if someone asked her to do something and she wasn't busy or scheduled with something else, she should do it. This kept her very busy doing things for other people, and she had built up a reputation as being very helpful and nice, but it left her with no time to work on her own life. At the same time she didn't feel she could say no to friends and acquaintances. We took a few minutes to craft some responses so Jean would have them ready when someone called. We decided she would say, "Thank you so much for thinking of me. I feel honored that you would want me to [serve on the board at the local children's hospital, manage the charity booth at the craft fair, etc.], however I must decline. Perhaps so-and-so would be interested." Jean used to think she had to have an excuse, but she didn't want to lie to her friends. I told her she didn't have to lie, and she didn't have to give any reasons or justifications. It is sufficient reason that she just doesn't want to. If one of her friends pressed her, she could simply say, "I'm not interested in working on that project," or "I'm working on other projects at this time."

We worked on the broken record technique, an idea from Manuel J. Smith's classic book, *When I Say No, I Feel Guilty*. No matter how the other person responds, you just keep repeating your statement in a neutral, low-key tone. For example, "Oh, but we really need you and you did such a great job last year." Jean would simply respond again, "Thank you. I was glad to help out last year, however I must decline this year." "Oh, but what will we do without you?"(She is laying a guilt trip on Jean.) "Thanks again for thinking so highly of me, however I really must decline." Jean felt really comfortable with this manner of saying no because she wanted to honor her friends, but she also wanted some time to work on her own life. The next day she received a call from a friend asking her to help plan her daughter's wedding, and Jean gracefully declined. Her friend wasn't hurt, and Jean didn't get burdened with yet another project.

Out of the blue, two friends Jean hadn't seen in over a year called and said they realized how much they had enjoyed her company, and would she like to renew the friendship? She did, and they made plans together. It seems uncanny, but it works. Try it yourself and see who comes into your life. If it isn't who or what you wanted, just say "No thanks."

Now, I'm not suggesting that you don't do any volunteer or charity work. I often encourage my clients to volunteer in order to find the fulfillment missing in their daily work. It is good and incredibly rewarding to help others for the pure joy of it. Just make sure you aren't volunteering to the detriment of your own life. One client, Theresa, was volunteering full time and working on her business part time. She had racked up $10,000 in credit card debt in the process. I pointed out that she needed to take care of herself before she devoted so much time to others. She couldn't afford to volunteer and needed to get a paying job until she could get her business off the ground. Once she paid off her debts and got her business into good shape, she could start volunteering again. This coaching program will help you free up time, space, and money so that it will be natural for you to give generously to the charities and organizations you want to support.

19. UPGRADE YOUR ROLODEX

"As if you could kill time without injuring eternity."

HENRY DAVID THOREAU, *WRITINGS*

Don't hang around with people just to kill time or because they happen to be the only friends you have. Either you fully enjoy them or you don't spend time with them. Do not accept anything less. This may mean that you need to let go of some relationships, which isn't always easy. It could be that you have grown and changed; while your friend was fun to be with at one time, this may not be true anymore. Sometimes we end up staying with people out of habit and stay in a relationship much longer than necessary. This costs you vitality and will make it harder for you to attract people you really enjoy. You don't need to make a big deal out of it. Just drift away, stop hanging around with them, even if it means doing things by yourself for a while.

One client, Joe, had a friend who was loads of fun to hang around with but had turned somewhat flaky over the past year. She would cancel plans at the last minute or say she would come to dinner and never show up. Joe decided he didn't need a friend like this so he used the four-step model (Tip 6) to inform his friend that her behavior was not acceptable. Unfortunately, the friend didn't change so Joe stopped making plans or calling her. They still bump into each other occasionally, but there are no hard feelings, he has just moved on. A few months later, Joe met a new and terrific friend, and then two old friends from college moved into town. He found himself with an abundance of truly great and loving friends.

If you actively engage in this coaching process, it is highly likely that you will be letting some old friends go and making new friends. Life is too short to waste with people who aren't willing to treat you with love and respect. Create the space for new friends and colleagues who inspire you and love you.

20. Feng Shui Your Home and Office

"No money is better spent than what is laid out for domestic satisfaction."

Samuel Johnson

Feng shui (pronounced "fung shway") is an ancient Chinese art of arranging your environment so that it is most favorable to your well-being physically and financially. Word is getting out in the western world about feng shui, which has been practiced for thousands of years in the East. A feng shui master knows what you need to do to create a harmonious environment that will increase your energy and success.

After attending a course on feng shui, I discovered that I needed to move my office desk to the opposite side of the room. The northwest wall was the most favorable direction for business success. Since moving my desk, my business has grown exponentially. In addition, this particular furniture arrangement turned out to be the best yet. The room feels more spacious than before even though there is more furniture. This is the magic of feng shui.

Anne, a psychiatrist, was worried about her business and always felt financially strapped. She hired me to help her increase her business and make more money. She had recently moved into a new home, and I suggested that she hire a feng shui master to really make it the best for her. The week after the master's visit, Anne called, ecstatic with the results. She had made some minor, relatively inexpensive changes in her home, and it had made a huge difference in how she felt. In one week she had three new therapy clients, and they were all on the intensive program, which meant she would be seeing each of them three to five hours a week. This was a tremendous leap in her business practically overnight. She felt prosperous, successful, and happy. Her new feeling of prosperity and success has given her a burst of energy, which she is using to create a marketing plan for her business.

Here are a few practical tips that come from feng shui:

- Make sure all your doors open and close easily without obstruction. This includes closet doors that might not open fully because of clothes hanging on them. (I had to move a shelf in the bathroom because the bathroom door only opened partially before hitting the shelf. Now the bathroom looks much more spacious.)
- If your windows look out at a cemetery or hospital, cover them with shades or curtains.
- If you do not have a window in your bathroom, put a mirror on the opposite wall facing the vanity mirror. This is said to increase air circulation.
- Never design or buy a house with the bathroom in the center of the house; it will drain out all the energy.

- The front entrance door should never open to face a bathroom. If it does, make sure you keep the bathroom door closed and put a mirror on the outside. In fact, it is a good idea to always keep the toilet lid down and the bathroom door closed regardless of where the bathroom is located.
- Make sure there are no cracks in the ceiling above your bed, and do not sleep under any exposed ceiling beams.
- Eliminate all the clutter in your home, office, and garage (Tip 11). Make sure there is always room for more—space on your bookshelves for new books, room in your closet and dresser for new clothes and shoes, and room in your fridge for more food.
- Put wastebaskets wherever you might need them around your office and home and every morning or evening go around and empty all of them. (My grandmother always did this instinctively right after breakfast because it made her feel good and seemed to be a fresh start to the day.)
- Repair, replace, or discard anything that is broken or damaged in your home or office. Do not waste valuable energy tolerating a fax machine that always jams, broken appliances, stained or ripped clothing, etc.

These are just some basic tips that do not do justice to this ancient art. For a thorough evaluation of your home and office, find a feng shui master (see Appendix D, the Resource Center). The right environment will energize you and increase your ability to attract opportunities and success.

My client John is a well-known professional speaker. He hired me because he had trouble focusing and for years had talked about writing a book. He had tons of ideas, but couldn't seem to get started. The first thing we started working on was getting rid of all the annoyances and clearing out the junk from his life. Every week he would get rid of at least one pile of papers. He even got rid of old books and clothes. He went one step further and hired a feng shui consultant to come to his home and reorganize. The feng shui master merely rearranged the existing furniture and made a few simple suggestions. John couldn't believe the immediate difference it made. He felt more comfortable in his office, and he wasn't as distracted because he had moved his desk to a more favorable position and gotten rid of all the piles of paper. For the first time in years, he was able to focus on his writing, and in six months he had already written half of his book.

Another client was running a thriving consulting business out of her small apartment. When she hired my company, she not only wanted to take her business to the next level, but she also wanted to start dating again. She was a vivacious and attractive young woman who could easily attract a man. I asked her what was under her bed, and sure enough, since she had used every available space in her apartment for storage, she had bed boxes filled with business supplies and mailing envelopes. She was literally in bed with her business. When she realized this, she immediately cleared out the business supplies and moved them to a closet in her office. By the next week she was dating again. The amazing power of feng shui—don't ask me to explain it. I just do it because it works. Try it for yourself and see what happens.

III.

MAKING MONEY
WORK FOR YOU

"There are people who have money and people who are rich."

Coco Chanel

It seems pretty obvious that having lots of extra money will help you become more successful. It isn't so much that you have the money, but rather that the money doesn't have you—or for that matter, that the lack of money doesn't have you. It is just as unattractive to make your life be about the lack of money as it is to make it be about the abundance of money. The goal here is to make money a detail in your life, not the main concern. Easier said than done.

Lack of money is the most common reason (perhaps "excuse" would be more accurate) people use to explain why they aren't happier or why they aren't doing what they love to do. I've heard it plenty of times. "If I only had more money, then I'd do XYZ and then I'd be happier." I've seen the very same people get more money and not do the thing they thought they wanted to do and remain just as miserable, so we know this isn't true. It's clear more money is not the key to happiness. On the other hand, less money isn't the key to happiness either. The trick is to learn to manage your money so that you have enough and can stop worrying about it and start feeling a sense of freedom in relationship to your finances.

There are basically two ways to create extra money: spend less and earn more. Follow the ideas and suggestions in this part, and you will soon be on the way to financial independence (Tip 29). I'm not talking about being able to pay your bills by yourself; I'm talking about having enough money saved and invested or enough income streams that you don't *have* to work for a living. You may *choose* to work for a living, but you don't have to if you don't want to.

Now that may sound completely impossible to you at this point, as you sit there with your massive credit card debt, mortgage, and car payments. If so, don't skip around through the money part. Do the tips in order. Just like lifting weights, sometimes what looks impossible is easy if you work up to it in small increments. Financial independence is possible for just about everyone—even you.

21. TELL THE TRUTH ABOUT MONEY

"Money, it turned out, was exactly like sex, you thought of nothing else if you didn't have it and thought of the other things if you did."

JAMES BALDWIN

What is money anyway? We know it isn't a magic cure-all—it doesn't buy happiness, love, or health. It isn't scarce even though most people seem to feel it is. It isn't a measure of how brilliant or talented you are; there are plenty of poor geniuses and just as many rich idiots. Money is simply a tool. Like any tool, it can be used for good or evil. The subject of money is emotionally charged for most people. It is still a taboo topic for many and often people feel uncomfortable even talking about it. The way you handle your money can tell you a lot about yourself. Your spending patterns often reveal your needs and what you truly value.

First, figure out what your own beliefs are about money. Our beliefs are the source of our actions, and our actions are the source of the results we get in life. So if you want different results in the area of money, it pays to look closely at your personal relationship to it. Here are some fill-in-the-blank questions to get you thinking:

I believe that money is . . .

My greatest problem or difficulty with money right now is . . .

One of the ways I handle money well is . . .

Financial success means . . .

If I could change one thing about my relationship to money, it would be . . .

If I had all the money I could ever want, then I would be . . .

The biggest change I would like to make in regards to managing my money is . . .

My parents taught me that money is . . .

Limited beliefs create limited finances. If you believe you have to work hard to make money, you probably won't have an easy time getting rich. Miranda believed money was evil. She would never have said so directly, but she associated having lots of money with all that she didn't like about the country—greedy, corrupt, fat-cat bureaucrats, and right-wing politicians. I wasn't surprised to find that she not only had no savings but had racked up quite a bit of debt and frequently bounced checks. Thinking that money was inherently evil, she naturally avoided having anything to do with it. Once Miranda uncovered her hidden beliefs about money, she decided to change them. She decided money was simply a tool, and she could use it to do good things in the world. She began to change her behavior. She started paying off her debts, opened a savings account, and even learned to balance her checkbook.

Some of the most common beliefs about money are reflected in expressions such as "filthy rich," "It takes money to make money," "Money is the root of all evil," "Money can't buy you love," "You can't take it with you," "The best things in life are free," "Money isn't everything." Write down all the beliefs you have about money, and then write down all the new beliefs you would like to replace them with. For example, "I enjoy my money. I am grateful for money. I use money to live my dreams. I have enough money to be generous and do great things." Shifting your limiting beliefs to expansive beliefs is the first step toward financial freedom.

Sometimes telling the truth about money isn't easy, but you may have to do it anyway. One client, Jeff, vice president of human resources at a large financial services company, signed up for one of my monthly Tele-Classes on attracting money. Like most people, he thought making more money would solve his problems and his credit card debt. We discovered in the course of this three-hour program that Jeff believed his job was to provide for his wife without question. I told Jeff that he had to tell her the truth about their financial situation and determine their financial goals and objectives as a couple. This wasn't easy, but Jeff sat down and had a conversation with his wife, Mindy, and the truth came out. After some calculations, he figured out that they were spending $2,000 to $4,000 per month more than he was earning. Annually, they were spending $50,000 a year more than they had. At that rate, it doesn't take long to get into really hot water. They had racked up massive credit card debt and were living far beyond their means.

They sought the advice of a financial planner who agreed to work with them for free as "guinea pigs" in a program to help couples turn around their financial situations. They cut up all their credit cards, stopped being overly generous with friends and family, stopped eating out all the time, cut back on dry cleaning, stopped taking expensive vacations, and started paying cash for everything. The amazing part of this all is that Jeff reports they aren't suffering, that it is a game to them to see how little they can spend. Every day they sit down together, chart their expenditures, and divide them into three categories: 1. Necessary; 2. Discretionary; and 3. Wish we had the money back. Mindy has done a complete turnaround and is now his biggest supporter in cutting expenses. She clips coupons and goes to a few different stores to get the best deals on groceries. She has always enjoyed cooking, and now they find that eating at home is healthier and more peaceful than eating out all the time. They aren't depriving themselves either. On their fifth wedding anniversary they did go out to an expensive and elegant restaurant, where they spent about $200 for dinner. But instead of putting it on credit, they felt tremendous satisfaction in whipping out the cash. And because they weren't going out every night, it was a truly special occasion.

Then, out of the blue, they got an unexpected inheritance of $2,000 from an uncle. Already they have started attracting money. They were tempted not to tell their financial planner of this windfall and go blow it on a vacation, but they decided that they were indeed committed to their financial goals and instead used the money to pay off one of their credit cards. They did all this in one month, and I can tell by their energetic enthusiasm for the process that they will soon be out of debt and on their way to financial independence.

If you really feel stuck in a bunch of limiting beliefs you just can't seem to shake, you may want to try using the subliminal tape *Attracting Infinite Riches*, produced by Alphasonics™ International. It suggests such positive messages as "I create prosperity"; "Earning money makes me feel good"; "Multiplying money is fun"; "I am happy about my wealth"; "Rivers of riches are flowing to me." The tape sounds like a pleasant babbling brook, so you can play it in the background at home and at work and no one will have any idea what you are doing. In fact, when a friend of mine was over visiting while the tape was playing, he commented that my house was so relaxing and that somehow the city noises seemed to blend into a calming stream. I have found it to be working in my life—whenever I play it I seem to get a new client or speaking opportunity. Although there are naysayers who pooh-pooh subliminal tapes, if we are only using a small percentage of the brain, why not try using the rest of it? It certainly can't hurt.

22. Be an Instant Billionaire

"After a time, you may find that having is not so pleasing a thing, after all, as wanting. It is not logical, but it is often true."

Spock, "Star Treck"

Every now and again it is a good idea to play the Billionaire Game. Ask your friends and family members the question, "If you had a billion dollars, what would you do?" Then go around the room and see what everyone says. This is an excellent exercise. I recommend that you take out a pen and paper right now and make a list of at least 100 things you would want to do, be, or have. Don't limit yourself in any way. Money is no object. Just start writing down everything that pops into your head. Do not censor anything right now. You can do that later. If you always wanted to have a house on the beach, write it down. If you have always wanted a Mercedes Benz or a Rolex watch, write it down. What about taking private dance classes, going to Hawaii, learning how to scuba dive? Write down every wish, desire, fantasy, dream, and hope that you can possibly think of. Most people pick up their pads and start writing and pretty soon they get stuck and can't even come up with 100 things they would want to do, be, or have. Push yourself past your limit and invent some more stuff. Don't worry, you don't actually have to do all this.

Now that you have your list, let's go through it. First of all, how many things on this list do you really want? Do you really want that Mercedes? What would having a Mercedes do for you? Are you willing to maintain it? We often forget that the real price of having something is the cost of maintaining it. Have you ever driven one? My client Richard spent one summer driving a Mercedes around East Hampton and realized by the end of the summer that he didn't want one. First of all, it was slow to accelerate. Second, it only took diesel fuel so he had to drive out of the way to find gas for it. Third, its electric window kept getting jammed, and he had to keep taking it to the shop, where they would charge a ridiculous amount for any repairs or parts. Fourth, he was terrified of getting a ding or scrape on it. No thanks. Who needs all this headache and fuss? Richard realized he was much happier driving his beaten up old Honda because he never worried about anything happening to it or anyone stealing it. Now do the same for the activities. Do you really want to become a famous opera singer? Or, given the time and training it would require, are you perfectly content to sing in the shower?

From this list, pick the top ten items that you really want to do, have, or be in this lifetime. If you were on your deathbed looking back at your life, these would be the things you would regret not having done. "Oh, I always wanted to see the Acropolis in Greece and I never went." By the way, I've never yet heard of anyone on his deathbed saying he wished he had bought that Rolex watch. Usually we regret not *doing* things or not *saying* things—forgiving people, apologizing for any harm we've done, not spending time with our loved ones, or missing out on a great experience in life. So you could save yourself a ton of money by realizing this right away. Make sure every remaining item is aligned with your values. I don't mean moral values, but what is really important to you. Now that you know what you really want, pick one lifetime goal and get started on that today.

You will notice that once you figure out what your needs are and get those met (Tip 43) you will want a lot less stuff than you did before. I did a variation on this exercise when I was writing this book. To keep me inspired when I felt like tossing the whole thing, I made a list of everything I wanted to buy with my book advance (this was before I had even found an agent, let alone a publisher). I ended up with a surprisingly modest list for a former shopaholic. I wanted a beautiful winter coat, a brown cashmere sweater twin set, lounge chairs and plants for the patio, designer eyeglasses, and a new rug for the living room. I wrote down this stuff along with the approximate cost of each item then forgot about it until I actually got an offer from a publisher. I went back to my list to see what I had wanted and was amazed to find that I already had gotten most of it for a fraction of what I had expected to pay. A friend had given me planters for the patio, my aunt the flowers, and my cousin the new rug. I had found a brown cashmere twinset on sale and realized afterward that I didn't like cashmere so much after all—it's itchy (sometimes things aren't as fabulous as we think they are). I had bought a camel hair winter coat that was perfect. The only thing I didn't have was the designer eyeglasses, and I realized I didn't really want them because the ones I had were just fine and I hardly ever use them. I could make a whole new list of things for the advance.

Take a few minutes to play the Billionaire Game and then write down your list of things just for fun. Pick your top ten and see what you end up attracting.

23. Plug the Money Drains

"Money isn't everything as long as you have enough."

MALCOLM FORBES

The most common mistake I see when coaching people in the area of money is believing that the quickest and easiest way to solve financial problems is to figure out some way to make more money. This is why suckers fall for get-rich-quick schemes every day. This is why people play the lottery. Maybe this time the big ticket will come in and all my problems will be solved. The problem with thinking like this is that money is not the answer to most problems. A study evaluated lottery winners and the impact winning the lottery had on their lives six months later. The same researchers also studied another interesting group—people who had recently been in accidents that made them paraplegics for the rest of their lives. The study revealed that, six months after winning the lottery or six months after becoming a paraplegic, both groups had the same levels of happiness. So winning the lottery will make you just about as happy as becoming a paraplegic. Nice thought. With that in mind, the fastest way to solve your money problems is to solve your money problems. And I mean to get to the root of why you are overspending or in financial trouble in the first place. If you don't figure this out, any extra money you make will just get washed down the same old drain. If you plug the drain, any extra money you make will add up quickly and begin working for you.

So what are the typical money drains? Curiously enough, having unmet emotional needs is typically the hidden source prompting people to overspend. Culturally, we are conditioned by the media that if we need something, we just go out and buy it and voilà! we'll feel fine. Unfortunately, this is an illusion. Ads appeal to our emotional needs more than our actual needs. However, the only way to fill an emotional need is to figure out what that need really is and then go get it met. No amount of money will ever be enough to fill your emotional needs. There is just no getting around this one.

Let me give you an example. Linda, a very ambitious, single advertising executive in Chicago, made plenty of money by most standards. When she started as a coaching client she had over $19,000 in credit card debt, and every paycheck simply paid off the overdraft on her checking account. She lived in a large and beautiful apartment by herself and was paying $1,100 a month in rent. She had expensive tastes and wore designer clothes and shoes, which she justified saying that it was important in her work to look up-to-date for her clients. At age thirty-four, Linda's only savings were the company retirement plan, which she had recently taken a loan against to reduce one of her high-interest-rate credit cards. She was living on the edge, and it kept her trapped in her job and stressed to the max, always juggling one card to pay off another. She knew she had to do something because she was at the end of her rope. When she started the coaching she had no idea that she was overspending because she had a need to be cherished. Every time she bought a beautiful new sweater or pair of shoes she felt, for a moment, special. Unfortunately, the spending high was short-lived. Oftentimes she never even wore the stuff she bought. It was more about the spending than the having.

Once Linda realized that what she really needed was to feel cherished, she began to think of ways she could feel cherished that wouldn't cost much money. Her coaching assignment was to find five people who would gladly cherish her. The very thought of asking people to cherish her made her feel uncomfortable, which just confirmed that it was, in fact, her unmet need (if you don't feel awkward and uncomfortable asking someone to fulfill one of your needs, it probably isn't the real need driving your behavior). After a little prompting, Linda asked her mother to call her every week for the next month or two and tell her how much she loved her. Then she asked her brother to send a postcard once a week saying some way he appreciated her. She even asked her boyfriend to give her back massages once a week. The point of this assignment was to overdo it—to so fully and completely satisfy her need to be cherished that it no longer drove her behavior. Don't worry, you don't have to do this forever, just for six to eight weeks, until you begin to feel your need disappearing. As Linda started to feel completely cherished, she noticed an interesting thing: she could now walk into a store and not feel compelled to buy something. Her desire to shop was disappearing naturally. Linda saw that the excessive shopping was simply a symptom of a deeper need (most unusual behavior patterns have an unmet emotional need at the source). Linda realized that she could never buy enough new shoes or blouses to fulfill her need to be cherished. You just can't get enough of what you don't *really* need.

Now Linda was ready to make some lifestyle changes. She agreed to keep a detailed spending log tracking every single purchase down to the penny for one month so she could see where her money was going. She listed all her fixed monthly expenses (rent, electric, gas, groceries, insurance) and added up all of her variable expenses (eating out, going to the theater, buying clothes, getting manicures, etc.). She was shocked to realize that she was spending about $10,000 a year on clothes and shoes. She also saw how little daily expenses were adding up. She spent $5 to $10 a day eating lunch out at the office. Even if she just went to pick up a sandwich and soda it would end up being about $5 minimum. This was $1,200 a year for lunch! The morning coffee and bagel, at a seemingly insignificant $1.50 a day, added up to $360 a year. Linda decided to make some small changes to her lifestyle. She took lunch to work, ate breakfast at home, and decided to buy only one or two key pieces of clothing to update her wardrobe each season. Then she looked at finding a smaller place to live, but decided she loved her apartment and would rather take in a roommate. She found a roommate who traveled frequently and was happy to split the rent. With just a few small changes Linda was suddenly saving $1,400 a month. She put $1,100 of this toward her debt and the other $300 into a savings account. Linda felt more in control of her life than ever before. She had another interesting revelation: she had been waiting for a man to come and rescue her and pay off all her debts. Of course, now that she had her debts under control, she started attracting wealthy and successful men. You are much more likely to attract people if you don't *need* them. All of you out there waiting for your Knight in Shining Armor or Rich Princess to make your life easy—get your own financial house in order first.

24. PAY OFF YOUR DEBTS

"So, if you have not been trustworthy in handling worldly wealth, who will trust you with true riches?"

LUKE 16:11

In the past twenty years, it has become socially acceptable to have debts. It used to be that people saved money for what they wanted and then bought it; now it is the other way around. We want something now, so we charge it and then pay it off at a ridiculous interest rate. The cost of our "gotta have it now" culture is high, and I'm not just talking about the interest. It goes much deeper than that. It is stressful to have debt. You may be so used to having debt and using credit cards to purchase things that you don't even realize how stressful it is. In fact, until you are completely debt-free, you won't believe what a relief it is. Right now it just sounds like a nice fantasy.

When I started my first job after graduating, I was already making more money than my parents did, and for the first time in my life I felt rich. In no time I had tapped into five different credit cards and a line of credit. Just about every week a credit card bill would come for one or the other of them. I dreaded opening the bill, never knowing exactly how much it would really be and always a bit shocked because it was more than I thought. I had no idea how stressful all this was until I paid off my credit cards and student loan using the plan described by Jerrold Mundis in his book *How to Get Out of Debt, Stay Out of Debt and Live Prosperously.* This is the best, most inspiring little paperback of its kind. It took me about two years to pay off thousands of dollars of debt, and now whenever I use my credit card, I make sure to pay the balance in full each month.

All that debt is stressful and drains your energy, making it very difficult for you to be your best and attract the people and opportunities you want. When you are debt-free it is natural to be carefree and light. However, it isn't easy to be relaxed and fun-loving if you are burdened by the weight of debt. A bank vice president who was very financially savvy had been carrying around a couple thousand in credit card debt and didn't think much of it until she took my seminar and realized that it might be costing her more than she thought. She promptly took money out of an investment and paid it all off. She later called to tell me what a difference that made and thanked me. She felt lighter and freer. This small action spurred her on to do some other things she had been wanting to do for years but had been postponing. She finally bought the cherry bedroom set she had coveted and started remodeling her home to her specifications. Unlike most people who would do this on credit, she chose to use her savings so as not to incur new debt. Of course, not everyone has the savings to instantly pay off their debts. I certainly didn't. It may take some time, but stick with the debt payment schedule and eventually you will be free and clear.

Let me use my client Barbara as an example to explain what I mean here. Barbara loved to shop. She thought that if she were rich, she'd be happy because she would be able to shop without a care in the world and never have to worry about money again. So Barbara spent her time making more money, staying in a job she didn't love because she was making decent money, and using that money to pay off the credit card bills she had racked up thanks to all that shopping. When she had tapped all her credit cards to the max and had used all of her checking account, Barbara began to see that there was a problem. She fantasized about meeting some wealthy guy who would fall in love with her and pay off all her debts in one fell swoop. Finally, when she couldn't even get a loan from her local bank, Barbara realized she had better stop daydreaming and figure out how to get out of the mess.

We set up a debt payment plan that would work for Barbara, but she was terribly discouraged. At the rate she was paying back her cards, she would end up paying thousands of dollars in interest and it would take about seven years. I told her not to worry, that it wouldn't take that long if she followed the plan carefully. The place to start was not to pay off her debts (that was only a symptom), but to get to the source of the problem. What unmet need was Barbara trying to satisfy by shopping? Once she identified the unmet need—to be appreciated—and figured out how to get it met, Barbara discovered she didn't need to go shopping anymore. For the first time since high school, Barbara could go into a store and not feel compelled to buy anything. This was a major breakthrough. In the past, she almost always bought something, even if it was just some small item like a note card or a bottle of nail polish. If she hadn't taken the time to figure out what she *really* needed, she'd still be out there on the shopping/debt treadmill. Find out what your needs are and how to satisfy them once and for all (Tip 43). It will change your life.

If it looks like you may be in way over your head, contact a credit counseling service in your community or the Debt Management Program run by the federal government. They will take all your credit cards and arrange a regular payment plan with the companies. You will pay them a fixed amount every month and they will then take that and divide it amongst your creditors. The two great advantages of this service are 1) they will make all the arrangements with your creditors and you can tell any bill collectors to contact them, and 2) you make a smaller monthly payment. This is a tremendous relief for many people and oftentimes the only way they can dig themselves out of debt and still keep a roof over their heads. The disadvantage is that you may not learn from the experience. Some people need to feel the pain in order to make the necessary changes in their spending habits.

Paying off your debts is the foundation for building a financial cushion. The skills and habits you develop to pay off your debts are the same ones you will need to build a financial reserve. Don't be discouraged. If you feel buried under debt get Mundis's book. The more closely you stick to the plan outlined in the book, the sooner you'll be out of debt and the easier it will be to attract the things you want.

25. Go on a Money Diet

"Wealth consists not in having possessions but in having few wants."

Esther De Waal

It is easy to forget in our consumer-based society that money can't buy happiness. But the latest research indicates that it may be even worse than we thought. According to the *New York Times* article "In Pursuit of Affluence, at a High Price" by Alfie Kohn, "Not only does having more things prove to be unfulfilling, but people for whom affluence is a priority in life tend to experience an unusual degree of anxiety and depression as well as a lower overall level of well-being." The psychological researchers cited in the article found that "pursuing goals that reflect genuine human needs, like wanting to feel connected to others, turns out to be more psychologically beneficial than spending one's life trying to impress others or to accumulate trendy clothes, fancy gizmos, and the money to keep buying them. The latter quest may amount to using compensation to try to compensate for something more meaningful." Dr. Richard Ryan concludes, "The more we seek satisfactions in material goods, the less we find them there. . . . The satisfaction has a short half-life; it's very fleeting." This is a strong case for abandoning extrinsic material goals and instead focusing on developing better relationships and becoming a better human being—the heart of this coaching program. And what's more, as you identify and fulfill your emotional needs, your need to spend will decrease (Tips 43 and 44). However, as the lure of commercialism is undeniably potent, you may need to take some drastic action to break your buying habit and start discovering the deeper pleasures in life.

One of the fastest ways to break the spending habit is to go on a money diet. Or you could call it a spending fast. For thirty days, stop spending. Make no purchases whatsoever other than the bare essentials like toilet paper, toothpaste, groceries, etc. Hold off on all other purchases. It is okay to make a list of the things you'd like to buy, but during the thirty-day period, DO NOT BUY ANYTHING. Try to go grocery shopping no more than once a week, and do not buy that pack of gum or that magazine at the checkout. The best thing is to make sure you have all the essentials on hand before you begin the money diet. If you want to buy gifts for weddings or birthdays coming up, buy those in advance too. That way you will decrease the temptation of going into the store. It is okay to keep your housekeeper and other assistants unless you are feeling financially strapped. At the first sign of financial stress, immediately cut all your extraneous expenses, and you will feel much better. When your financial situation improves, you can always resume your services. It isn't worth the stress to live on the edge.

Rebecca, a stay-at-home mom with three kids, was quite a shopper. The idea of the money diet intrigued her though. It was a challenge— could she not spend for one month and live? This would be a major breakthrough for someone who needed a regular shopping fix. When she tried the money diet, she realized that spending is the quick, but not necessarily creative, solution to a problem. Spending is a habit that can easily turn into an addiction. Rebecca had been doing fairly well at not spending money and was finding a wealth of resources that she had never noticed before. Since she couldn't buy books, she found herself at the public library and discovered an amazing and underutilized resource. She could check out books, try them out at home, and return them at no cost. This solved two problems: she didn't have to pay for them so it helped her save about $80 a month in book purchases; and she didn't have to find a place to store them. What a deal! For entertainment, she couldn't go to the movies at $8 a pop, but once again, she could check out videos for free at the library. They even have CDs and records to check out. She almost slipped and bought a canvas book bag for $15 on sale at the library until she realized that she could carry the books in a plastic grocery bag just as well and save the money.

Then, since she couldn't grab bagels and muffins for the kids for breakfast, she decided to make breakfast at home and made a much healthier meal of buckwheat pancakes and fresh fruit. This became a pleasant family ritual, and Rebecca felt better knowing her family was eating a healthier breakfast. She was beginning to discover that spending wasn't all it was cracked up to be.

What about exercise? Rebecca wanted to take a yoga class and discovered that there was a free one once a week at the gym. Then she checked out a yoga video at the library for free and got her kids involved too. She packed a few sandwiches and went for long walks along the beach with her husband instead of going to dinner and a movie. They found time to talk about their life and make plans together, which improved their relationship as well. She traded one night a week babysitting with a friend who also had kids so she didn't even have to pay for a sitter.

Rebecca thought it would be nice to have a pet for the family. Instead of buying a pet, she made friends with the neighbor's cat, who meows at her door every time it is in the mood for a good petting. She would give Murphy a good scritchy scratch around the ears for about fifteen minutes and both were satisfied. Best of all, she didn't have to clean out the cat litter. The same neighbors also had two dogs and were grateful that her kids would take them out for walks and play with them. Remember, even if you adopt a pet for free, maintaining a pet costs a couple thousand dollars a year when you include shots, food, licensing, shampoo, kennels, etc.

Going on a money diet helped Rebecca get in touch with the simple pleasures of life that are so rich. She discovered all sorts of free and wonderful activities that she would have missed if she hadn't been on the money diet. And she found it was fun to come up with creative solutions. In fact, she had so much fun the first month, she decided to try it for another month and see what else she could learn. Oh, I almost forgot—Rebecca saved $500 dollars on this diet. Anyone who has been on a food diet will find the money diet a piece of cake.

Once you have broken the spending habit, you will discover the joy of saving. Extra money is a very nice thing to have. It gives you a wonderful sense of security along with the freedom and independence to do what you want—and who wouldn't want that?

26. EARN WHAT YOU DESERVE

I bargained with Life for a penny,
And Life would pay no more,
However I begged at evening
When I counted my scanty store.

For Life is a just employer,
He gives you what you ask,
But once you have set the wages,
Why, you must bear the task.

I worked for a menial's hire,
Only to learn, dismayed,
That any wage I had asked of Life,
Life would have willingly paid.

JESSIE BELLE RITTENHOUSE

Now that you've cut your expenses, it is time to get to work on the second half of the money equation: increasing your income. If you work for someone else or for a company, you can ask for a raise. If you own your own business, you may be able to raise your rate or fees or perhaps add another product or service. If you are already making more than the market rate, then perhaps you could moonlight to increase your income.

Let's start with how to ask for a raise. Start by doing a little investigating and find out what people at similar companies doing your job are earning. Many business magazines publish national salary averages. You can find this out at a local library, or you can call friends who work for other companies and ask them. You may be surprised to learn that you aren't even earning a competitive market rate. If you discover you earn more than average, don't let that stop you from asking for a raise. An excellent employee is well worth retaining.

Second, write down a list of all your accomplishments over the past six months to a year and type it up in a memo: Accomplishments to Date. You want to build a strong case for why you deserve a raise. Use as many concrete, numeric figures as possible and demonstrate how your performance helped to improve the bottom line. Cite projects and committees you worked with and their results. More often than not, your boss will not remember everything you did. When you think how often *you* forget what you've done, you can imagine that a manager with even a few employees to supervise will not remember everything you've done. For many employees it makes sense to write a quarterly memo of your accomplishments and keep a copy for your own file. This way, when your boss writes up your evaluation, she will have all your memos on hand to refer to. *Never* list any failures in these memos. Your manager may have forgotten that you were the one responsible so please don't remind her. Stick to the positive facts.

Many companies have a policy of asking employees to write a self-evaluation. Be very careful when it comes to the area of improvement. Don't provide them with negatives they may not even be aware of. Unfortunately, most salary decisions are based on perceived performance, not on actual performance. Don't shoot yourself in the foot. On the other hand, you don't want to look like you aren't trying to improve. A safe bet would be to mention an area where you would like to further develop yourself. For example, if you work in the operations side of the business and want to learn more about sales, write that down as the area for improvement and request the opportunity to develop your sales skills by taking a sales training class. This makes you look like a very proactive employee. Large companies do their salary planning way in advance. This means that your boss estimates your salary increase anywhere from nine months to a year before you get it. All the more reason not to wait until the last minute to keep your boss informed of your results.

Third, after you've written up the memo for your boss, request a meeting to discuss your performance in person. If your company already has quarterly performance reviews, great, but don't let a quarter go by without some feedback from your boss. You want to make sure you are on track and meeting the expectations of your company. How are you going to know this if you don't ask? If you aren't meeting expectations, far better to know sooner than later so that you can course-correct. If this is the case, document your improvements in any problem areas as soon as possible and set up another meeting with your boss to discuss this and assure her that you are doing a great job.

Fourth, ask for what you want. If you are a great employee, you should be making more than the industry average. You may not get what you want, but you should at least ask. Since most people are afraid to ask for a raise, this will put you in a special category. When the boss is looking at the amount of money she has to distribute amongst her staff, who do you think has a better chance of getting a bigger percentage of the pie? The person who asks and makes a solid case is much more likely to receive a raise than the person who may be working just as hard, but never states his or her case.

So those are some tips on asking for a raise. Now, what if you own your own business? If you are self-employed, there may be any number of ways to make more money. The first and easiest is often to simply cut your expenses, but since you've already done that, it may be appropriate to raise your fee or rates. I encourage my clients to charge whatever the market will bear and to raise their rates every year or six months depending on their business. In order to do this you may need to be continually adding value to your services so that the increase is worth it for your current clients. Or you may simply maintain existing clients at a grandfathered rate and charge new clients your new rates. Again, so much depends upon the type of business, the market rate, and the level of service.

What about moonlighting? This can be a great way to make extra money while at the same time experimenting with a different field. Many clients are not fulfilled in their current work but are not sure what they would really enjoy. Moonlighting can be a safe way to try out a business idea or to work part time in the field you are interested in. Just make sure you don't overdo it. Sometimes people spend too much time and energy moonlighting, and it negatively affects their work at their day job. Call human resources to find out about your company's policies in regard to part-time work and get the appropriate permission if needed. Working for some companies may be a conflict of interest, and you could unwittingly jeopardize your current job. If you are wondering where you will find the time to moonlight, try turning off the TV. The average American watches more than twenty hours a week—enough for a part-time job.

What are other creative ways you could increase your income? Perhaps a hobby could net a little extra income if you got creative. Perhaps you are a great dancer and love going out dancing in the evenings? You might be able to get paid for it if you start giving classes or teaching private lessons. What about leveraging one of your natural strengths? You are super-organized and love straightening out a mess—you could moonlight as a professional organizer. Unless you are a naturally gifted salesperson who loves making cold calls and has a huge network, I would stay away from multilevel marketing programs. Most people don't have the sales skills to really make money and run out of prospects after they've tapped into their network of about two hundred friends and colleagues. Take a moment to write down ten possible ways that you could increase your income.

27. Set Up a Reserve Account

"The want of money is the root of all evil."

Samuel Butler

"Money does not make you happy but it quiets the nerves."

Sean O'Casey

My old idea of a reserve account was a credit card that still had some room to spend on it. I had no savings except for my company 401K, and I had even taken a loan against that. I never saw the point of having savings. After all, at 3 percent interest I wasn't going to earn any significant interest. And it was a whole lot more fun to spend than to save. So why bother?

That's the funny thing about having a cash reserve—you can't appreciate it until you have it. It is just something you have to experience, and once you do, you'll never go back to your old ways. My first savings goal was to have six month's living expenses in a money market account. Living in Manhattan, this came to about $15,000. At the time, it seemed like a huge and impossible amount that would require years of saving, but I got there in one year. Money came in from unexpected sources—the accountant found a tax refund, my sales team made goal every quarter and we got bonuses. In addition, I set up an automatic savings plan and $500 a month was automatically deducted from my paycheck before I could get my hands on it. Now the purpose of this reserve account is not to buy a new car, take a trip to Europe, or go on a shopping spree at Macy's. You need a different spending account for that stuff. A reserve account is a cash cushion to protect you from the unexpected bumps in the road of life.

You might be wondering what good all this money is if you can't use it for a trip to Europe. It is for the time when all four tires go out on the car at once. For the plane tickets to see your grandmother who slipped and broke her hip. It is to help you through those tough times in life so that you can do what you need to do without worrying about the money.

Having six months to two years of expenses socked away will give you a tremendous advantage at work, whether you own your own business or whether you work for someone else. People who have savings are much less likely to work with an annoying client. I work with all my business clients to develop an ideal client profile. This way they can tell prospective clients exactly whom they work best with. The business owners who have substantial reserves find it much easier to let go of clients that don't fit this profile and refer them to someone else who may be better suited to their needs or personality type. If you are desperate for cash, you'll be more likely to compromise your standards and work with anyone who comes along.

If you work for a company, you will be more likely to enforce your boundaries (Tip 5) and maintain your standards if you know that in a worst-case scenario you can always quit and find a better job. A financial reserve is the key to your confidence. So many times I've worked with clients who feel trapped in their jobs because they have major credit card debt. These are typically the same clients who are afraid to inform their bosses when they have crossed a boundary and, ironically, to ask for the raise they so badly need. Stop living in fear and start saving.

A cash reserve will help you attract success by giving you peace of mind and a sense of security. You'll be more relaxed and confident and less worried or anxious. Grace under pressure is attractive, and reserves make it easy to be graceful. But don't believe me; you must experience this yourself to know what I'm talking about.

28. Start Saving 20 Percent of Your Income

"I do want to get rich but I never want to do what there is to do to get rich."

Gertrude Stein

Most people have a natural tendency to be either savers or spenders. The good news is that although you may have a natural predisposition to save or spend, you can change this—but you may need a compelling reason to do so. My client Lou was a big-time spender. He loved antiques shopping and bargain hunting. He didn't really see the point of saving. Didn't you save so you could buy something later? Savers are probably quivering at this point, but this was his basic outlook at the time. Since action follows thought, it should come as no surprise that Lou had credit card debt and nothing in savings. He was completely tapped into his overdraft checking line so that every time he got paid, it just paid back the line of credit.

This turned around for Lou when I explained the concept of financial independence—having enough money or income streams so that you don't have to work for a living (Tip 29). What an appealing idea! Lou had never thought this possible. After all, he wasn't from a wealthy family; he wasn't going to inherit a business or money. He was making a decent salary but spending more than he made. Lou had always thought that financial independence was for "those other people." He, on the other hand, would always have to work for a living. But here was this coach already well on the way to financial independence telling him that he could do it too. Lou's whole perspective changed. For the first time in his life, he had a reason to save that appealed to him. He wanted the freedom and security of knowing that he didn't have to work for a living.

The real key to financial independence is to start saving 20 percent of your current net income. Have it automatically deducted from your paycheck or checking account to go into a mutual fund or secure investment. You are now on your way to financial independence. Now *that* is a goal worth saving for! Either cut your expenses by 20 percent or increase your income by 20 percent. Better yet, do both and get there twice as fast (the fastest way to start is to cut your expenses).

One of my colleagues who is now in his late fifties said that when he got his first job at eighteen he figured he should be able to live just fine on 80 percent of his income and save the other 20 percent. He continually stashed away that 20 percent, and without any struggle, with just his regular jobs, he is now a multimillionaire. That was all it took. Just 20 percent of his net income went into savings. He figured out how to live on the rest. The secret formula for financial independence is consistent savings over time. If at age twenty-two you took advantage of your annual $2,000 IRA contribution and put it in a stock mutual fund every year, by age sixty-five you'd have $409,000. I am always amazed at the number of people who don't know they can sock away $2,000 a year into a tax-free IRA account. The fact that it is tax-free until you withdraw is a big bonus, and the interest will add up that much faster. And now you can take advantage of the new Roth IRAs and enjoy tax-free withdrawals too. To find out more about IRAs go to your bank and ask for a brochure. You should also talk to your accountant to see whether it makes sense for you to convert your IRAs into Roth IRAs. This decision will depend on your individual circumstances. (See Appendix D, the Resource Center, for more information.)

The tremendous payoff in security, freedom, and confidence is well worth the minor lifestyle changes you need to make in order to save 20 percent. If you really can't save 20 percent, then start with 10 percent and work your way up to 20 percent. Shop around for the best interest rates and ask the bank to set up your automatic savings plan and IRA so you don't have to worry about the details. Then you can forget about it and relax knowing that you are being responsible for your future.

29. Play for Financial Independence

"I've been rich and I've been poor. Believe me, honey, rich is better."

SOPHIE TUCKER

Once you create a six-month reserve (Tip 27) and have gotten into the habit of saving 20 percent of your income (Tip 28), the next step is to start playing for financial independence. Don't go crazy on me—I said *play*. Make this a game and just see what happens. If you haven't done the previous steps, this may seem overwhelming, in which case skip it for now and come back later when you are ready. The game will still be here waiting for you. Financial independence means you have enough money or revenue streams that you never have to work again. You can live comfortably off the interest. If you work, it is a choice—you do it for the pure joy of it. Now this is a game worth playing. You may have nothing to lose except a load of debt.

The first step is to realize that anyone (yes, that means you!) can play this game. You don't have to make a huge income, inherit money, be born into wealth, or win the lottery to play this game. Second, decide how much money you really need to be financially independent. Most people tend to overestimate this number and think in terms of millions. But I'm not talking about living the glamour life. If you lived very simply, you could live on the interest of $250,000. This would generate $1,250 a month at a very conservative interest rate of 6 percent. And if you did any work at all, your lifestyle would go up. If you think this idea is crazy, read the book *Your Money or Your Life*, by Joe Dominguez and Vicki Robin. It will help you shift your thinking in this area. One of my clients figured out that if she and her husband saved $2,000 a month for fifteen years they would be able to retire at age forty and live off an annual interest income of $30,000.

Just by being on the path toward financial independence you will start attracting better opportunities. You'll soon find that you'll also have the money to invest in other moneymaking projects. I made an audiotape program, *Irresistible Attraction: A Way of Life*, that I would have been reluctant to invest in if I didn't have the financial reserve already in place. The tape is a handy income stream. I did the work once and now I make a profit every time I sell a tape. Not only is it a moneymaker, but it has paid off in other ways: people who like the tape usually want to take a workshop or start coaching. The audio program is an inexpensive way for potential clients to get a sense of what my company has to offer.

Another benefit of having extra money is that you will start thinking bigger than you ever have, and since your thoughts lead your actions—hold onto your hat—you may be in for an exciting ride. (Avoid get-rich-quick schemes or multilevel marketing plans. I discovered that most folks involved in these programs have big debts and are often under-earners. That's what many of these programs are banking on—the deadly combination of desperation and greed.)

Let's assume that $250,000 is your figure for financial independence. How will you get there? If you created a way to save or earn an extra $100 a day, you'd be there in ten years and still have weekends off. You could start a sideline business, moonlight, get more education or training for a higher paying job, or cut your expenses by 50 percent and invest the savings. Or do all of the above and get there in record time. This is not rocket science, just consistent savings over time, and it adds up. The operative word here is *consistent*.

Open a separate savings or mutual fund account and call it your financial independence account. Even if all you can save is $10 a day, start playing the financial independence game. More ideas will come to you once you get started. And remember that cutting your expenses is usually the fastest way to have more money. Most people get fixated on making more money when it is actually much faster and easier to simply cut your expenses. Look at your big ticket fixed items such as rent, mortgage, car payments. One of my clients in her early sixties and her husband are selling their large family home and building a smaller one that perfectly meets their needs now that the kids are all grown and have their own homes. They will eliminate the last of the mortgage, build the new, smaller house to specification, and still have some money left over to put into savings. A great idea! Don't get trapped into thinking that downsizing means suffering—reducing your costs often improves your quality of life. My client and her husband are thrilled that they won't have to do so much work to maintain the new home.

Do not worry if you can't come up with $100 a day. It is perfectly okay to start small. If you spend $5 on eating lunch out, bring your lunch to work instead and put the money you save in the financial independence account. Lots of small changes add up quickly.

The good news is that you don't have to wait until you reach your financial independence goal to start reaping the benefits. Just knowing that you are taking consistent action toward your goal, that you are on the plan for financial independence, will dramatically reduce the stress and anxiety you may have over money. You won't fear getting old and having to rely on your family to take care of you. You will be calm and secure in the face of crisis knowing that there is a cash reserve to tap into. This is essential to attracting the things you want in life. The more money you have, the more opportunities you will attract. Your confidence will go up because you can say, "Take this job and shove it," and not worry about paying the mortgage. You will be more attractive to employers because you don't need the job—you are doing it because you love it. You have nothing to lose by playing this game and everything to gain.

30. Protect Your Stuff

"You don't need to pray to God any more when there are storms in the sky, but you do have to be insured."

Bertolt Brecht

Given Murphy's Law, if you have insurance you'll never need it, but if you don't, disaster will strike. I am always amazed at the number of people who don't have major medical insurance. I know it is expensive, but so is getting hit by a bus. No joke, one of my friends was recently hit by a bus and survived with a broken knee and no front teeth. She was lucky. It is bad enough when disaster hits, but worse when you have no insurance. And it will always get you right between policies. One client had just moved from one apartment to another and hadn't had time to set up renter's insurance. He was burglarized and lost thousands of dollars of electronics and irreplaceable family jewelry.

Renter's or homeowner's is a must. Major medical is a must. Life insurance is not. You only need life if you have a spouse or children who will need a lump sum if you unexpectedly die, or if you are going into business with a partner and rely on his or her assets. If that person dies will you be able to buy out the business? Make sure he or she has life insurance that covers the business investment. Whole-life, universal life, and variable life insurance are generally a waste of money—go for term. Term insurance provides death benefits only and provides no build-up of cash value. With any cash value policy, your early payments go primarily to sales commissions and overhead so in most cases, you would be better off investing the difference in premiums yourself. If you have no confidence in your ability to save and want to be sure there is money for your family when you die, then you might want one of the permanent whole-life or flexible policies. However, as Burton G. Malkiel, Chemical Bank Chairman and professor of economics at Princeton University, recommends in his excellent investment book, *A Random Walk Down Wall Street*, if you have the discipline to save, buy renewable term insurance so you can keep renewing your policy without an annual physical. "So-called decreasing term insurance, renewable for progressively lower amounts, should suit many families best, since as time passes (and the children and family resources grow), the need for protection usually diminishes." Malkiel cautions that "term-insurance premiums escalate sharply when you reach the age of sixty or seventy or higher. If you still need insurance at that point, you will find that term insurance has become prohibitively expensive. But the major risk at that point is not premature death; it is that you will live too long and outlive your assets." Of course, always take the time to shop around and look for the best deal as policy rates vary widely from company to company.

What does insurance have to do with attracting what you want? *Peace of mind is very attractive.* Plus you don't want to lose your hard-earned cash reserve unnecessarily.

A single-engine plane crashed in Phoenix, Arizona, and with all the beautiful insured homes around, it just happened to land on an uninsured home. The pilot bailed out, and no one was home so no one was hurt. However, the homeowner's insurance that came with the original mortgage didn't exist because the mortgage had been paid off. The owner of the small plane didn't have insurance either. The house was left in its burned and crispy shape for years. The homeowners were plain out of luck. One of the best ways not to court disaster is to have insurance.

Let's not forget the most important insurance of all—protect your children and/or your estate with a will or a revocable living trust. As every state has different laws, it is wise to consult an attorney or a Certified Financial Planner (CFP) to make sure your trust or will is valid and written so that your intentions will be properly executed. Have you legally identified guardians for your children in the event that you and your spouse both die? Prepare for the worst possible disaster, and you will be more relaxed knowing that your children will be well taken care of. A good attorney or (CFP) will help you address these and other issues in your trust or will. Even if you are single, you may want to set up a living will so that if you should happen to become a vegetable, they won't leave you plugged into life support forever, depleting whatever resources you might have had.

Another commonly overlooked item is disability insurance for self-employed people. When you own your own company, you are the most valuable asset the company has. If you become disabled, you may be unable to perform the functions necessary to run your business. Most employees who work for a company have some disability insurance, but this doesn't provide coverage if you leave to start your own business. And the thing that people don't know is that it is harder to qualify for disability insurance once self-employed, so make sure you have your own disability insurance a few months before you leave your company to start your own business.

And don't forget to protect your valuable documents. Most of us have our own peculiar ways of storing important papers and valuables: the title to your house is in a desk drawer in the secretary, the gold coins are stashed in a decorative box under your sweaters, the passports are in a file drawer. This is all well and good until a pipe bursts and floods the basement where all the papers are stored in cardboard boxes, there's a fire, a tree crashes through your house . . . stranger things have happened. Then you discover just how valuable those papers were. Don't wait until lightning strikes. Mark your calendar and set aside a Saturday morning to protect your stuff, and do it right this time. And if you are running a business from your home, do the same for all your business documents and important records. One client would have lost his entire client database of over 700 client names, addresses, phone numbers, and other pertinent information when his computer crashed if he hadn't wisely made a backup copy on a disk. All that vital information was preserved. Back it up and keep an extra backup in a safe-deposit box or another safe location just in case your whole house burns down.

The first step is to make copies of all your valuable documents, including your birth certificates, car titles, property deeds, lease agreements, legal documents, wills, financial records including all your bank account numbers, credit cards, investments, loan documents, IRAS, 401K plans, property and life insurance polices, passports, citizenship papers, and don't forget your social security card. Make copies of them all and keep your copies separate from the originals. Store your originals in a fireproof home safe or bank safe-deposit box (you can usually rent a small one for $25 to $30 a year). If you travel frequently you may want to keep your passport handy at home and put the photocopy in the safe.

While you are at it, make an inventory of your valuable possessions, including those gold coins, the antique armoire, your grandmother's diamond wedding ring, and all your electronic and other appliances—computer, television, stereo—with the serial numbers. List the approximate value of each item and save the receipts as proof of value. If you don't have the receipts or if you think something is now worth more than the receipt, obtain written appraisals for artwork, antiques, and jewelry that you want to insure. It is very difficult to prove the value of something once it has disappeared. As a final measure, videotape or photograph your valuable items. Organize the list of possessions and the receipts, appraisals, and photographs in a binder and store this at the bank or in your safe. If you are using a home safe, make sure it is built into the wall or securely bolted into the floor so it can't be carted off by a burglar. Be aware that banks don't always offer insurance on your stored valuables, so make sure your homeowner's policy covers any items in there as well.

The next step is your computer. It is very unlikely that anyone would come into your home or office and steal all your paper files, but it is likely that they would steal your computer. Even if your computer is insured, the data on it may be irreplaceable. Make a regular backup of all your important files on a disk, tape, or cartridge. Store one copy at the bank and another at home and remember to update weekly or as necessary. You may want to make your computer harder to steal with a security cable that locks to your desk. Portables are, well, portable and very easy to run away with. While this sounds like a lot to do, once you get your documents in order you will prevent hours of headache in the event of accident or misfortune. I learned this the hard way—my computer got zapped in a lightning storm (always unplug everything during a lightning storm; surge protectors cannot protect you from a direct hit). I sent it to the shop for repair. Even though I got a new computer, I lost all the data on the hard drive except for the few things I had backed up. If you ever hear of a friend's computer crashing or something terrible, immediately make a backup—it is always wise to heed these subtle messages as warning signs from the universe that you may be next.

One last reminder: let someone close to you whom you trust know where your valuable documents are stored and how to retrieve them in the event that lightning or some other disaster strikes. All of this will only take a few hours, and once it is done, you can easily do an annual update to include the new valuables, changes to your will, etc. Take these preventive measures and, given Murphy's Law, you are less likely to get hit. There's no point in saving all your money to watch it go down the tubes due to some freak event.

IV.

....

MAKE TIME WHEN
THERE ISN'T ANY

"The trouble is that you think you have time."

BUDDHA

EVERYONE COMPLAINS THAT there isn't enough time. We act as though time were a fixed quantity, and it isn't. Time expands and contracts depending on what we are doing. The irony is that being overly busy makes time seem to go even faster. If you want to feel like you have more time, do less. When I was leading a seminar in Kansas City, I met a musician who, in his travels around the world, lost his passport and his wallet and ended up living with a few people on the beach in Hawaii, picking fruit and catching fish and mussels. He felt that he had all the time in the world. He had no calendar or watch and the weather was always lovely. After what seemed like a couple of years, he went in search of civilization and found his way back to the mainland. He was astounded to discover that he had only been gone for four months.

One of my clients, Richard, had a fear of dying. This was understandable because his father died at the age of forty-five and Richard was now forty-six. The older he got, the more he ran around like crazy, packing as many activities as he possibly could into his already jammed schedule.

Richard seemed to have it made. Tall, blonde, and fit, he carried himself with the easy assurance of a Southern California surfer—which he once was. He was a dynamo in his field, business consulting. He drove a bmw. He was at the top of the tennis ladder at the local sports club and also played a respectable game of golf. Things didn't look so great from where Richard sat. In fact, he rarely just sat. And although he liked keeping himself busy, he felt scattered. He knew he was accomplishing a lot, but he was losing ground financially. He had run up huge debts while maintaining two households, and the debt gnawed at him. His new business ideas had enormous potential but were a long way from spinning any real profits. He was freelancing for corporate clients, a stopgap measure. His brother, an architect, offered him a part-time personnel job, but he feared taking it would mean giving up on his business ideas. There were other problems as well. Since he'd left his wife, his daughter had turned cold. He didn't even know how he felt about himself. One day he would feel arrogant, the next in despair. "I have shut God out," he told me.

I took a deep breath and said, "Richard, what I want for you is a life complete from your past so you are free to live your own life." There was a long silence. Then he said that his wife had wanted him to leave things just the way they were when they were married, with the same house, the same car—as if nothing had happened and they weren't separated. "How long have you been living like this?" I asked. "Over seven years," he replied. "It is time to complete this relationship," I said. The next week Richard reported that he had hired an attorney to begin the divorce. As for the business side, I asked that he focus on one or two projects guaranteed to generate an immediate income. I also asked that he design a budget and cut his living expenses by 50 percent.

As we talked we kept returning to the question of time. Richard was always running late. Usually he had a good excuse. Just as he was getting ready to go see a client, another prospect would phone. "It's hard to leave a situation I'm handling that's important," he explained. He'd end up arriving late for his appointment. He could live with that; didn't it just prove how busy and successful he was? But he could see that he was overbooking himself. What may have hurt most was when, tired from a hectic round of interviewing clients, he briefly lost the top spot on the tennis ladder.

I made two simple recommendations. Take twenty minutes every morning to plan the day and to reflect (Tip 35). And make a firm rule to arrive at every appointment ten minutes early. Here was my pitch: Have you ever observed that the really senior executives always seem to have plenty of time? When you meet them for lunch, they'll be waiting at the table, calm, composed, and having a drink. Who has the advantage?

It paid off right away. The next week, Richard scored a major new account when he arrived early to interview a prospect, was ushered into the office to wait, and noticed photos of the executive playing tennis and golf. At ease, the two began talking about their shared love of the sports and ended up making a tennis date. The long-term gain looks even more promising. That little twenty minutes for reflection gave Richard the perspective he had been missing. He has begun to use the time for meditation, "thanking God for what went on the day before," as he put it. It allows him to "let the day come to me," he said. Richard has taken the job with his brother and is well on the way to clearing his debts. He pushed for and got a clean break with his ex-wife—a divorce. He and his girlfriend have joined a church and are now engaged. He is preparing to launch his new company. His daughter has even warmed up, and they are speaking again. Best of all, he no longer veers between elation and despair. "You saved my life," he told me. But all he really had to do was take the time to think about it.

The following are some simple ways to create more time in your life.

31. Track Your Time

"The more a person is able to direct his life consciously, the more he can use time for constructive benefits."

ROLLO MAY, *MAN'S SEARCH FOR HIMSELF*

"We spend, I am very certain, the half of our time among people that we do not particularly like and on things that do not particularly amuse us, and consequently have no time for the people and things that do really matter to us."

ALEC WAUGH, *ON DOING WHAT ONE LIKES*

When you can't figure out where all the money goes, it helps to do a spending log for a month and see exactly where it is going. The same goes for time. Do you work like crazy, come in early and leave late, and still don't have time to do all there is to do? Do you feel like there aren't enough hours in the day to get everything done? Do you spend too much time managing the routine tasks and don't have time for the big important projects at work and at home? If you have the feeling that time is going by too quickly and just don't know where it is all going, it is time to take a closer look. Take one week and track your time in fifteen-minute increments. Write down everything you are doing from the moment you get up until you go to bed at night, from phone calls to coffee and bathroom breaks. Yes, I realize this is a tedious assignment, but you only need to do it for one week and then you can extrapolate the data and rearrange your life accordingly. To make this assignment easier, get an inexpensive diary that already has a schedule in fifteen-minute intervals so you can just write in the activity. Also, pick an ordinary week that reflects your typical schedule, not a vacation week. Now you are ready to start tracking.

You are the only one who will see this time log, so don't change your schedule to try to make it look good. Just record as accurately as possible what you really do during a regular week. This will include things such as shower, dress, blow dry hair, prepare breakfast for the family, eat breakfast, read the paper, drive to work, chat with colleagues, plan the day, answer E-mail messages, meet with clients, go out to lunch, read memos, write reports, return phone calls, send a fax, etc. Write it all down. At the end of the week you will have a precise record of where your time is going, and you will be able to make some intelligent decisions based in reality. Most people are appalled to discover how much of their time is spent in seemingly important tasks that in the end are not fulfilling or could be easily delegated.

Here is what one client, Michael, a human resources manager, discovered after reviewing his time log: Michael lived with his wife and two kids in a lovely home in the outskirts of London and had a commute of 1 hour and 40 minutes each way. That totaled 16.6 hours a week just to get to work—almost enough for a part-time job. Michael talked to his boss about the lost time and was able to negotiate working from home two days a week, saving himself 6.6 hours a week. In order to maximize his commute time in the car, Michael played books on tape or listened to self-improvement tapes that he checked out from the local library.

Another big time-waster was phone calls. He spent 11 hours a week on the phone. Michael realized that a big part of his job entailed being on the phone, but he also discovered that he was repeating the same information to employees. He also spent a lot of time on small talk and personal calls. Michael found that the two-minute conversations were often more productive than the twelve-minute calls. He decided to start advising his callers right from the start that he only had a few minutes. This eliminated the chitchat and people got right to the point.

Then Michael was amazed to discover that he spent a good 2 hours and 15 minutes faxing documents and hovering over the fax machine to make sure all the documents went through properly. His computer had built-in fax capability, but he hadn't taken the time to learn how to use it. He asked a colleague to show him how it worked (which took ten minutes), and he started using technology to his advantage.

Michael was mortified to find that he spent a good 3 hours a week looking for memos and other things that he needed on his desk. He had Post-it Notes plastered all over his desk and computer and so many stacks of paper that there was only a small space left on his desk for working. He thought he was pretty organized because he could find things quickly, but the time log revealed that he wasn't quite as organized as he thought. Michael decided to put this 3 hours to use and spent an hour each day eliminating the piles on his desk, setting up hanging files to keep projects in, and sending old documents to the archives or discarding them (Tip 17). He took down all the Post-it Notes and decided to use his computer to keep a running to-do list.

The other big chunk of wasted time was due to interruptions from his boss and his coworkers. He was a well-liked manager and prided himself on having an open-door policy, so his staff was in the habit of popping in at any time during the day. This added up to 4 hours and 15 minutes a week. Michael decided that he wanted to keep the open-door policy, but that he would also implement a closed-door policy. When he was working on a project that demanded his focused concentration, he closed the door and put up a "work in progress" sign. He told his staff that when the door was closed he would prefer not to be disturbed unless it was an emergency. He got so much accomplished in the two hours his door was closed that he encouraged his staff to do the same. Productivity in the department increased by 25 percent.

As for his boss, Michael began a file called "Meet with Boss" in which he would jot down any questions or issues to discuss. If he had a question about something in a memo, he would just write the question directly on the memo, slip it in the file, and bring the whole file to the meeting. He requested a weekly half-hour phone meeting and during this time would address everything in the file. He saved 2.5 hours a week by doing this.

On the home front, Michael realized that he would come home exhausted, flick on the TV, and watch about a half hour before dinner and then another two and a half hours after for a total of 15 hours a week (see Tip 32). A huge time-waster! He decided he would rather spend his time doing something more fulfilling and satisfying. He decided that after dinner he would take a walk with his wife and kids for some exercise. Then they would read books or play chess or Scrabble with the kids when their homework was done instead of watching television. This turned out to be much more relaxing and fun for the whole family.

Track your time and see what you are really doing. Ask yourself whether this is how you want to be spending your life or not. Then start automating, delegating, and deleting the time-wasters and start using that time for working on one of your big lifetime goals (Tip 51).

32. TURN OFF YOUR TELEVISION

"[Watching television] is a one-way transaction that requires the taking in of particular sensory material in a particular way, no matter what the material might be. There is, indeed, no other experience in a [person's] life that permits quite so much intake while demanding so little outflow."

MARIE WINN

In his book *Flow: The Psychology of Optimal Experience*, Mihaly Csikszentmihalyi shares decades of study on "optimal experience"—those times when people are happiest that make all life worth living. His investigations have revealed that genuinely satisfying experiences occur in a state of consciousness called "flow"—a state of focused and intense concentration in which there is a feeling of transcendence. Csikszentmihalyi outlines numerous different activities and determines whether they are "high-flow" or "low-flow." High-flow activities require focus and concentration; your mind is actively engaged in what you are doing. Not surprisingly, watching television is one of the lowest-flow activities.

This study confirmed what I always suspected: TV drains your energy. When have you switched off the television after watching a program and said, "I'm going to start writing that great American novel now."? In fact, do you ever feel like doing *anything* after watching TV? The same goes for other insidious TV-based time-wasters that can take over our lives before we know it—playing computer games, watching videos, etc. After you've tracked your time (Tip 31) you'll know how much of your life television is eating up.

Television is addictive in much the same way that food, caffeine, gambling, alcohol, or any other overused substance or activity is addictive. Not only is watching television a socially acceptable addiction, like caffeine, it is socially encouraged. Even if you don't enjoy it, you may find yourself watching television just because everybody else is. The typical American watches over six hours of TV a day. That adds up to an extra forty-two hours of time a week—enough for a full-time job! And you thought you didn't have enough time. Just give your TV to a friend for a week and see how much time you'll have.

One client used to watch a morning news program while he was getting ready for work. He thought this was an efficient use of his time— he liked the program, got the news and weather—a great way to start the day. Just as an experiment, I suggested that he stop watching TV in the morning for one week. He was amazed. He felt more peaceful and organized. He thought he'd miss the news, but he didn't miss it at all. Now he enjoys his peaceful mornings and feels less stressed throughout the day.

Another client, who lived alone, was embarrassed by the amount of TV she was watching. She went cold turkey and took the TV to a friend's house. She soon found she had replaced the TV with another addiction— murder mysteries. She felt that wasn't much progress. However, she noticed that reading novels didn't sap her energy the way TV did. There were no commercials. She could put the book down at any time and go mow the lawn or fix dinner. Looking back on it, she realizes how much TV drained her energy.

Joanne, a forty-something recent divorcée, complained that she didn't have any dates. I asked her what she did in the evenings and wasn't terribly surprised to hear that she watched TV. Even if she was just puttering about the house she would leave the TV on so the house wouldn't seem so quiet. The danger of watching TV is that it can give you the illusion that you are with other people because you are watching them while the TV, in effect, keeps you company. Obviously, this isn't fulfilling because you aren't interacting with anyone. I suggested that Joanne cut out all TV cold turkey for one week. She couldn't do it. She was clearly addicted. So we came up with another plan. I told Joanne to make a list of all the fun activities or courses she had always wanted to do, but never seemed to have the time for. She wanted to do some volunteer work, take dance classes, and run a marathon. She joined a marathon training program that raised money from sponsors for charity. This accomplished three of her goals (she wanted to get in shape too). Then she signed up for a dance class in the community even though none of the guys there looked very appealing. Now she didn't miss TV at all, and her social life started to percolate. She had more energy and even got up the nerve to answer a personal ad. On the way to the restaurant to meet the fellow, she got lost somewhere in Soho and two attractive Italians helped her find the place. Somehow they got her phone number in the process. The next day they called and invited her to a party in the Hamptons, where she met a very handsome film producer. They hit it off and she is now in a wonderful relationship.

Try limiting your TV viewing to consciously selected programs and turn the set off when they are over. Decide how many hours a week you will watch and stick to it. Don't fall into the habit of watching the next program just because you have the television on. Beware! Television is more costly than you realize and actually reduces your ability to attract what you want in life.

33. ARRIVE TEN MINUTES EARLY

"Punctuality is the politeness of kings."

A FAVORITE SAYING OF KING LOUIS XVIII

If you already do this, good for you; if not, the fastest and simplest way to create a reserve of time in your life is to show up ten minutes early to every business and personal appointment. It sounds like a waste of time. After all, you could use that ten minutes to make one more phone call.

In this case, by doing less, you gain more—more time, peace, and awareness. By arriving ten minutes early you actually have time to compose your thoughts, take in the environment around you, and relax. As an experiment, try showing up ten minutes early for one week.

I recommended this to one client, Dexter, a very busy, successful businessman who was always rushing around, seeing how many things he could get done in a day. Dexter thought that if he could squeeze in one more phone call before an appointment he was being more effective and efficient. It wasn't surprising that he usually ran a few minutes late and arrived rushed and a bit harried with a ready excuse on his tongue about traffic or some such thing. When I suggested that he arrive ten minutes early, Dexter wasn't too keen on the idea. He felt it would be a waste of his precious time. I persisted and asked him to try it for one week and see what happened. He could always go back to his old ways. He agreed to do it.

To make sure he would arrive early, I asked Dexter to write down in his calendar the time he needed to leave instead of the time he needed to be there. When he looked at his schedule, he would get up and go regardless of the ringing phone and let his assistant handle the calls. This wasn't easy for Dexter, but he succeeded in arriving ten minutes early for a lunch appointment to discuss business with a prospective client. The executive he was meeting wasn't even there yet, so the maître d' showed Dexter to his table, and Dexter had a chance to sit, take in the surroundings, and compose his thoughts. So who has the advantage already? Dexter only had to wait five minutes before his prospective client arrived. That short time gave him a sense of peacefulness and enabled him to relax and focus on the client. The lunch was a success, and Dexter saw the immediate benefits of this simple strategy. He realized that he had been spending his commute worrying about what excuse he would make for arriving late instead of thinking about his objectives for the meeting. A reserve of time gives you an opportunity to slow down, to think about who you are going to be talking to and what you are going to say. It is the sign of a true professional.

Die-hard late folks like Dexter can simply write in your calendar the time you need to *leave* your home or office in order to be at the event ten minutes early. If you are not sure of the commute, factor in more extra time in case you get lost. Some people focus on the time of the event, and that is when they start getting ready to go, which explains why they are always late.

Under-promising is another way to help you show up ten minutes early. Instead of saying, "I'll be there in twenty minutes," say thirty minutes. That way if you get stuck in traffic your client won't be waiting around for you. If you don't get stuck and arrive early, use that ten minutes to relax and breathe deeply or just sit and do nothing. One client always carries a bunch of blank postcards with her and uses odd moments to keep up with her correspondence.

Of course, different cultures manage time in completely different ways. In Latin American countries you would never show up for a party at the stated time or risk catching the hostess in the shower! You'll need to make adjustments depending on the customs of the country.

34. GET YOUR WORK DONE IN HALF THE TIME

"Work expands so as to fill the time available for its completion."

C. NORTHCOTE PARKINSON,
PARKINSON'S LAW

If work expands to fill the available time, the solution is to reduce the amount of time you have to get the work done. When pressed, most people can get the job done in half the time they are currently using. I'm not kidding. Have you ever noticed that the day before you are leaving for a week of vacation you always manage to clean out an entire in-box that has been jammed for weeks? There is nothing like an incentive to get a body moving. How could you get your work done in half the time? It may take some creative thinking, but it is well worth the effort. You could use your spare time to work on your own projects, create a vision for your life or business, catch up on your correspondence, or send thank-you notes. A word of caution: not every workplace lends itself to this possibility; you might be closely supervised. Try this on the job only if it works for you.

You can also apply this principle to the work you need to do at home. How can you get the chores done in half the time? (See *Speed Cleaning*, by Jeff Campbell, for some great tips.) If you have a pile of paperwork on your desk, set an alarm for one hour and see if you can beat the clock. Tons of files to clean up? Set a morning aside and get a buddy who wants to work on a project of his or her own. Every hour call each other up for a two-minute progress report. For three weeks one of my clients kept saying she was going to clean up all the piles of papers in her office. It just wasn't getting done so we set up a Saturday morning from 9:00 A.M. until 12:00 P.M. to blast through it. I worked on my in-box and she worked on hers. She called me every hour to report her progress, and I gave her a pep talk to keep her going. In three hours she cleared her desk and two file drawers. She felt terrific! She had a clean slate that was easy to maintain with just a few minutes of filing every day. I did this with another one of my clients, who wanted to get some home improvement work done. I was cleaning up my files in New York, and she was painting the kitchen in Arizona.

Somehow this turns a dreary task into a fun game. You'll be amazed at how much you can accomplish. Afterward you'll feel great that you've gotten it out of the way, and you'll have more time to do the things you really love. The ultimate goal is to have as much time as possible for yourself and for the fun things in life. People who are having a great time easily attract success; opportunities come to them. So get your work done in half the time.

35. Ask Yourself, "What Is Important About Today?"

"The present is the point of power."

KATE GREEN

It is easy to become so preoccupied that you forget what really matters most. When a reporter asked Peter Lynch, the super-successful investment banker, why he left his high-powered job on Wall Street, he said, "When I am on my deathbed I'm not going to be saying, I wish I had spent more time at the office." He wanted to pack lunch for his two daughters and be there while they were growing up.

To help cut your work time in half, before you get caught up in your work every morning ask yourself these three questions and take a few minutes to jot down the answers:

1. What is important about today?
2. What must get done today?
3. What is important about the future?

By asking yourself, "What is important about today?" you may discover that today's important event is your son's third birthday, and you want to leave work at 3:00 P.M. to go to his party. It may be an important sales call that you need to spend an hour preparing for. Answering this question makes planning your day easier and helps you focus on the important things without getting distracted by everything else. Next, ask, "What must get done today?" You must meet with your manager at 1:00 P.M. to discuss a project. You must call this customer. You'll start to see that most of the time relatively few things *must* get done today. This can be very liberating. If you have a lot of "musts" then you haven't been in the practice of asking the third question, "What is important about the future?" This question forces you to plan. What is coming up that you could prepare for today, once you are done with today's "musts"? The report due next week? Your grandparents' fiftieth wedding anniversary coming up in two weeks? Keep asking these three questions and you'll soon catch up with the "musts."

Whole books have been written on the concept of time management. If you focus on these three questions, your life will not only become easier, but you'll save yourself the time of reading all those books. Time management is an oxymoron. You can't manage time, you can only manage your activities. As for the items that aren't on this list of three questions, they are generally a waste of time so just skip them.

I highly recommend to all my corporate and business clients that they set up a "Reading" hanging file folder in their desk drawer and regularly toss in long memos, reports, and articles to read later. One of my clients tried this and discovered that he never had to read 90 percent of the stuff that crossed his desk. He would file a lengthy memo, and before he'd even had a chance to read it, he would receive a new memo replacing the old one with some updated policy. On rare occasions someone would actually refer to a memo, and he would simply say, "Yes, I'm sure I've seen that, hold on a second." He'd flip through his file, pull it out, and be right up-to-date. After about a month, he would quickly sort through the pile, skim anything that looked interesting, and toss the whole lot.

36. Do One Thing at a Time

"Grasp all, lose all."

FOURTEENTH-CENTURY PROVERB

Rushing around trying to do ten things at once is not efficient. Give yourself permission to do one thing at a time. In reality, that's all you *can* do. You might as well accept it and focus on doing one thing consciously and well. I hear you protesting already that you not only *can* do multiple tasks at once, but you *have* to; you work in a busy, stressful office. Let's take a look at a typical busy day. You are working on a report, and the phone rings. You answer the phone while still looking at the report. You are talking on the phone and looking at the report when someone comes up to interrupt you. Now you are doing three things at once—a normal day at the office. No wonder you feel exhausted at the end of the day.

Now imagine the same situation in slow motion. You are working on the report, the phone rings, you STOP working on the report and pick up the phone, you START a phone conversation. Now someone comes in with a question, and you have a choice. Either you STOP the phone conversation, "Could you please hold?" and START a new conversation, or you STOP the interruption with a hand gesture, complete your phone conversation, hang up, and START the new conversation. You STOP that, then you START your report again. Your life is a series of starts, changes, stops. Since you really can only do one thing at a time, just do one thing at a time consciously and deliberately instead of pretending that you are doing three things at once. It is wonderfully liberating. When I consciously did one thing at a time at the office, I felt in control instead of harried and put upon. It is obviously stressful to try to do more than one thing at a time, and there is nothing attractive about stressed-out people. You will miss great opportunities if you are too busy to see them. This week make a point of only doing one thing at a time.

Lauren, a very busy and successful salesperson, was in the habit of eating, making calls from her cell phone, and putting on her makeup in the car on the way to work—all while she was driving, mind you. She was constantly juggling to get as much as possible crammed into every moment. She thought she was saving time this way. I asked Lauren to experiment for one week and just drive to work without doing anything else at the same time. She had to get up ten minutes earlier in order to put her makeup on, and she decided to bring her breakfast to work and eat it at her desk. It took everything she had to resist making phone calls, but after the first few days, she discovered a certain sense of calmness and peace. She realized that she wasn't saving as much time as she was stressing herself out. When she drove to work (I wouldn't even let her turn on the radio) her thoughts roamed free, and she came up with some creative ideas to find new clients. She gained a sense of control and peace that lasted throughout the day and was well worth the ten minutes in the morning.

37. Do It Now!

"He who hesitates is last."

MAE WEST

Responding immediately is attractive because it is still very rare even though it seems so obvious. It is so rare because most people procrastinate. In fact, you may need to upgrade systems, streamline, and change your whole manner of responding to people in order to provide an immediate response.

How can you respond immediately? My mantra is "Do it now." When I catch myself holding a piece of paper and thinking, "I'll look at this later . . ." I say, "No, do it now." Otherwise I waste a lot of time shuffling paper around. I received an E-mail notice that the boyfriend of one of my colleagues had died. I thought about sending a sympathy card. Then I caught myself postponing the activity and said, "Do it now!" I wrote a note on the spot. It was done, and I deleted the E-mail instead of saving it to handle another day or, worse yet, forgetting about it.

My client Rebecca had recently moved into Manhattan and was working as a salesclerk at a clothing store. The prospects for advancement weren't great so she began looking for a career in the fashion world. She was looking through the want ads and found one for a position with Giorgio Armani. The deadline for applications was that very day. She immediately typed up a résumé and faxed it over to them. Then she decided she would follow up to make sure they had received it. Did she just pick up the phone? No, she walked over to the store on Madison Avenue and very politely let the human resources manager know that she had just faxed over her résumé. Rebecca knew that her personal appearance and gracious manner were her greatest assets—attributes that would not be seen on the résumé. I am certain they were impressed with her immediate and personal response. This is the kind of personal attention that their high-end customers would demand. They were willing to give her a chance even though she had only three months of retail experience in New York, and they were looking for someone with three years of experience. After a week of interviews, she got the job and jumped from a dead-end job making $7.50 an hour to earning over $50,000 a year.

Where are you delaying? It may be costing you unnecessary time and energy. Anything you don't do now is something you will just have to do later. If you wait, the knowledge that you have to do it will be taking up valuable mental space and burdening you with the weight of trying to remember to do it later. If you really can't do it now, put it in a pending file and log the time and date that you will do it in your calendar or tickler file. What changes do you need to make to restructure your life so that you can respond immediately? You may want to post a little sign over your desk that says, "DO IT NOW!"

38. DO COMPLETE WORK

"There's only one real sin, and that is to persuade oneself that the second-best is anything but the second-best."

DORIS LESSING

"When we do the best that we can, we never know what miracle is wrought in our life, or in the life of another."

HELEN KELLER

It may seem that the way to save time is to get the job done as quickly as possible. While that may save time in the short run, doing complete work saves time in the long run and gives you the mental space and clarity to tackle the next project. Complete work is done so well and so thoroughly that it won't come back to haunt you. What would that look like on the job? Suppose a customer calls in and complains that an erroneous fee was charged to his or her account. The customer service representative politely responds, "Not a problem, I'll have it taken care of immediately." The customer hangs up, pleased with the service. The customer service representative does indeed reverse the charge, and a credit appears on the next statement. But there is also a new charge for that month's statement. The representative did take care of the fee, but being pressed for time, did not get to the source of the problem. Why was the fee assessed in the first place? With a little more research, the source would have been identified: the account was not encoded correctly. But this didn't happen so the client calls in, this time irate, and wants to speak to the manager. Then the client writes a complaint letter to the president's office, and ten other employees get involved from the top on down, memos must be written, etc. The solution is to do complete work the first time. Make this a company policy and watch your problems disappear.

On the home front, suppose you decide to wash the car. Instead of using a bucket of soapy water, you buy long-lasting polish designed to protect the car's finish. You polish the chrome, vacuum out the glove compartment, and put specially designed window cleaner on that repels the rain. You do a complete job. If you really go all out on a project, and do a super job, it is personally fulfilling. You'll be proud of your work. This alone is reason enough to do complete work.

You can do this in relationships too. What would your relationships be like if you said everything that needed to be said and made sure that nothing was left hanging? One of my friends always made a point of saying goodbye and hugging her parents whenever they left after dropping by for a visit. Then one time she was hosting a party and her parents left early. She was busy handing out appetizers and didn't have a chance to say goodbye. That night her mother died of a sudden heart attack. My friend was distraught, but never forgot it. She realized that nothing is more important than expressing your love to your family and friends. She could just as easily have taken a few moments to say goodbye and then gone back to the party. Of course, she is lucky that she had been telling her parents how much she loved and appreciated them all along. I have talked to many people who have never thanked their parents for bringing them into this world or told them that they love them. I usually ask my clients to do this.

Sam was in his late fifties, divorced, had three grown children, and still had some unresolved issues with his own father. He felt that his father had been super-critical of him while he was growing up and that there was nothing he could do to please him—nothing was good enough (Sam by this time was a highly successful businessman and sat on the boards of a number of corporations). I pointed out to Sam that his father was critical because he loved him so much and wanted nothing but the best for him. I encouraged him to talk to his father, who was now in his eighties, before it was too late and to tell him that he loved him. Sam wasn't too keen on the idea and said that it was too late, that his father wouldn't understand. I told him it didn't matter what his father did, what mattered was what Sam did. Far better to express your love and forgiveness while your parents are still alive. Sam did finally tell his father that he loved him. His father was his typical gruff self and passed over it, but Sam felt good about it anyway. He was finally able to forgive his father after all these years of resenting him. You will free up plenty of mental space when you make a standard of doing complete work and tying up loose ends in all areas of your life.

39. Procrastinate with Purpose

"Tomorrow is often the busiest day of the week."

Spanish proverb

"'Never put off until tomorrow what you can do today.' Under the influence of this pestilent morality, I am forever letting tomorrow's work slop backwards into today's and doing painfully and nervously today what I could do quickly and easily tomorrow."

J. A. Spender, *The Comments of Bagshot*

Tip 37 ("Do It Now!") notwithstanding, procrastination has an undeservedly bad reputation. Many people consider procrastination one of their weaknesses, and they beat themselves up and feel just terrible about how they procrastinate so. Perhaps they have it all wrong. What if procrastination was not the bad guy, but the good guy? What if your procrastination simply showed you the way to living your dreams and reaching your true goals? Hmm . . . we don't usually hear it presented this way.

First of all, let's take a moment to distinguish the various types of procrastination—we have a lot lumped into one big fat category. There is procrastination because you don't enjoy the task; procrastination because you lack information or knowledge; procrastination because the task is too overwhelming; procrastination because you don't have the right goal in the first place. All of these are excellent and valid reasons to procrastinate. Procrastination is a lot more complicated than it appears at first blush. Once you figure out *why* you are procrastinating, the rest is easier. Begin with the basic premise that procrastinating is a very good thing.

Why do you procrastinate?

1. You procrastinate because you don't like the task, job, or duty, so you put it off as long as possible.

I'm a firm believer that if you don't like doing something, you probably shouldn't be doing it. How the heck are you going to have a great life if you are doing all manner of tasks you don't enjoy? Exactly. Suppose you hate doing expense reports so you wait until you hit the limit on your company credit card before you start collecting the receipts and filling in the report so you can get reimbursed. Instead of wasting all that mental energy and getting into potentially awkward situations with clients, you just need to admit that you hate doing this task and delegate it to someone else. Train your assistant to do it, or if you don't have an assistant, pay a bookkeeper to do it for you. It is worth it. There, that one's handled. What other ugly tasks are you putting off? Most of the time, you shouldn't be spending your precious time doing that task anyway so delegate it or automate it.

You can also try isolating the part of the project you don't like and delegating or automating that. A client hated doing her weekly activity report. She realized what she hated about it was going back and thinking of all the things she did during the week. She couldn't delegate that because she had to collect her own thoughts. So she decided to use a mini tape recorder and take a few minutes at the end of the day to record her accomplishments. Then she gave the tape to her assistant to transcribe, and she edited the memo in about five minutes. What a relief!

On the home front, a client realized that he procrastinated with the housecleaning because he didn't like dusting. He decided to hire a house-keeper just to dust because he didn't mind doing the other stuff. This was an affordable solution for him and he was happy.

Suppose you hate leading meetings and as a sales manager you are expected to have one every week, but keep postponing it. Perhaps your team is self-reliant and doesn't really need a weekly meeting so it is just a waste of everyone's time anyway. Or try delegating it to someone else. Who says the manager always has to be the one leading the meetings? One sales manager I coached ended up delegating the leading of the sales meetings to a different salesperson each week. It turned out to be a highly effective technique, and everyone began to take more responsibility for the success of the team. Very few managerial tasks can't be delegated, so start training your team to do every aspect of your job. What if you don't have a team and you have an icky task to do? Try swapping with a col-league. I'll fill out the expense reports if you calculate the sales figures. Or recommend to your boss that the really nasty jobs no one likes be rotated regularly. That way one person isn't stuck doing the dirty work all the time, and the manager ends up with a team of people who are thoroughly cross-trained. A win-win for everyone.

2. You procrastinate because you don't know how to handle something.

A sticky issue arises at work and you aren't sure how to handle it, so you don't and just hope it goes away. You tell your boss or whomever that you need some time to think about it. Sometimes this head-in-the-sand approach actually works, and the issue resolves itself. Sometimes you have to get involved, but giving yourself a night to sleep on it may pro-duce the solution you were looking for. Or perhaps you need some addi-tional information before you can really make the best decision. Postponing the decision will give you the time to think about what is miss-ing for you to make the decision. Many times the information will just present itself out of the blue, and then you'll be able to proceed. Or maybe you are procrastinating out of ignorance. You may need more training in order to handle something, in which case make the request of your man-ager. Or perhaps you just need to do a little more research and check how someone else handled it or get some advice from your boss on how to deal with it. One client who ran a printing business was procrastinating about learning how to work his computer. He didn't even know how to plug it in, but knew that the computer would improve his effectiveness in the business. He was procrastinating out of ignorance. I recommended that he hire a specialist to come over and help him set up his computer, show him how to plug it in and how to use it. He also signed up for a basic computer class at a local business school.

Another client was procrastinating with the bookkeeping for her business. She had an entire year's worth of figures to enter and dreaded the task. She had purchased an accounting software program over a year ago, but hadn't even removed the plastic wrapper. She had no clue how to set up the program. I referred her to a bookkeeper who specialized in that program and who came right to her home office, set up her program, entered all her data, and taught her how to use the program. That solved that.

3. You procrastinate because you can't find the time.

Now perhaps it isn't that you hate the task, and it isn't that you don't know how to handle it, but you just can't seem to find the time. The project looks overwhelming and you don't know where or how to get started. One client, a professional trainer and speaker, had been wanting to write a book for years but just couldn't seem to find the time. He knew a book would help him take his speaking business to the next level and would generate more income. He had always wanted to write a book so it wasn't that he didn't want to do it. He even knew what he wanted to write and had collected a number of ideas. His problem was in getting started and getting the momentum. The overwhelming size of the task left him at a complete standstill. And the truth of the matter was that he hadn't carved out the space and time in his life to write a book.

First, I got him clearing off his desk, where he was buried in mounds of paper. Then we started carving out blocks of time reserved for writing. He decided that the best time for him was for the first three hours before lunch. We set a goal of just writing for those hours and not worrying about the end result. He had to sit and write even if he thought it was no good. The object was to write for three hours, not to worry about quality. His schedule was erratic, but when he wasn't booked to lead a training or seminar, he used those hours to write. In six months he had already completed half his book.

4. You procrastinate because you don't really want to do what you said you want to do.

This is called having the wrong goal in the first place, or if not the wrong goal, the wrong strategy. Take losing weight—why would anyone want to restrict calories and suffer and do all the horrible things there are to lose weight? Just mentioning the goal "lose weight and get in shape" depresses most people. They are procrastinating because they don't really want to do it, they just think they should. This goes back to dumping the old goals and getting rid of the "shoulds" (Tip 4).

5. You procrastinate because you are stuck and need a boost to get yourself going and create a little momentum.

Once you get started, you find the energy to do the whole job. One client did this with a remodeling project at home. He wanted to replace the light fixture in his dining room and knew that if he did that, he'd have to repair and repaint the ceiling as well. This is a case of the task seeming monumental. So he decided he would just go to the store and buy the supplies. He did that and then he decided, well, I'll just remove the old light fixture. He did that and said, well, I'll just start with the taping. He did that and said, well, I might as well do the replastering so it will have time to dry. He did that and then he said, I might as well just try a coat of paint and see if I like the color. Before you know it, he had talked himself into completing the entire project one little step at a time. Give yourself permission to do just one tiny piece of the project and quit. More often than not, you'll do a whole bunch more because of the natural momentum created.

6. You procrastinate because you need time to mull things over.

This is what I call creative procrastination. If you are an artist, writer, or painter, or perhaps are just trying to think through some thorny problem, you may find yourself procrastinating. This is not only appropriate, but necessary. You may find yourself suddenly doing the ironing or mowing the lawn or some other menial task you normally abhor because it suddenly looks more appealing than your current project. This is just fine. You need the time to get your thoughts together before you embark. At some point you will be ready and will start to paint or write, and everything will pour forth effortlessly.

A computer consultant friend was helping me straighten out a problem I was having with my database, and he couldn't figure it out. After scratching our heads in frustration for a while, I got fed up and said, "Let's go to the movies and forget about it." Sure enough, in the middle of the movie, he prods me with his elbow and has a big grin on his face—the solution had come to him. After the movie, he came back to my office and fixed the whole thing in five minutes. So while going to the movies might look like procrastination or slacking off, your brain is still ticking away at the problem.

You now have six reasons why procrastinating is a very good thing if you do it with purpose. Make a list of all the things you are procrastinating about and figure out why—then you have the solution.

40. SET ASIDE SACRED EVENINGS

"To survive we must begin to know sacredness. The pace at which most of us live prevents this."

CHRYSTOS

A sacred evening is just that: an evening you reserve for yourself to do exactly as you please, whether that is going for a stroll in the park, taking a bubble bath, getting a massage, reading a book, going to a concert, or just doing nothing at all. It is a time for you to be by yourself, to play, to rest, to relax. You have nothing planned or scheduled. It is sacred because you must hold it as inviolable time. That which is sacred is separate from mundane activity and set apart for a higher purpose. If you don't take sacred time for yourself, it will get scheduled away like the rest of your life.

If you have kids, it is ten times more important that you give yourself sacred evenings. You need time to engage in adult activities and time to be totally selfish (Tip 87). Then, when you are with the kids, you'll find that you are glad to be with them. I have two sisters, one a year older and one a year younger, and my mom stayed home to raise us. I just recently found out that when we were little, on occasion she would go to the grocery store just to be around other adults and hear adult conversation. You *need* these sacred evenings—it's not optional.

Look at your calendar, take out a yellow highlighter, and block off those free evenings. Block off at least one night a week. Married with children? This is not a problem. You can each give the other a night off once a week. Make this a legitimate evening off rather than sneaking out and feeling guilty about it. Let your partner do whatever he or she wants. Then when you are together, you'll be relaxed, refreshed, and happier.

V.

· ·

BUILD POWERFUL
RELATIONSHIPS

"He can attract it best by not being attached to it."

DONALD J. WALTERS, *MONEY MAGNETISM*

ASK SUCCESSFUL PEOPLE how they achieved that success and they will tell you they didn't do it alone. We need other people for support and encouragement, we need them for ideas and friendship, and we need them for love and kindness. Having the right connections and knowing powerful people will greatly increase your chances for success. Now I'm not going to go through the standard stuff you've heard repeatedly about the importance of networking and joining the right associations. Anyone can run around and collect a bunch of business cards. Lots of people have huge databases, but few have a strong network of supportive and powerful friends. Part V is about creating deep and lasting alliances with great people, not superficial acquaintanceships. We will go right to the heart of the matter and look at what it is that really attracts people to one another in business and personal relationships.

When it comes down to it, we want to work with people we like and trust, even if someone else may be offering a better service. We are most attracted to the people who aren't needy. Thus, one of the key elements to being successful and attracting the best people and opportunities is to identify and then fulfill your needs. In Part III, you handled your financial needs; now it is time to fulfill your emotional needs and develop powerful, lasting relationships.

For starters, just as you need more money than you think, you also need more friends and love. We are used to getting by with just enough. Always living on the edge and just getting by is inherently stressful. If you want to attract success, you need *more* than enough—an abundance of loving friends and supportive colleagues. Getting more than you need may be the single most important thing you can do to attract everything you want and draw success to you like a bee to a flower. You want enough to completely stamp out any feelings of neediness. We've all seen relationships in which a needy person ends up repelling the very person he or she is trying desperately to attract. The one who doesn't need you is always more attractive.

This principle of "not needing it" works in all areas of your life, not just relationships. If you don't need money, it is easier to attract money (this explains the saying "the rich get richer and the poor get poorer"). Try going to the bank and getting a loan when you are in desperate need and want to consolidate your credit cards with a low-interest loan. You will probably be declined for having "excessive obligations." However, if you have money in savings and go in for a loan (you really don't need it) it is easy to get one. When you don't need it, you are most likely to receive it; when you do need it, they smell the desperation and run from you— life's big catch-22. The same with friends. If you don't need more friends it is easy to attract new ones. We are naturally attracted to the friendly and confident person who is liked by everyone.

Satisfying your needs also dramatically reduces your stress. Running around in survival mode is not particularly attractive behavior. Most people aren't even aware of what their needs are, and even fewer people take action to get their needs met. Yet this process is essential to attracting success and will change your life. If you don't take the time to figure out what your needs are, you may spend time chasing things that you *think* make you happy, but ultimately leave you unfulfilled.

Fortunately, it is easier to get more than you need if you've increased your energy first. If you find that the tips in this part are too much of a struggle, go back to Part I, Increase Your Natural Power, and see what you might have missed. Asking others to meet your needs is one of the most challenging and difficult of all the coaching tips, as it makes most people feel uncomfortable. Don't let that stop you from doing this part. The payoff is well worth any initial discontent.

41. Make Amends

"If you haven't forgiven yourself something, how can you forgive others?"

Dolores Huerta

The best way to start attracting great people into your life is to clean up the relationships you already have. This should sound familiar. Maintain what you have before you expand is a key principle in coaching. Let's start with the most intimate and important relationship of all—the one with yourself. What are your less than desirable traits? Perhaps you are too critical and judgmental of others? There is nothing, absolutely nothing, attractive about judging others. Quite the contrary. Nobody likes being judged, so if you want to be successful, this may be an area to work on.

Naturally, I wanted to eliminate this negative personality trait and, after some investigation, discovered its source—me! People who are judgmental are usually hard on themselves. They hold themselves to a high standard, and when they don't make it they beat themselves up about it. You are judging and evaluating yourself all the time and my, what a harsh critic you are. You can't help yourself, but you end up holding your loved ones to the same high standards you have for yourself, whether they have agreed to these standards or are even aware of them. Not exactly fair, is it? This is why you may come across as judgmental toward the people you love most. Acquaintances may not feel the brunt of this because they aren't so close. The magic cure for this unpleasant trait is to forgive yourself first. When you stop being so hard on yourself, you will have room in your heart to forgive others too. It starts with you.

Another way to think about this is to realize that you are doing the best you can at the time. You had a rough day at work, you didn't have time for lunch, you come home, and the kids want you to take them for ice cream. You snap back, "Can't you see I've had a bad day!?!" Not the best thing you've ever done, but the best you could do on an empty stomach after a rough day. Forgive yourself first. Then go apologize to the kids. So now when people snap at you, or do less than you expected, you can already forgive them in advance because you know they are doing the best they can at that time. This does not mean that you condone unpleasantness; rather, that you stop judging it. You can let someone know, "Do you realize you just snapped at me?" in a neutral tone of voice without being judgmental. It is not right or wrong, good or bad; it simply bothers you.

Most people have a whole list of things they have been carrying around that they haven't forgiven themselves for and are still beating themselves up about. To err is human. So get out your pen and paper and start listing all the things you haven't forgiven yourself for. Think back to when you were a little kid and got your brother or sister or friend in trouble for the "crime" you committed, and work your way up to the present when yesterday you said something derogatory to a colleague at work. Now go through that list and see whom you can contact to apologize. I still haven't located Jeffrey, whom I blamed for stealing my blue pencil in the third grade only to discover later that I had left it at home. In some cases it may be enough to apologize and in other cases you may need to make reparations or amends. If someone spilled red wine all over the beautiful white sweater you loaned me to wear to a party and I came back and handed you a ruined sweater with my sincerest apologies, that wouldn't do it. I need to get you a new sweater just like or even better than the one I ruined. So go out there and make apologies and amends as appropriate. This is an amazingly liberating exercise and will free up an incredible amount of energy. Apologize, make amends, and above all, forgive yourself.

42. FORGIVE IN ADVANCE

"The weak can never forgive. Forgiveness is the attribute of the strong."

GANDHI

Bearing a grudge, being angry or resentful, is a *huge* energy drain. If you want to relieve a tremendous weight and feel ten pounds lighter instantly all you need to do is call somebody you hurt or wronged in some way and apologize. Yes, do this even if it wasn't your fault. In fact, take this one step further and call up everybody who has hurt you and forgive them. This takes a great willingness to forgive and to give up being right about stuff (yes, do this even if you are right and they are wrong). The whole point here isn't who is right and who is wrong, but that it is affecting you and your ability to attract what you want in life. You don't need any past burdens and grudges weighing you down or slowing you up—and they will if you don't do something about it.

My client Karen had divorced her first husband three years ago and was happily remarried. Her ex-husband had also remarried. She had just started the coaching program with me and the first issue that came up was the fact that she was still upset with some hurtful things her ex-husband had said during their marriage. (Whenever you have something unresolved from the past it will rear its ugly head when you start taking action on your dreams.) I told her to call him right up and inform him (Tip 6) in a neutral tone of voice what he had said and how it had hurt her. Just stick to the facts without any embellishment. Then ask him to apologize and then forgive him. Karen did not want to do this. "Why not?" I asked. She didn't want to dredge up the past. "Well, that's too bad. You've already dredged it up, so you can sweep it back under the carpet where it was before and wait for it to pop up again in the future, or you can deal with it now and get on with the rest of your life. The whole call will take all of five minutes. It's your choice, but let's make sure you are aware of the costs of not clearing this stuff up. First, it will keep popping up at different points in your life until you handle it. It isn't going to go away. Second, by not resolving this you get to be a victim in the relationship, and he gets to be the ogre. Is that how you want to remember your first marriage? Third, by keeping this unresolved, you are, in effect, hanging onto this old relationship, and it is getting in the way of your current relationship with your husband. This will all disappear the moment you forgive him. This is just a five-minute conversation." She hesitated, then said she would think about it.

The next day I get an ecstatic phone message. Karen called him up. They had a great conversation, she told him what was bothering her without blaming or judging, and she forgave him. She was bouncing off the walls with all the newfound energy. Freed at last from the weight of the past, she was now ready to get going with her dreams and goals. The key to freedom is forgiveness.

Don't let the past weigh you down. Forgive everyone. Forgive yourself. Now that you know you need to forgive people in the end anyway so you can be free of them or the incident, you might as well just forgive everyone in advance. This will save you tons of time, heartache, and energy. Think about it; wouldn't you want to be forgiven in advance? Make a list of the people you are holding grudges against, the people you don't want to talk to or see, and get on the phone or start writing letters. Remember, you can say just about anything to anybody if you do it in a neutral tone of voice. And don't make the mistake of thinking you have forgiven someone when you still have some small rancor or resentment. As for the truly egregious stuff, get the therapy you need to start coming to grips with your anger—a little progress can go a long way toward freeing up your energy and your life. Another thing: not forgiving somebody doesn't hurt anybody but you. They probably don't even remember what it was that you were so upset about in the first place. Start making amends today.

43. IDENTIFY YOUR NEEDS

"Everything comes to the man who does not need it."

FRENCH PROVERB

How do you figure out what your needs are in the first place? Your emotional needs are what you *must* have in order to be your best. When your needs aren't being met you will probably feel irritable, unloved or unappreciated, angry, resentful, jealous, deprived—any or all of these unpleasant feelings indicate that some need of yours is not being met. Everyone has different needs. Take Michelle, who has a strong need for independence. When this need is met, she does her best work. When Michelle worked under a boss who micromanaged her, she very quickly became irritable and resentful and started complaining to everyone who would listen. Left to her own devices she does a great job, which is one reason why now she prefers owning her own company—it meets her need for independence. Another person might have a need for clarity and would prefer to work under a manager who spelled out exactly what to do and how to do it. Neither need is better or worse, good or bad, just different. It makes your manager's job easier if you tell him or her how you need to be managed to perform at your best. If you work best with lots of feedback, tell your manager and set up a system so you can get the regular feedback you need. Perhaps this could be done in a ten-minute weekly meeting with your boss.

My client Paul has a need for approval. He starts to doubt himself and his abilities if he doesn't get regular doses of approval from friends, colleagues, and supervisors. This explains why he majored in accounting even though it went completely against his natural inclination. (Paul is a gregarious, fun-loving people-person and is now much happier as a professional speaker.) Paul's father wanted him to be an accountant because he was an accountant, and Paul very much wanted his father's approval. Needs are so powerful that they will have us doing bizarre stuff in an attempt to satisfy them, even if it obviously doesn't make sense or is to our own detriment.

Behind just about any bizarre behavior or addiction is an unmet need. If you were starving you might dig through trash to find food or you might even beg or steal for food. Well, most of us are starving in terms of getting our emotional needs met. Men, this part is for you too. Although in our culture we don't want our men to have needs, they have as many as women do. It is a part of being human to have emotional needs, and pretending not to have them won't change the fact that you do. A client, Raymond, had a need to be in control. Small wonder that he was a judge. When he told his wife about his need to control, she wasn't the least bit surprised, but by articulating it, they got it out in the open and could come up with healthy and acceptable ways for him to meet this need. For one thing, she decided on the spot to let him have the remote control for the TV.

Here are some of the most common needs. Keep in mind that there are hundreds of different needs, and yours might be some version of one of these. Most people have some variation on the need to be loved. I say "most" because some people have this need so fully met that it doesn't even occur to them as a need, just like after Thanksgiving dinner it doesn't occur to you to eat. Variations of the need to be loved include: to be cherished, adored, approved of, acknowledged, cared for, accepted, included, valued, treasured, saved. Read through this list and see if any ring true for you.

Other needs are: to be certain; to control, dominate, command, or manage; to communicate, share, be listened to; to be comfortable, protected; to follow; to be free, independent, self-reliant; to feel needed, important, useful; to be noticed or remembered; to improve, please, or satisfy others; to do the right thing; to have a cause or vocation; to work; to be busy. You may need honesty, sincerity, loyalty; order, consistency, perfection; peace, quietness, calmness, balance; power, strength, influence, acclaim; abundance, security.

Pick your top two or three needs (what you *must* have to be your best) or invent your own. If nothing pops out at you after reading the above list, try this approach: When are you feeling cranky and irritable? Is it when you find yourself saying yes to something when you really wanted to say no? Or when someone is taking advantage of you? Look at the flip side and perhaps you have a need to please others or be liked so you find it very difficult to say no. Identifying your needs isn't easy. Most of my clients balk at this step and want to quickly move on, but I don't let them because this is a critical element of attracting success. You have experienced how unattractive neediness is, so don't gloss over this one. If you are having trouble figuring this out, you may want to work on this with a coach or someone who knows you well. Now you are ready to start asking for what you really want (Tip 44).

44. ASK FOR WHAT YOU REALLY WANT

"Ask, and it shall be given you; seek, and ye shall find; knock, and it shall be opened unto you."

MATTHEW 5:1

A lot of time, heartache, and energy would be saved if we just asked for what we really wanted. I know it sounds simple, but for some reason, most people are reluctant to do this. Somewhere we got this idea that our colleagues, friends, family, and loved ones should just *know* what we want without our having to ask for it. Perhaps we think our loved ones have the same needs and desires that we have. Whatever we think, it just isn't so. We all have unique needs and unique ways to meet them.

Once you discover what your unique needs are, you will be much more aware of them. Stephen, who worked as a sales executive in an upscale retail store, discovered that he had a need for appreciation. He had been doing great work and had racked up a terrific number of sales but hadn't heard a peep about his stellar performance from his managers. Stephen was getting miffed and a bit cranky. Instead of just pouting or complaining to his colleagues about how unappreciative his managers were, Stephen realized he was responsible for getting his needs met. In their weekly meeting, Stephen addressed this very simply by informing his managers that he'd like more positive feedback on his results. The two managers immediately apologized and thanked him for letting them know. They both admitted that they were terrible at giving positive feedback and needed to do it more often. Stephen got permission to prompt them occasionally, and they were appreciative. When Stephen called he was thrilled. He didn't realize how simple and easy it was to get this need for appreciation met on the job.

One of my clients realized she had a need to be treasured so she casually mentioned this to her boyfriend. Soon he was bringing her beautiful bouquets of flowers, gifts, and chocolates. He thought that was what she meant by being treasured. Believe it or not, this client complained to me that this wasn't making her feel more treasured, although it certainly was very impressive. I asked her what did make her feel treasured, and it turned out to be the small gestures—a secret squeeze of the hand, a loving look, and sweet nothings whispered in her ear were what she really wanted. She asked very specifically for what she really wanted, and he was pleased to know. Her boyfriend started to treasure her the way she wanted to be treasured. So if you like being held tenderly instead of getting a big bear hug, say so. If you like getting tulips instead of roses, ask for them.

Somehow we have this crazy notion that it isn't the same if you have to ask for it; that people should magically know what you need and want, especially your significant other. Well, the first thing to realize is that people don't know. They just don't. More often than not, our bosses don't know how we prefer to be managed, and our friends don't know how we need to be appreciated. Most of us give what we'd like to receive. While this may work some of the time, it certainly doesn't work all of the time because we are all different and we all have different needs. If we don't even know what makes us feel special, how on earth can we expect someone else to figure this out? Second, it is not true at all that asking ruins it. That is a huge myth. You'll have to experiment with this for yourself. I gave my boyfriend permission to go right ahead and give me foot massages at any appropriate opportunity. He got into the habit of putting my feet in his lap and massaging away. And believe me, it felt just as good! The people who love you and care about you will want to make you feel great, so don't hesitate to ask for what really makes you happy.

Once you've identified your needs it is time to ask your friends and family and sometimes even your colleagues to satisfy those needs. Be very specific in doing this. Ideally you should ask five different people to meet a given need in different ways. The point of the exercise is to overdo it and get so many people meeting your needs that you feel completely satiated. For example, Martin discovered he had two key needs: to be respected and to be loved. He asked his wife to give him a romantic kiss when he got home from work and say how much she loved him. He asked his father to call once a week to tell him something that he admired about him, like, "I'm proud to have you as my son." Martin asked his sister to E-mail him a "love note" once a week. Now Martin wasn't about to ask his boss to kiss him or send a love note, but it was certainly appropriate to ask his boss for positive feedback on his work. He also asked his colleagues for feedback. This may sound like Martin is exceptionally needy, but that is precisely the point of this coaching assignment. You are supposed to overdo it—the point is to get *more* than enough. At first you will probably feel embarrassed and awkward asking someone, even close friends and family members, to fulfill your needs. That is perfectly normal. Don't let that stop you from going ahead with the assignment. The key to making your needs "disappear" is to get lots of people to fulfill them in a variety of ways. Once you've done this assignment, you won't come across as needy anymore. In fact, you'll be much more content, satisfied, and confident.

You can also set up ways to meet your own needs. Martin finds he feels more respect for himself when he works out and takes excellent care of his health and body. I felt cherished by hiring a housekeeper (Tip 15), a massage therapist (Tip 84), and a personal trainer (Tip 85), and by setting aside time for myself with sacred evenings (Tip 40). After about four to six weeks of all this pampering you will begin to feel satisfied. You won't be as needy anymore because you have gotten an overdose of fulfillment. You won't need your friends and family to call you each week forever, although if they enjoy doing it, why not continue?

One of my clients had a friend call every week just to tell him one thing that he appreciated about him. They have been doing this for three years now and have formed a powerful and supportive relationship in the process. Another client, Barbara, used to call her mother once a month—they loved each other and had a good relationship. In order to fulfill her need to be loved, Barbara asked her mother to call her every week and tell her that she loved her. This weekly phone call created a deeper relationship and gradually Barbara became close friends with her mother—something she had never realized was possible. Her mother became one of her biggest supporters as she started her own business.

Opening yourself up and being vulnerable enough to ask someone to meet one of your needs isn't easy, but the payoff is often tremendous for both parties. The people who love you will want to meet your needs and will be happy to do so. Don't try to force people to meet your needs. Another client wanted her longtime lover to meet her need to be appreciated. The lover didn't want to do it. She suddenly realized that all these years it had been a one-way relationship with her constantly giving and her partner taking. When she wanted her partner to give it didn't happen. A few months later she ended the relationship, moved out, and started developing healthier relationships with give and take on both sides.

It is essential to find multiple sources to meet your needs. If you rely on yourself, you may forget or stop doing it. If you rely on one person to meet your needs, he or she will resent it after a while. We tend to assume that our significant others should not only meet all our needs completely, but do so without our even letting them know what our needs are—a pretty big burden. No wonder so many relationships end in disappointment or divorce. Can you see that by relying heavily on one person to meet your needs, you are potentially straining the relationship? When you are in love, your needs are getting met, you are both making a special effort. At first you are thrilled to give a massage, bring flowers, cook a romantic dinner. But over time, if this is no longer optional, it becomes a burden, not a joy. Meeting your needs is not optional; you must get them met to be your best, just like you have to eat in order to meet your basic physical needs. But don't expect one person to meet them all. The best relationships are those in which needs are met outside of the relationship as much as inside it.

This goes contrary to everything we have heard about love and needing someone else. For the most part, we have, as a society, confused needing with loving. They are two entirely different things. This probably explains the high divorce rate. People get married because the other person fulfills their needs. In a few years, the person gets sick and tired of fulfilling the other's needs, and begins to resent it. Then the unfulfilled person can justifiably say, "You aren't meeting my needs—you aren't the person I married," and they get a divorce and start looking for someone else to meet their needs. This is the danger of basing your relationships on mutual needs satisfaction. While a person who loves you should be glad to meet your needs, you don't want to rely solely on that person to meet them. Needing someone is not the same as loving him or her.

Ideally, you want to get your needs so completely satisfied that they "disappear." Think of having a stocked refrigerator. When you are hungry you can just open the door and get some food to eat. The same with needs. What would it look like to have one of your needs so fully met that you didn't worry about it anymore? When you feel a need for something, you will naturally ask for it. This doesn't mean that you won't want your loved ones to meet your needs. But look at the difference in a relationship. I want the man I marry to have both the willingness and the ability to buy food and take care of me. However, he doesn't *have to* do that because I can fulfill that need very well myself. If someone does feed me, it is a lovely gesture, a nice bonus, but not a requirement. I want a man to feed me not because he has to, but just because he wants to. The same with emotional needs. Obviously, I will not marry someone who isn't willing and able to cherish me, but I also wouldn't want cherishing to be a requirement, just as I wouldn't want his ability to feed me to be the reason I marry him. Love is a choice, not an obligation.

One of my clients realized that she had a need to be told she was beautiful. Whenever her boyfriend told her she was beautiful, she thanked him and said that made her feel really loved and appreciated. This is really smart. If someone accidentally or intentionally meets one of your needs, you can get more of that by reinforcing the action with an acknowledgment. In effect, you are coaching the people around you to treat you in a way that brings out your best. The more conscious you become of what your needs are, the more creative you will get in finding ways to meet them. At first it may feel awkward and uncomfortable, but soon you will be naturally asking people to meet your needs without even realizing it.

In working on the needs with clients, invariably I will hear that they can't possibly ask people to meet their needs. Well, you will be amazed at how people will want to meet your needs once you tell them those needs. Once when I was leading a seminar in London, I talked in great detail about needs and mentioned as an example my own need to be cherished. I told the audience that I kept on discovering new things that made me feel cherished, and one of them was having my hair stroked. (When I was little my father used to rock me and stroke my hair when I was sad, a tender gesture that made me feel loved and protected.) Well, at the end of the day a number of people came up to tell me how much they had enjoyed the seminar and actually reached up and ran their fingers through my hair. I was both mortified and amazed. I was amazed because these were supposed to be stiff-upper-lip Brits after all, and here they were lining up and patting me on the head, stroking my hair in public. I was mortified because I had left out an important detail—I like the *man* in my life to run his fingers through my hair, not just anyone on the street! So remember to be specific because you will get what you ask for.

The point of this exercise is to ask others to meet your needs. Just the act of asking should make you feel embarrassed, uncomfortable, and silly. If not, then you probably haven't identified a true need.

45. FIND YOUR OWN FAMILY

"Without a family, man, alone in the world, trembles with the cold."

ANDRÉ MAUROIS,
THE ART OF LIVING

It is extremely difficult to attract the success you want without close friends and family who love and support you unconditionally. What is success without loved ones to share it with? You may have the good fortune to be born into a loving and supportive family, but if not, it is essential to create your own family. Find people who will "adopt" you and love you just like a son or daughter. Not everybody is lucky enough to have parents who can offer this special love. Instead of spending time complaining about your parents or blaming them for your problems, it may be time to accept them for who they are and start looking for someone who *can* act as a mother or father to you. Fortunately, there are plenty of people out there with love to give so if you look, you will find them.

One of my clients realized that even though her own parents couldn't give her the love she needed, her in-laws could. They took her in just like a daughter, and she accepted and loved them like parents. Don lost both of his parents when he was fourteen, and an aunt took him in and raised him. He is thirty-three now, and although he loves his aunt like a mother, he still yearned for someone to be a father to him. I suggested that he visit a retirement home and find someone there who had love to give. Don met an elderly gentleman who shared his love of baseball. He went to visit him every week, and soon Don felt he had found the love and affection he had been missing. If you already have great parents, be thankful and acknowledge them often.

So often we assume that our parents will be around—that there will be time later to talk. This isn't always the case. A colleague of mine had always wanted to take her father to Sweden and had assumed that they would make the trip after her ailing mother died. Then her father unexpectedly developed kidney trouble and had to get dialysis treatments regularly. Things weren't working according to plan, and she realized that she had better take him to Sweden as soon as possible. He had been caring for his wife, but she agreed to let him go for two weeks. They had an incredible trip. He had never been in a hotel in his life; he had never traveled because his wife didn't enjoy it. He hadn't been back to Sweden since he had left as a teenager. They went to the old neighborhood and saw people he hadn't seen in years and looked at the house where he was born. My colleague hadn't heard her father let rip a deep belly laugh in years. He said that the trip was the best thing he had ever done in his entire eighty-three years. Do not wait to enjoy your parents. Let them know how much you love them with both words and actions.

46. DATE YOUR SPOUSE

"As is usual with most lovers in the city, they were troubled by the lack of that essential need of love—a meeting place."

THOMAS WOLFE, *THE WEB AND THE ROCK*

Most successful people have a strong supporter behind them cheering them on from the sidelines, someone who will hold them tight when they feel shattered, someone who will love them flaws and all. This is often a spouse or partner. How much time do you spend every week in one-on-one conversation with the love of your life? The national average is twenty-seven minutes. This is because we assume our spouse will always be there so we can talk when we have time, but of course, there never is time in most busy households.

If you want a nurturing, supportive, loving relationship it is imperative that you date your spouse or partner once a week. This will ensure that you break that appalling national average. Hire a sitter, trade a night with the neighbor, but whatever you do, make sure you have a romantic evening to enjoy your partner. It is important to keep the romance alive, to nourish the relationship. You don't have to go someplace fancy, but go out. Pack a picnic lunch, eat it in the park, and watch the moon rise. Or go to that cheap and delicious Chinese restaurant. Put on a great-looking outfit or suit and go out. This may be the only time you and your partner have to talk about your hopes and plan your dreams. Have fun! Be creative. Avoid topics you know will cause trouble and stick to the more romantic stuff. You deserve this special time together. It will enliven your relationship and remind you why you are together in the first place. It is also good to be a model for your children by showing them how much you treasure your relationship. You'll both be better parents the rest of the week.

My client Laura was complaining that her husband wasn't supporting her in her consulting business, which she was working on at home in the evenings in hopes of leaving the day job she hated. She also complained that he wasn't romantic anymore. He never brought her flowers or gave her gifts. They rarely did anything together since the two kids were born. I told Laura to hire a sitter one night a week and just go out with her husband alone. There was nothing wrong with their relationship that a little attention wouldn't fix. It is very hard to be romantic when the kids are screaming in the background and little Suzy has just spilled milk all over your shirt. Laura was skeptical, and her husband was reluctant to spend the money for the sitter, but I told her to do it anyway. It was essential to the success of their relationship that they spend some time simply enjoying each other.

The next week Laura called back to report that they had fun on their date. They went to a nice little restaurant, and they talked about their plans for building a new house and growing her home-based business.

Then they walked through a shopping mall together holding hands. She said it was so pleasant just being with him. Then later that week, she was in a store and a man came up behind her and put his hands over her eyes. It was her husband. She got excited to see him in the store unexpectedly and saw him for a moment the way other people would see him—this great attractive hunk of a fellow who was crazy in love with her. She felt so lucky to have him. They have been continuing their weekly dates and are now really working well together as a couple. Laura supports him in being successful on the job, and he has gradually become her most enthusiastic supporter, actively encouraging her to leave her job so that she can focus on her own business. Date your spouse, nurture the most important relationship in your life, and he or she will in turn give you the energy you need to be successful in your work.

47. BUILD A STRONG NETWORK OF SPECIAL FRIENDS

"We cease loving ourselves if no one loves us."

MADAME DE STAËL

What is success without friends to love, enjoy, and celebrate with? You need plenty of friends who love and support you. Many get by with one really close friend, but while that may be enough, successful folks typically have a number of really close friends. Robert thought he had plenty of friends—three lifelong buddies. However, one is in Washington, D.C., one is in Oregon, and the other is in Russia. He stays in contact with notes and calls and occasional visits, but it isn't the same as having someone in town whom he can actually play with. Obviously, you won't be able to go out and find five new friends for life in a week, but you can open up your heart and make room for more friends. And you can create a club, join an organization, or start a hobby where you will meet people with similar interests. Be aware of the people around you in business functions, networking events, and parties, and if someone there seems special and interesting, make an effort to get to know them.

One client, Lauren, met a very influential woman in media at a cocktail party, and they hit it off right away. The media maven asked Lauren if she would like to go out to lunch to get to know each other. Of course she gladly accepted. Lauren was torn though between becoming friends with this woman or trying to get her as a new client. She thought it would be great to have such an influential client. I recommended that she forget about the business side of the relationship and focus on developing the friendship instead. Remember that true friends are rare and treasured finds; clients may come and go. Lauren did exactly that, and in the long run this friend gave her numerous business opportunities and referred all sorts of clients to her. If Lauren had tried to pursue the business relationship right away, it might have backfired on her.

On the other hand, don't try too hard to get close to people—either it is effortless or it isn't worth it. (If you've met your needs—Tip 43—this probably won't be an issue.) Friendships and good working relationships happen naturally, and while you may need to make an initial effort to get the relationship started (such as a phone call to invite someone out to lunch or to get together), you don't want to push yourself on other people either.

Successful people typically are at the center of a strong and supportive community. Very few people these days stay in the same place they were born. The easiest way to be a part of a community is to stay in one place for a long time. You become a part of the town and people get to know you. In small towns almost everybody knows everybody. Built-in communities of this sort were once taken for granted. People have forgotten that being part of a loving and supportive community is an important part of life. You will not be your best if you are not part of a loving community.

These days you usually have to create your own community, and this is actually a very good thing. Instead of being stuck with the people in your geographic area, you can pick and choose the right group for you and find people you truly enjoy. Work environments or church groups frequently serve as communities, but not always. I never did feel a part of the banking crowd, but I immediately liked and respected my fellow coaching colleagues. Keep looking and experimenting until you find a group of people you really love. You'll feel right at home when you find the right group.

One of my clients has a beautiful life that most people would envy—a happy, thirty-year marriage to a loving and supportive husband, two lovely and successful children, two gorgeous homes, and a successful retail business—the ideal American dream life. For twenty-three years she has belonged to a book club of fourteen women. They meet once a month to discuss a book, but over the years they have become a tremendous support to one another. They have helped each other through two husbands' heart attacks and deaths, teenagers on drugs, breast cancer, you name it—all the horrible things that can happen in life. Not one of them has ever needed to see a psychiatrist because each has the tremendous love and support of thirteen other women. Of course, most of the time they just have a grand time and are there to whoop it up for all of the celebrations in life—their children's weddings, grandchildren, new business ventures, successes, birthday parties, and anniversaries. The book club ensures that, no matter what happens, they will all be there for each other. An insurance policy for loneliness.

If you don't already have this sort of powerful and supportive group, now is the time to start one. Create your own or join an existing club. Once you find the right group, stick with it like glue. Closeness and trust will build over time.

48. Create Your Own Mastermind Group

CRYSTAL: *"Do you realize that most people use two percent of their mind's potential?"*

ROSEANNE: *"That much, huh?"*

"ROSEANNE"

The more you want to accomplish, the more help you'll need. Successful people don't get there all by themselves. You need more support, help, advice, and encouragement than you think you need, especially if you are going to do something big. The most successful people have a team to help them, to give them sage counsel—a mastermind group. The president has his cabinet to advise him. CEOs have boards of directors. If you want to accomplish something that looks too big and difficult to accomplish, why not create your own mastermind group? This special group of people with different talents and backgrounds will help you brainstorm on ideas and provide suggestions on how you can reach your goals. Left to our own devices, we can quickly get discouraged or succumb to the

"Oh, I can't do this; who do I think I am anyway to even attempt it" mentality. A support team won't allow this to happen and will be able to play devil's advocate, possibly preventing costly errors on your part. These are the people who love and support you and who are not afraid to tell you the truth. On your part, you must be willing to hear what they have to say and willing to hear the truth even if you don't like it. However, make sure these people really want to see you succeed.

Just to give you an idea, on my team I have a magazine editor who gives me feedback on my writing and ideas. I also rely on the insights of the president of an advertising company, a former client. A good friend of mine has worked in marketing and public relations and always has great ideas to share. Another friend is good with computers and helps me when I'm having system problems; I give him a quick call, 90 percent of the time he can tell me what the problem is over the phone, and I'm back on track. These days, if you aren't technologically savvy you definitely need a computer friend or two. My coaching colleagues are always willing to share their experience and provide suggestions. I hired a producer to help me with an audiotape I created instead of trying to do it all by myself, and now she is a ready source of new ideas for marketing my business. Another friend works in publishing and has been a great help throughout the process of getting my own book published. I have a mentor who is a self-made multimillionaire. He regularly gives me advice and encouragement and prevents me from making costly mistakes. And of course I have a coach to help me work on improving my own life. I constantly rely on my own family and friends for love, support, and encouragement.

The bigger and scarier the project you are working on, the more support and advice you will need. Instead of trying to figure out the Web myself, I hired a great guy to design and set up my company website. Most of the people in my mastermind group are friends and colleagues and offer their advice for free. However, don't be afraid to pay for services that you need. If you expect friends to provide their professional services for free you'll soon find you are out a valuable friend. More often than not, people are willing to give you great information, advice, and feedback on your ideas if you simply invite them to do so or invite them to lunch. Sometimes people are willing to barter. Your skills and services could be of great value to the other members of the group.

A mastermind group can be an informal arrangement in which you call people individually, or you can set up a regular monthly meeting in which all the members of the group support each other. If you start a formal mastermind group, the purpose will be to support *everyone* in the group, not just you, so don't hog the time. Each week or month that you meet ask who has an issue or problem that they'd like to resolve and brainstorm from there. The most effective groups include people with very different backgrounds—a lawyer, an accountant, a marketing person, an artist, an entrepreneur—so that everyone will benefit from the synergy of the group and have a different perspective to share.

49. GIVE GREAT GIFTS

Why is it no one ever sent me yet
One perfect limousine, do you suppose?
Ah no, it's always just my luck to get
One perfect rose.

DOROTHY PARKER

Give special gifts spontaneously, for no reason whatsoever, as it occurs to you. While you are picking up new filler paper for your daily planner, pick some up for a friend who uses the same system. If you bake a batch of lasagna, make it a double batch and bring the other half over to a friend or neighbor who loves your cooking. When you subscribe to a magazine, order a subscription for your friend too. If a client has just given you a big order, send a thank-you gift and note.

I tend to think that if I like something, then the receiver will like it too, but this isn't always the case—you may have very different tastes. So think about what someone would love and get that, even if it isn't your own style. The best gifts are those that you didn't even know you wanted but are thrilled to have. Giving spontaneously makes the whole year feel like a holiday and a cause for celebration. Keep a bottle of champagne in the fridge to crack open at a friend's success—a job promotion, an engagement, or any possible excuse. Stock up on special gifts so that if you are invited to a last-minute birthday party, you won't have to worry about shopping and can pull out and wrap a little treasure on the spot. Have fun and play Santa all year round.

Barbara, a regional marketing director, was trying to win over some new accounts. She had taken the chief financial officer out for lunch and submitted a proposal, but it wasn't accepted. She reworked the proposal, and wanted to resubmit it, but wasn't sure how to proceed. She wanted to give the financial officer a gift of some sort along with a personal note, but was worried that it might appear she was trying to buy him. I told her not to worry, that giving one small paperweight would be perfectly appropriate. Everybody likes to get a gift. We came up with the idea of sending the beautiful paperweight with a funny note underneath it reading, "I thoroughly enjoyed our last lunch and would love to take you out again as soon as your busy schedule permits. I figured I'd better send along this paperweight so that this note wouldn't get lost in the shuffle! Looking forward to seeing you again!" This did the trick. He called her to thank her for the gift, they set up a lunch, and this time he accepted her proposal. She gave the gift with the hope that it would improve their relationship, but with no expectation. A true gift is given with no strings attached.

Let's get this gift-giving thing down straight. The *only* reason to give a gift is because you get pleasure from giving it. So often people think that the recipient is the one who is getting all the fun, but the real pleasure goes to the giver. Giving is actually a selfish act. If you aren't giving gifts for the pure joy of it, then it probably isn't much fun for the receiver either so you might as well stop doing it. This week make a list of everyone in your life you would like to give a special gift to and start giving. Give a gift to the supportive people in your mastermind group. Give a gift to a family member you'd like to acknowledge. Send a thank-you gift to a client for no particular reason, just to say thanks for being a client. They will be surprised, and you will feel terrific.

50. SEND FIVE THANKS A DAY

"Who does not thank for little will not thank for much."

ESTONIAN PROVERB

One of the most effective ways to build powerful relationships and attract great people is to thank them for all that they do for you. Make it one of your daily habits (Tip 3) to send at least five thank-you notes a day. It may surprise you, but it actually takes much less time to jot down a simply thank-you and mail it than it does to make a phone call. A note is more thoughtful than a phone call because it will never catch someone at an inopportune time. A handwritten note is also more personal and more likely to be remembered and appreciated. It doesn't have to be a long-winded letter. Just a simple line or two of gratitude is all that is required. Buy a box of stationery and some stamps to keep handy in your desk at work for thanking clients, colleagues, mentors, and managers. Keep another box in your desk at home for thanking friends and family members. You can also keep a handful of stamped postcards in your daily schedule or agenda, and when you have a few spare minutes while waiting at a restaurant or bus stop you can be jotting down a thank-you note or two to pop into the nearest mailbox.

You will be amazed how many little things people in your life are already doing to help you out. If you take just fifteen minutes a day to write a few notes and acknowledge them, they are even more likely to want to help you out again in bigger ways in the future. If you don't acknowledge a small favor, why would anyone feel inclined to grant you a large favor?

Think of clients who just bought services from you or your company. When I worked in sales at the bank, I had to buy my own thank-you notes because the bank didn't want to run the expense of buying them for the salespeople. But I knew that thanking my customers was one way to keep them coming back for more, and it made my job easier. Sending a thank-you note is a piece of cake compared to making a cold call. A few years later, the bank launched a customer service campaign and started requiring that the salespeople send out thank-you notes to all new customers. Don't wait until your company figures this one out. Do it yourself.

And don't forget to thank colleagues: the one who switched days off with you so that you could spend time with an unexpected out-of-town guest; the assistant who typed your report for you at the last minute even though he already had an in-box overflowing with work; the mentor who told you the ins and outs of the office politics. Take the time to acknowledge your boss. Most often managers get picked on and criticized; rarely are they thanked for the good things they do. Did your manager give you credit for the work you did on a big project? Don't expect this. Your manager has every right to take full credit. Send a short one- or two-line note thanking your boss for acknowledging your efforts. Be sincere, thoughtful, and concise. This not only will make your boss feel good, but it will also remind him or her of the good work you did. When you take a few minutes to think about it, you will start to realize just how much help you get every single day of your life.

If you had a rough day at the office and don't feel particularly grateful, think of five friends or family members you haven't appreciated in a while. If they haven't done anything special lately, don't let that stop you. You can thank your mother and father for just being there for you or for giving birth to you and raising you. Thank someone for an invitation to a party even though you couldn't attend. You can get creative with this and thank people you might not normally thank. How about thanking the chef at your favorite restaurant for the fabulous meals? Don't worry, you can never give too much thanks. More often than not, people are starved for a little acknowledgment. Can you imagine how much fun it would be if you received five notes of gratitude every single day? So start the trend yourself and get writing.

This tip has an unexpected bonus. In the process of writing these simple notes, you will feel a wonderful, warm feeling of gratitude. Done day in and day out, you will begin to develop a constant and natural sense of gratitude and appreciation for all the people in your life. This is an incredibly magnetic and attractive quality. When you start looking for things to be thankful for, you end up attracting even more favors and more friends. Give and you shall receive.

VI.

· ·

DO WORK YOU LOVE

*"If you can't find the truth right where you are, where else do
you think you will find it?"*

BUDDHA

AT THIS POINT in the coaching program you have increased your natural energy, have more time and space than you have had in a long time, are surrounded by supportive and loving people, and are on the path to financial independence. Life should be looking pretty good at this point. So now the question is what do you want to do? Some people seem to be born knowing what their natural gifts and talents are, and they know exactly what they want to do in life. I was always a bit jealous of these people because I was born with a strong sense of purpose, a feeling that there was something important I was supposed to do, but no clue as to what that might be. I was pretty good at a lot of different things but not so extraordinarily good at any one thing. It just wasn't obvious what I was supposed to do. If you are searching for what to do, Part VI will help you discover your natural gifts and talents. But even if you already know what to do with your life, read on.

No one attracts success more than someone who is doing what he or she loves to do. When you are doing what you love, your eyes sparkle, you are happy and excited about life, you are full of energy and joy. You feel satisfied, content, turned on. Given all this, why don't we do what we love? It is perverse how much time we spend doing what we *don't* love to do. The latest research indicates that 50 percent of the western world is in the wrong job. Given the amount of complaining I hear at cocktail parties, this seems to be a fairly accurate assessment. And I used to be one of those complainers.

The happiest people get paid for doing what they love. But don't wait to be paid before you start. You may never get paid so you had better start now, or you'll go through your whole life without experiencing the joy that comes from doing something you thoroughly enjoy. Doing what you love rejuvenates you; it gives you more energy than it requires. The people around you will love you more because you are relaxed and happy, and that positive energy will rub off on them. The following tips will help you tap into the energy that is already out there, leverage your natural gifts, and move effortlessly in the direction you want to go.

51. DESIGN YOUR IDEAL LIFE

"Is life not a hundred times too short for us to stifle ourselves?"

FRIEDRICH NIETZSCHE

"There's got to be more to life than sittin' here watchin' 'Days of Our Lives' and foldin' your Fruit of the Looms."

MAMA, *MAMA'S FAMILY*

Before you even begin to design your ideal career, you need to design your ideal life. And before you design your ideal life it is a good idea to play the Billionaire Game (Tip 22) to expand your thinking beyond the norm. Most people set goals that are much too small because they don't believe something bigger and better is possible. Now is the time to go beyond your current limitations and beliefs and find out what you really want to do in life. The biggest mistake people make is trying to design their lives around their careers. It really works much better the other way around. Start by designing your ideal life and then figure out what sort of career would support it.

I should probably warn you that most of my clients find it isn't so easy to design an ideal life. I'm giving you a blank slate, and you can invent absolutely anything you want. Your ideal life is ideal. It doesn't have to look anything like your current life. Consider these questions:

- Where do you want to live?
- Who do you want to be?
- Who would you like to be spending your time with?
- What sort of home would you like?
- What sort of work would you like to be doing?
- What would you do for fun?
- What would a normal day look like?

Review what you wrote in the instant billionaire exercise (Tip 22), but also think more deeply about what you really want in life. Is there someone you envy? Great. Take a look at his or her life and see what specifically you envy about it. A great and fulfilling career? A lovely summer house on the beach? Wonderful, loving relationships? Envy can be very useful in helping you determine what you want your own life to look like.

Now describe your ideal life in glowing and vivid detail. You can write it down in a journal or special notebook. You can draw or paint pictures of it. You can type it into a computer. If you aren't much of an artist or writer, you can cut and paste. One client decided she didn't like the looks of her own drawings—they were less than ideal, in her mind—so she cut out magazine pictures that represented various aspects of her ideal life and made a scrapbook. She used rubber cement to glue the pictures, and in the margins she wrote a description in the present tense of what each picture meant. For example, one of her goals was to get married and have children so one of the pictures was of a good-looking man sleeping in a hammock in the backyard. There was a white picket fence, a golden retriever lounging on the grass, and sound asleep on top of the man, cradled in his arm, was a little brown-haired boy about five years old—the very picture of domestic tranquility and happiness. She felt this "snapshot" was a perfect representation of her ideal life. Below the photo she jotted down some descriptive notes such as, "My wonderful husband, our son, and the family dog taking a break on a beautiful Sunday afternoon. Aren't they adorable! Even the dog is happy," just as if she were married at the moment. Two months later she met her ideal man, and it looks like they are on the road to marriage. Have fun with this exercise. Remember it is your ideal—it doesn't mean that your husband and child will look like that or that you will even have a white picket fence.

On the other hand, it doesn't mean you won't either. She did the same for her career and cut out a picture of a well-dressed professional woman with briefcase in hand kissing a man goodbye at the airport. Below the photo she wrote, "My honey just dropped me off at the airport, and I'm off to Paris to go to the annual sales convention—I just love my work." This photo captured the client's desire to travel to foreign countries as part of her work and to have a supportive, loving husband. You get the idea. Make a scrapbook if you like or invent some other creative way to design your ideal life.

Many clients find this assignment difficult. If you are still stuck, try describing just one ideal day in your ideal life. This is an excellent exercise to help you figure out what you really enjoy doing. Start in the morning when you wake up. Where do you wake up? Is someone bringing you breakfast in bed, or are you going out for a run along the beach? Imagine that you can have anything you want; money is not an issue. Keep on writing until you have described the entire day until you fall asleep at night.

When my client John did this exercise he realized that his ideal day was within reach. He would wake up, have great sex with his lovely wife, eat breakfast with his son and daughter, go golfing, and meet his golfing buddies for lunch. Then he'd hire a limousine to take his family into Manhattan to enjoy an incredible dinner and a show. They would come home and talk about what a fabulous day they had and go to bed. Once he wrote down this ideal day, he knew that he wanted to spend more time enjoying his family and playing golf.

I pointed out that his ideal day was easily within his reach and suggested that he try living it to see how it felt. For some reason, it always astounds people that they can actually live one of their ideal days. Usually, once you experience one ideal day, you realize that you probably wouldn't want that day all the time. Go on to the next assignment and design an ideal week. Include both play and work time. I had one client whose ideal day was to loll around on the beach sipping margaritas. She was worried that her whole life would become a waste if she started to indulge in her ideal. I asked her when was the last time she had been to the beach. It had been a few years. I recommended that she book a trip to some exotic island and get it out of her system. She realized that after one week of beach bumming she was bored and ready to do something else. Don't worry, as lazy as you think you might be, most people get restless by week two and are itching to do something. We are meant to make a contribution. We need a challenge to really feel fulfilled.

Start incorporating as many aspects of your ideal as possible into your life right now. Okay, you may not have the man and boy in the photo right now, but you might be able to get the golden retriever. You may not have a maid to bring your croissant and coffee in the morning, but you could make them for yourself. You may not be doing any traveling on the job, but you could book your next vacation to Paris and let your boss know that if the opportunity for travel arises, you'd like to be the one to go. Start making even the smallest steps in the direction you want to head, and you'll soon be there.

52. ALIGN YOUR VALUES AND VISION

"Men for the sake of getting a living forget to live."

MARGARET FULLER

"So far I've found that most high-level executives prefer the boardroom to the Bahamas. They don't really enjoy leisure time; they feel their work is their leisure."

WILLIAM THEOBALD

The key to having fulfilling work is to do something that is in alignment with your highest values. I'm not referring to values in the moral sense of right and wrong, but rather in the sense of doing what you truly love to do—that which is of intrinsic worth to you personally. When you are living in accordance with your values, you are most fully alive and most fully yourself. For example, you might value creativity and invention. You might value travel and adventure. Or perhaps peace, being spiritual, or honoring God. You might value risk, speculation, experimentation. Or perhaps grace, beauty, or elegance. Maybe you value improving others, contributing, serving, encouraging. What about leading, being a catalyst, inspiring others? Maybe you feel most alive when you are part of a community and feel connected to others, or perhaps when you are playing games or sports. People value different things. When do you feel most fully alive? What are you doing? Are you planning and designing? Are you coaching and energizing others? Take a moment to reflect on the peak moments in your life. Look back and see what the highlights of your life have been.

One client realized that one of the highlights of his life was giving his high school graduation speech. He valued inspiring others. Now he is a professional speaker, and his work requires that he constantly inspire others. He couldn't be happier and is thrilled with his work.

The most rewarding careers are those that allow and perhaps even demand that you express your values fully. We are our best when we are fully living our unique values. Take a few minutes to review your personal history and list the peak moments of your life. Next to each, write down why that moment was important to you. Now write down the value it reflects. One client wrote that she had a terrific childhood; she used to explore the woods and spend time playing outdoors. She realized that she valued being surrounded by natural beauty and missed it terribly in her job at an advertising agency. She decided to spend more time out in nature and took a weekend job as a volunteer park ranger. She loved it, and after a few months she decided to find full-time work in the National Park Service. Write down your top four or five values.

53. INVENT FIVE ALTERNATIVE CAREERS

"It's pretty damn hard to bring your uniqueness into actual being if you're always doing the same things as a lot of other people."

BRENDAN FRANCIS

Now that you've designed your ideal life, you are ready to start figuring out what work would enable you to live that way. Many people seem to get stuck in one field or career. If they apply for a job in another field, there is always the problem of not having the right experience. Here is another coaching assignment to help you consider various options. Pretend that your current job has been eliminated from the face of this earth, and you now have to do something completely different. What might you like to do? Have you always thought it would be great to become a professional dancer? Or perhaps a composer, mathematician, judge, scientist, reporter, restaurant owner? Pick any five careers that you fancy. Don't worry if you don't have the training or education. Write a paragraph about why you'd want this career. Then go on to the next career. Why would you want this one? This will also help you figure out what you really value.

One client, Jenny, a hard-working, forty-five-year-old human resources executive, did this exercise and came up with a rather unexpected result. She had selected the following five alternative careers:

1. garden designer
2. painter
3. creative writer
4. interior designer
5. photographer

Jenny was surprised when she realized that she'd like to look after other people's gardens. Somehow it just didn't fit with her idea of the executive life she had. But, she said, "There is a thing inside of me that loves to tidy up and make things look nice." The five alternative careers revealed a strong creative side that had been stifled. She said, "I've never allowed myself time to try them out." I told her it was high time to get started, that there was a whole creative side of her dying to get out.

Jenny admitted that she had put it to one side in following a serious professional career. She had always done the right thing in her life. We started to consider other options, and she began to explore courses that she could take. I asked that she take one day at home and make it her creative day. I told her to go out and get a paintbrush and start. Play with it. Buy a canvas. Tend someone's garden. Volunteer to do the interior design on a friend's house. Just start. Even if it seems tiny and all you have is half an hour, pick up a paintbrush or snap a few photographs.

The next week Jenny reported that she had gone out with an artist friend and purchased some paints, brushes, and a canvas. She hadn't actually started painting yet, but just getting the supplies had been great fun.

The week after that she had an offer from a friend to go into the interior design business with her. The next week she had finished a painting and liked it so much that she hung it in her living room. Her friends admired it and thought she had purchased it from a "real" artist. She is now selling her home and moving into a less expensive apartment in anticipation of quitting her executive job to pursue these new interests. She felt stuck, unfulfilled, and dissatisfied, and now she is more vibrantly alive than ever. The future looks promising and exciting instead of dull, drab, and routine. Jenny feels that anything is possible now.

54. Discover Your Unique Talent

*"There are two kinds of talent, man-made talent and
God-given talent. With man-made talent you have to work
very hard. With God-given talent, you just touch it up
once in a while."*

PEARL BAILEY

We all have some special talent, skill, or gift—something we do or some way we see things that is different or better than anyone else. Very often what comes naturally to you is so much a part of you that you don't even notice it. People tend to think that if it is easy for them, then it is easy for everyone else too. This just isn't so. You might think that if it is this easy or fun, then you shouldn't get paid for it. We like to think that work is hard—that if we don't sweat and struggle, we don't *deserve* to get paid for it. Again, this just isn't so. In fact, it is more often the opposite: the people who make the most money love what they do and have some natural ability for it that they have honed and developed.

If you can't figure out what your special talent is, interview your friends, family, and colleagues. They will tell you. It really is this easy. Here are some questions you can ask them:

1. What do you think is my greatest strength?
2. What is my biggest weakness? (Ask this only if you feel up to it, and ask them to tell you in a constructive way. Do not comment

on anything they say, just write it down. You are simply gathering opinions.)

3. What do you see as my special talent or gift? What do I do naturally and effortlessly that is special?
4. If I were on the cover of a magazine, what magazine would it be and what would the story be about?
5. When am I most fully expressing this gift or talent?

The next step is to begin to honor your gift. By that I mean that you fully express it, share it with others, do it, be it, live it. Remember, your own special skill comes so easily and naturally that you probably take it for granted.

Steve hired me because he wanted to make more money. He was in a banking career working as a benefits administrator, and although he didn't mind the work, he was frustrated with the low pay. I gave Steve the homework of finding out his special talent. Steve typed up the questions listed previously, handed them out to friends and colleagues, and came back with surprising results. Steve's greatest strength was his personality. Across the board people loved his warmth, his sense of humor, his ability to get along with everybody. Yes, he could solve problems and was analytical, but that wasn't his special talent. As for the magazine, *Golf*, *Golf Digest*, and *Sports Illustrated* were the winners, and the best story was about how Steve used golf to quickly move up the corporate ladder. So we started to make this fiction a reality. What if we could leverage Steve's personality out there on the golf course courting clients? He'd be in seventh heaven. Steve talked to his manager, who really liked him, about learning the sales end of the job. Then Steve volunteered to organize a golf outing for senior management and the top clients. He started looking at every way that he could to honor his gift for people and his love of golf. His manager soon put him in charge of a big account and started training Steve to make the transfer to sales with a salary increase in six months. Now he is not only happier on the job, but he is in a job with much higher income potential. Just start. Do one thing that will allow you to fully express your unique gift. Then see how you can incorporate that into your life today, and the universe will pull you in that direction.

55. DO WHAT YOU LOVE

*"To live is the rarest thing in the world. Most people
exist, that is all."*

OSCAR WILDE

Everything in life is some form of energy. If you want to have an effortlessly successful life, it makes sense to go *with* the current of energy, *with*
the flow of life, rather than against it. Going with the flow means that
you align yourself with the natural forces rather than against them. Put
your canoe in the river headed downstream from where you want to go,
and you'll reach your destination a whole lot faster. How do you know
if you are living in the flow of life? Good things come to you easily, and
you enjoy what you do. There may be hard work involved, but it doesn't
have to be a struggle. When Michael Jordan played basketball, he worked
hard, but he wasn't suffering and he wasn't miserable. When you are working hard at something you are passionate about it is a joy, even when you
are sweating bullets. You still have to work to direct a raft downstream,
but it isn't the tremendous struggle that going upstream is. Work can be
tremendous fun. Some of the most highly paid people in the world make
their living playing games. Look at sports stars like Tiger Woods, Brett
Frasier, Mark McGwire, Martina Hingis. The most successful people are
not only doing what they love to do, but what they are naturally good
at. Then they get even better at it—they master their skill.

   One way to find out what you would love to do for a career is to
start doing more of what you love to do in life. If you love dancing, sign
up for a regular class. If you love reading, consider joining a book club
or starting one yourself. If you love investing, take a class on it. Whatever it is, start incorporating it into your life. The more you are engaged
in the "flow" activity, the one that lights you up (see Tip 32), the more
you'll attract the good things in life. This doesn't mean that you have to
stop what you are doing and make a living off dancing if that is what
you love. You may find that the activity is only fun if it isn't a career.
Start small with a flow activity and see where the current takes you. One
friend in pharmaceutical sales was interested in the stock market; he
started taking courses in the evening, reading books on the topic, and
setting up a paper trading account. After one year, he started trading small

amounts of his own money, and now he is working on Wall Street as a trader. Another client started taking dance classes and soon realized dancing was all she wanted to do. She quit her job as an accountant, became a dance teacher, and loves it.

Start taking the path of least resistance. Work for a company that produces something you can be proud of. Do a job that suits your natural talents. Marry the partner who shares your goals. There's a lot of energy in the world; you can go with it or against it. It's your choice. If whatever you are doing really seems difficult and you are dragging your feet, it probably isn't the right thing for you. When it is right, you will want to do it, no matter how difficult it is. One of my clients, Sam, was berating himself for failing to organize his business finances. He was a smart and successful computer consultant, but he couldn't seem to get his act together. Every year he paid hundreds of dollars in fines to the government for failing to pay his taxes on time. The truth was that he just wasn't good at organizing little details. He finally admitted this and gave the whole task of bookkeeping and accounting to his accountant. Sam even had his bills and checking statements sent directly to the accountant's office so that he wouldn't misplace them. This was a tremendous weight off his mind and freed him up to do more of the computer work he loved and enjoyed. Sam ended up attracting a new consulting client that paid him thousands of dollars. He made up for the accountant's fees and then some, and is happier working on the things he is naturally good at and enjoys. Create the time and space for more of the activities you love by eliminating the activities that are a struggle (Tip 16).

Another client, Anton, is an incredibly gorgeous man built like a ton of bricks who loves fitness and health. When Anton hired me, he was working extremely hard doing three different jobs and was suffering from insomnia. He was up every morning at 5:00 or sometimes 4:30 and usually didn't get to bed until 1:00 or 2:00 A.M. His primary focus was a multilevel marketing business that sold health and fitness products like shower filters that remove chlorine. He spent most of his time attending their events, hosting meetings, and calling prospective people to get them involved in this business too. In addition, Anton taught aerobics at a couple of gyms and had a few clients whom he worked with one-on-one as a personal trainer.

In spite of all his hard work, Anton wasn't making it. He had incurred over $40,000 in credit card debt while trying to build his multilevel marketing clientele. His girlfriend was frustrated that he never had any time to spend with her and that he was always broke. He hadn't talked to his mother in years because he had borrowed money from his little sister and hadn't been able to pay her back. Yet he was convinced that if he just tried harder he would make a success of it and the big bucks would roll in. I asked Anton just how long he needed to suffer before he realized that this multilevel marketing business was killing him. We took a hard look at the numbers, and Anton realized that he was spending more money going to weekend trainings and workshops than he was making. It was a losing business. I asked him if he could make money just selling the products and he said he could make some, but that the real money was in getting new people into the business. Right away this should tip you off. If you can't make enough money selling the product then you shouldn't be in the business.

Yet Anton couldn't let it go. He had invested so much time and money over the past two and a half years that he was certain success was right around the corner. So we made a deal. I told him that he needed to bring in money and do it fast, and that he must only engage in activities that would generate income now—not some day, maybe, in the future. He was not allowed to invest another dime in training until he had a positive cash flow. Anton agreed to this plan. I also asked him to consider filing for bankruptcy. He needed a fresh start and it wouldn't be easy with all that debt hanging over his head. He saw a doctor about his insomnia and found out that physically, he was perfectly sound. I suggested that the stress of not having money and his huge debts were keeping him awake at night. Anton didn't feel right about filing for bankruptcy, so I didn't press it.

Anton soon discovered that the only surefire way to make some money right away was to do personal training. He loved doing it and was great at it, but he just didn't see how it could make enough money for him. He was still fantasizing about the get-rich-quick scheme that the multilevel marketing firm kept dangling over his head. Making just $35 an hour (his cut after the gym took a percentage) wasn't going to help, but at least it was some money. I asked him to design a brochure to leave out on the counter for new clients. He did this with a simple computer program and some preprinted paper—it looked terrific. Within the space of three months, Anton went from training three clients to twenty-three. He was still doing the multilevel marketing business at night, but more and more of his time was spent making money at the gym. He decided to see an attorney about bankruptcy. He came to terms with the fact that many new businesses go bankrupt and that this was not a personal failure, but a poor business decision. He decided he wouldn't make the same mistake twice. He started spending more time doing the things he loved—playing soccer and taking his girlfriend out on Friday and Saturday nights. Things were falling in place, and life was getting easier and easier every day.

One week Anton called to report that he'd had a perfect day. Everything went so smoothly. He slept for a solid six hours and woke up refreshed. He caught the train into town without a wait. His clients were all on time, and his sessions were upbeat and powerful. He had time to eat a good lunch. That night he even had people calling him for a change to order some products, and he took his girlfriend to the movies. This is living in the flow of life. A year later, Anton has moved into a lovely apartment in the suburbs and is engaged to his girlfriend. He is on good terms with both his mother and sister. He is debt-free, sleeping at night, and has a thriving personal training business. His next project? To start a gym for kids. Life wasn't meant to be brain surgery. Just do the things that come naturally and easily and let the good things come to you for a change.

56. Work on a Special Project

"We must be the change we wish to see in the world."

Gandhi

One way to discover your special gift or talent is to work on a special project that really lights you up. Design a project at work, at home, or in your community that would be fun and exciting. In fact, why not really liven up your life and have a special project at work and at home? At work, you could create a special task team to resolve an issue that bothers you. Sign up for a course in something that you've always wanted to learn, like computers, a foreign language, negotiation skills, or effective delegating. Or create a system to automate as much drudgery as possible. Learn a different side of your business. If you are in the marketing department, make some sales calls with one of the sales reps. Whatever you choose to do, make sure it really interests you (and that you have permission from your manager).

You could also create a special project on a more personal side. Decide to run a marathon and take up daily training. Commit to having a washboard stomach and do 500 crunches a day. Start writing a novel. Paint a wall mural. Start a project to enhance your community. Or you could take a personal love to work. One client loved gardening and got permission to plant a bed of flowers in front of her sterile office building. She organized a team of colleagues, and they planted it together. Now every day she looks forward to seeing the fruits of her labor as she walks into the building.

My special project was called "Neat Street." I was tolerating two big things about living in New York City—the dirty streets and the homelessness. I didn't like the way my block always looked trashy even though it is in a nice residential neighborhood in midtown Manhattan. I also didn't feel right about the homeless people. I didn't want to give them money because I thought it would go to drugs or alcohol, but I didn't feel right about just walking by either. Then an idea popped into my head: why not ask the homeless people to clean the streets? I was so inspired I went down to the nearest ATM and as always, there was a homeless man with his cup extended. I asked him if he would be interested in working. He said yes. I told him the idea. If he would volunteer to sweep my block on both sides of the street every day, I would ask each resident on that block to give him at least $1 a week donation. (This is a city block, so there are over 150 people on our block.) I told him there was no guarantee how much money he would make, but that he had nothing to lose. He showed up on the block the next morning at 7:00 A.M., and I gave him a broom and a dustpan. This was the birth of "Neat Street." James, the homeless man, ended up being photographed for an article in the *New York Times* and was also on television. He became a regular part of the community, sweeping the block rain or shine, and ended up making enough money to share an apartment with a friend. Now "Neat Street" has spread to other blocks, and all sorts of organizations have created partnerships with the homeless to provide them work cleaning the streets. Who knows, maybe one day New York will be a remarkably spotless city.

What special project would you like to start? Or, if you aren't the starter type, how about joining someone else's project that you believe in?

It doesn't matter if your project is a little teeny tiny one. It still makes a difference. Consider what's known as the Hundredth Monkey Phenomenon. According to Ken Keyes Jr., the author of *The Hundredth Monkey*, some natural scientists were observing monkey behavior on the island of Koshima. These monkeys lived primarily on some sort of sweet potato that they dug out of the ground. One day a scientist noticed that instead of just eating the potato fresh from the ground, the monkey washed it in the stream first and then ate it. This was a new behavior—none of the other monkeys did this—but "monkey see, monkey do," and before long all the monkeys on the island were washing their potatoes first and then eating them. A strange thing happened. All at once, all of the monkeys on another island started washing their potatoes too. There had been no transfer of monkeys; these islands were hundreds of miles apart. There was no rational explanation for this sudden change of behavior, so the scientists documented it as the Hundredth Monkey Phenomenon. New scientific breakthroughs are frequently made at the same time in different countries by completely different researchers. Studies in the United States indicate that the crime rate goes down in communities where more people meditate. I believe this is the same phenomenon. Go ahead and be one of the first monkeys. Start your project. It does make a difference.

As you work on a project that inspires you, you may discover what it is you truly love to do in life. Begin to orient your life around it. You may also find that in working on the project, you attract the next career opportunity. People who love what they are doing frequently attract great people and opportunities to them effortlessly.

57. Let Your Intuition Lead the Way

"Trusting our intuition often saves us from disaster."

Anne Wilson Schaef

Another way to find your dream job is to follow your intuition. It is simple, but not necessarily easy. First you have to learn how to distinguish those varying and often contradictory little voices. One is your head talking—the rational, intellectual part of you—and the other, the intuition, is from your gut. Your intuition always has your best interest at heart, while your head can get you into big trouble because it operates on the "shoulds" in life. Your intuition knows nothing of what society might think; it is only interested in you. If you are super busy, it will be harder to hear your intuition because the chattering in your head might be drowning it out. So if you don't hear your intuition very clearly, you may want to go back and work on Part II, Clean Up Your Act, and Part IV, Make Time When There Isn't Any. Sitting still for ten minutes to do nothing except give your intuition a chance to speak is also a great way to start (Tip 33).

Here is a perfect personal example of how your head can get you into trouble. I had the thought to check my E-mail again one evening, though I had just checked it an hour ago (intuition speaking—it isn't necessarily logical). I find a message that a colleague is vacating his bay-veiw penthouse on Cape Cod, Massachusetts, and is looking for a house-sitter for two months—all utilities included at no charge. I immediately thought (intuition speaking), "Yes! This is perfect!" The head voice steps in and says, "Don't be silly, you should be in New York building your business, not running off to some beach house. Besides, your boyfriend will miss you if you are gone for so long." Then my intuition came back and said, "Hey, just send an E-mail back saying you'd like to do it. If it is meant to be you'll get it, if not, someone else will. And if you get it and decide you really can't go, you can always say no afterward." My intuition won this discussion and off went my request. Sure enough, I got it and ended up in Provincetown writing this book in complete peace and solitude, very happy and as content as could be.

Shakti Gawain explains intuition beautifully in her book *Living in the Light*: "The intuitive mind, on the other hand, seems to have access to an infinite supply of information. It appears to be able to tap into a deep storehouse of knowledge and wisdom, the universal mind. It also is able to sort out this information and supply us with exactly what we need, when we need it. Though the messages may come through a bit at a time, if we learn to follow this supply of information piece by piece, the necessary course of action will unfold. As we learn to rely on this guidance, life takes on a flowing effortless quality. Our life, feelings, and actions interweave harmoniously with those of others around us."

As you develop your intuition and start following its guidance, you will start to listen less and less to your head, the "rational voice." You will start to go more by feel. You will listen to your whole body and let things unfold, even though it may go counter to logic. This is not airy fairy stuff. Scientist Candace B. Pert, Ph.D., explains in her groundbreaking and fascinating book *The Molecules of Emotion* the molecular connection to our emotions. There are actually different molecules associated with joy, sadness, fear, and each of our varying emotions. Essentially, those gut feelings you have are real. There are real molecules behind them. Given this is the case, it is time to start listening to what your whole body is telling you.

The more my clients trust and follow their inner voices and gut feelings, the easier and more exciting life becomes. Start following your intuition on the little things. For example, it is a clear, sunny morning, but a little voice tells you to bring your umbrella. See if you were right. Did it rain or not? My guess is that our bodies, with their billions of cells, can sense and feel things that we can't begin to grasp on a rational or intellectual level. I use my whole body when I am coaching. If I feel physically uncomfortable, am I sensing that a client isn't telling the whole story? And I do my coaching by phone! Let me tell you an interesting coaching story to give you an example.

Marissa had been transferred from Iowa to work in Colorado (where she had always wanted to live), and all her moving expenses had been paid, even the rent on a temporary house, while she and her family looked for a new home. But she was worried and stressed-out because they had not sold their old home in Iowa, and they couldn't afford to pay for both their new house and the old mortgage. While housing sales were booming in Colorado, they were stagnant in Iowa. Try as they might, the house just didn't sell, and time was running out. Marissa said, "I always did hate that house and now look what it's causing!" Out of nowhere I got this crazy intuitive flash that the reason their house wasn't selling was because she had all these negative thoughts about it. Nobody would want to buy an unloved house. I told her I had an unusual homework assignment for her that was completely off the wall. I asked her to think of all the good times they had shared in the house. The Sunday mornings when their two little girls would jump in bed and then they would all make pancakes together in the kitchen—that kind of mushy good stuff. Well, she was so desperate at this point she agreed to give it a shot. She even started asking her four- and five-year-olds what they had enjoyed doing at the old house and got her husband talking about it (she didn't tell them the coaching assignment). Two days later, I got an ecstatic call from Marissa. They had a buyer for the house, and—get this—the buyer needed to close by the end of the month and requested that they speed up the closing process. Was it coincidence? Well, just what is coincidence?

If everything is some form of energy, our negative thoughts are also energy and people pick up on them like a radio picks up radio waves. Our thoughts are boundless—not limited by time or distance. Okay, I know this may sound pretty loony, but why not start listening to your intuition and see what happens? You will find that you make better decisions and that good things will come to you.

58. FIND YOUR PATH IN LIFE

"Live all you can; it's a mistake not to. It doesn't so much matter what you do in particular, so long as you have your life. If you haven't had that what have you had?"

HENRY JAMES

People who know what they want to do in life, people who have a game plan or a vision or a purpose or even a big goal, are more successful than those who don't. If you have a sense of purpose, a direction to head in, you'll naturally attract people who are interested in going the same direction. Even if they aren't interested, they might become interested because you are having so much fun along the way.

What is your purpose in life? What are you here to accomplish and learn? What's in your soul, your heart, to do? This may be something as simple as to have fun and bring fun to those around you. Write your purpose in the form of a statement. Here are some possibilities:

My purpose is to learn and love as fully as possible.
My purpose is to be a catalyst for change and growth.
My purpose is to have a great time and laugh a lot.
My purpose is to become financially independent and raise a healthy, happy family.
My purpose is to be a happy traveler.

A purpose doesn't have to be earth-shattering in scope. You might have a big vision like Bill Gates's—a computer on every desk, running Microsoft software—or Martin Luther King Jr.'s—equality for all people. Perhaps you'd like to take a stand for the environment or take some action that furthers peace on the planet. You don't have to change the world. Start small with something for your family, your block, or your neighborhood (Tip 56).

Some of my clients find even thinking about a life purpose to be overwhelming, so instead I suggest they create a theme for the year. The theme can be anything you want—fun, adventure, romance, love, calmness, balance, play, joy, peace, laughter, work. Whatever you want. Pick a theme, any theme. If you don't like it, you can always pick another. This could be the year to have great adventures. Or perhaps you would like to have a different theme for each month. With a purpose for the month or the year, you know what to focus on, and it is easier to say yes or no as opportunities arise. Not sure what your purpose in life is? Then perhaps it is time to get some perspective (Tip 59).

59. GET SOME PERSPECTIVE

"The power that makes grass grow, fruit ripen, and guides the bird in flight is in us all."

ANZIA YEZIERSKA

"Every man has two journeys to make through life. There is the outer journey, with its various incidents and the milestones. . . . There is also an inner journey, a spiritual Odyssey, with a secret history of its own."

DEAN WILLIAM R. INGE,
MORE LAY THOUGHTS OF A DEAN

If you are still struggling to find your path in life, you may need to take a retreat from your current life and get a broader perspective. Sometimes we need to get outside of our lives to see what it is that really fulfills us. When we are caught up in daily demands and obligations, it can be difficult to imagine life being any other way. The ideal can seem so impossibly far away that it ends up depressing instead of inspiring a person. If this is the case for you, it is high time to head for the hills.

There are lots of different ways to take a retreat from your life. You could pack your bags and stay at a bed-and-breakfast or inn in a small town or a cabin in the woods. You might house-sit for a friend who has an empty beach house in the winter or an empty house anywhere. In general it is a good idea to leave your own house if you can because there always seems to be something to do in our own home—the laundry, the fridge lightbulb to replace. . . . When you are at someone else's house or an inn you don't have to worry about that stuff because it isn't your problem. There are all manner of places where you can get away from the hectic pace of your own life. The Sivananda Yoga Ranch outside of New York City has very simple, clean rooms and a vegetarian menu for a relatively small fee. When I felt stressed-out, just one weekend at the Yoga Ranch and I felt completely rejuvenated. Try to go away for at least three days if you can, but if you can't spare the time, even one day can make a difference. Many monasteries allow people to stay for free or for minimal donations. For a list of such retreats check out the book *Sanctuaries: The Complete United States: A Guide to Lodgings in Monasteries, Abbeys, and Retreats*, by Jack and Marcia Kelly. Pack a simple bag with minimal clothes, a journal to record your thoughts in, and that is about it. Avoid the temptation to bring too much stuff with you—remember, the point is to get away from it all.

Sometimes, however, you may not even have the energy or the finances to leave your home. Perhaps you don't have the vacation time available and still need to work. In this case, you can take a retreat in your own home or stay with a family member. If you live alone, this is fairly easy. You can tell your significant other and your friends that you are taking a retreat and you'll be away for the week. If friends know you are gone, they won't be calling you at home. Start your day with a special ritual, and when you come home from work, light a candle or meditate or do something that helps relieve the work stress and reminds you that you are on retreat. Try to eliminate most of the petty annoyances (Tip 1) and pay your bills and do other chores before you start your retreat, just as you would before leaving on a vacation. Use the evenings to think, read books, meditate, take baths, go for long walks, listen to music. Do not watch TV or engage in any other addictions. That defeats the whole purpose (Tip 2). Spend some time in nature and be sure to look at the stars.

After living in Manhattan for a year and a half, I finally left to go home to Arizona for Christmas. I fell asleep on the plane, and when I awoke, it was dark. I lifted up the window shade and gasped . . . there were millions of stars! I was shocked because I had forgotten about the stars. In Manhattan, because of all the city lights and pollution, you are lucky if you see two or three stars in the sky, if you even bother to look up at the sky. But in the desert, you can see billions of them. Seeing the stars in the sky made me feel humble—just a tiny speck in this huge cosmos. They gave me perspective, reminding me that my problems are insignificant in the grand scheme of things. I thought, "That explains why New Yorkers think they are at the center of the world, that everyplace pales in comparison—they can't see the stars and have lost perspective." The ocean does this for me too, with its huge peacefulness, the rhythmic, powerful, endless crashing of waves on sand. Nature is a great healer. If you feel stressed, overwhelmed, or out of balance, go out and enjoy nature—look at the stars in your own backyard. It will restore and rejuvenate you. It will put whatever problems you have in perspective.

What if you have a family? It may seem impossible to take even a weekend retreat, but you may be able to do so with a little help from your family. Ask grandparents or other family members to take the kids for one weekend and stay at home in peace and quiet. I recommend that you take a retreat from your relationship too. We all need time alone now and then, and when you come back, you will both appreciate each other more (Tip 40). Get creative, but find some way to get perspective on your life.

60. TAKE A SABBATICAL

"Reason may fail you. If you are going to do anything in life, you have sometimes to move away from it, beyond all measurements. You must follow sometimes visions and dreams."

BEDE JARRETT,
THE HOUSE OF GOLD

If a weekend or weeklong retreat just doesn't do it, you may want to go one step further and consider taking a sabbatical. Once reserved for academics, unpaid sabbaticals are now offered by 20 percent of U.S. companies as part of their employee benefits, and 3 percent of them even pay. Even if your company doesn't offer a formal sabbatical, you may be able to negotiate time off for work on personal growth or professional development. More and more employers realize that burnout is an issue, and they'd rather grant a month or two of time off than lose an employee altogether. If you've worked for the same company for years, you may need a big chunk of time off, from a month to a year, to reevaluate and redirect your life.

A sabbatical is more than a vacation. Yes, you will want to rest and relax, but it is a time to experiment with new skills and take some risks. Sabbaticals help you step outside of the day-to-day routine and find out what's most important to you. There can be some risk in taking a sabbatical, both to your employer and to you. You may discover that you don't want to go back your old job, or you may decide you do and return to find your old job has been filled, or you've fallen behind your peers. But more often than not, sabbaticals are a win-win for all concerned. If you decide you don't want your old job, ultimately your employers will benefit by not having a stale, burned-out employee on their hands. If your old job is filled, you may need to try out something new that will broaden your skills and experience.

Whenever my clients are switching companies, I encourage them to work in as much time off as possible before they start their new job. Sometimes all they can work in is a week, but I've also had clients work in two whole months between jobs. Lucy, a thirty-seven-year-old public relations manager, resigned from her job and managed to negotiate a later start date at her new job in a consulting firm. This would give her two months off. She had paid off her debts and had been building her financial reserves (Tips 24 and 27), so she could afford to take this extended time off. I encouraged her to use that time to fulfill one of her lifetime goals, which was to travel to Ecuador and study Spanish. She thoroughly enjoyed her trip and learned a valuable new language skill in the process. As an unexpected benefit, when she returned from the sabbatical, she also realized that it was time to end a personal relationship of seven years. Living and traveling on her own for two months enabled her to gain the independence and strength to do this.

Graham, a fifty-seven-year-old executive, took a three-month retreat to experiment with everything from studying software to climbing the Rockies and the Alps. During his sabbatical, Graham wanted to try things that were far removed from his duties as chief executive in a high-stress job addressing the country's economic and trade issues. He wanted to get away from the daily routine of work and reflect on his greater purpose in life. The first day of his sabbatical, he slept for twenty-seven hours straight. (Don't worry, this is normal. If you sleep excessively for the first few days or week, you are just repaying a very old sleep debt. Your body needs the rest, so don't beat yourself up about it. Enjoy the sleep and you will recover your natural energy very quickly.) Since his wife couldn't join him for much of the sabbatical, Graham did most of it on his own. His mountain treks left him in trimmer shape and renewed his love of the outdoors. When he returned to work, he felt revitalized. As a side benefit, since the office had run well during his absence, he found that people were now used to taking on more individual responsibility, and it was easier for him to delegate (Tip 62). He now valued his personal and family time more and was much better at saying no to evening and weekend obligations (Tip 18). He even decided to reserve Sunday as a day of rest free from business and even social engagements (Tip 89).

Here are a few tips on negotiating your own sabbatical:

- Point out how the company will benefit from the sabbatical. What new skills will you learn? How will you come back a better employee?
- Present a solid plan as to how your work will be handled in your absence.
- Remind your employer that in the information age, it makes sense for you to get an outside perspective, just as academicians do to study new ideas and get fresh insights on problems.
- If you are headed toward burnout, let your company know that this will be a way for you to recharge your batteries and come back with renewed energy and commitment. It is much more cost-effective to retain a good employee than it is to train a new one.
- If any of your planned sabbatical activities would directly benefit your company (new software skills you develop, for example), ask your employer to pay a partial salary and cover the costs of the training.
- If you plan to work for a volunteer, charity, or nonprofit organization, you may qualify for grants or fellowships. Do some research and you may be able to swing the sabbatical with little or no expense.
- If you will be gone for a long time, consider subletting your apartment, renting your home, or joining a home-swapping program.

- If you want to go overseas and are on a tight budget, go to places where the currency exchange works in your favor so that you can stretch your dollars.
- Before you begin negotiations, make sure you fully understand how the sabbatical may affect your employee benefits. Will you still have health insurance and be able to participate in retirement or 401K savings plans?
- Before you leave, make sure you have completed your work or trained someone to take over ongoing projects. You don't want to be worried about your work while you are supposed to be off exploring new worlds. And you certainly don't want to come back to find a bunch of angry colleagues or managers who didn't know what to do with xyz project while you were away.

Above all, use this precious time to learn more about yourself, try things you've always wanted to try and never had the time to do, go places you've always wanted to see. Live outside the box. Don't worry about what other people may think. This is your time to find yourself and renew your love of life. This is the perfect time to experiment in living one of your values (Tip 52). Listen to your intuition (Tip 57) and see where life takes you for a change. Sometimes we have to get off track in order to get on the right track again.

VII.

···

WORK SMARTER,
NOT HARDER

"It is no credit to anyone to work too hard."

E. W. Howe

It always bugged me when people would say, "Work smarter, not harder." If I knew how to work smarter, don't you think I would have been doing that? In Part VII you will learn how to become exceptionally efficient, productive, and effective by doing less, not more. You have probably heard the 80/20 rule—that 80 percent of your results comes from 20 percent of your efforts. If you could just figure out which 20 percent of your efforts was effective, theoretically you could safely eliminate 80 percent of what you currently do. This is working smarter. It goes back to the "less is more" principle. In Part II, we saw that having less stuff enabled us to attract more of what we really wanted; here you will see that less work often produces better results. When you are overly busy, stressed, and working too hard, you lose perspective on what is really important (Tip 35), you make careless mistakes, and you miss out on the really great opportunities all around you. When you are too busy and tired, you may ignore the subtle messages and end up creating a bigger problem than necessary (Tip 69). Put your nose to the grindstone and, more often than not, all you get is a red nose.

Now that you've identified your special talents and gifts in Part VI, you are ready to leverage these strengths and learn how to effectively delegate your weaknesses. You will find out how to get unstuck when you are in a rut and how to reduce your stress at work by under-promising. You may end up eliminating your to-do list (Tip 64) or eliminating goals altogether when you discover the power of not doing anything at all and just taking a nap or a break. In a culture that assumes being busy equals success, it is easy to fall into the trap of working too hard. So often I see people pushing harder and harder, and what they are doing is simply pushing the very thing they want away from them. One client was new in sales and was pushing hard to make the sale. She ended up scaring away her prospective clients. I told her to stop trying so hard (Tip 66). When she began to relax and have fun with her prospects, she immediately started booking deals right and left. She couldn't believe that the more fun she had, the more money she made. Don't get me wrong, there is work to be done, but not nearly as much as you might think. The following coaching tips show you how to work smarter while having more fun and success in the process, whether your goals are professional or personal.

61. STRENGTHEN YOUR STRENGTHS

"I think knowing what you cannot do is more important than knowing what you can do. In fact, that's good taste."

LUCILLE BALL

Many of us think we have to do it all and be good at everything. It's part of our independent spirit. We live in a time and in a civilization where you can actually afford *not* to do it all—welcome to the twenty-first century. Yet for some reason, we still think we should. We think we have to go to work, come home, cook the gourmet meal, clean the house spotlessly, take care of the children, have an extraordinary social life, take classes to improve ourselves—all in the same day or week. What if you just strengthened your strengths, really took a look at what you are good at, focused on that, mastered that, and delegated the rest? People who have really mastered something tend to easily attract the good life. Warren Buffett is a master investor. Barbra Streisand is a masterful singer. Doing a lot of things fairly well is not nearly as valuable as doing one thing *extremely* well. Mastery is an art, and even if you have the natural gift for something, it usually takes time, practice, and dedication to make that gift pay off. Tiger Woods may be naturally athletic and have a gift for golf, but he has honed the sport to an art form with practice, work, concentration, and coaching. Do we care if he can balance his checkbook? Of course not. Give up trying to be good at everything and focus on your strengths.

If you are still having a hard time letting go of all the things you could do, think of it in terms of how much energy something costs you. How much does it cost you in terms of your well-being and happiness? When you are agonizing over something or just procrastinating forever, consider what it is worth to you. Jonathan, a brilliant computer programmer, was smart enough that he could do just about anything he set his mind to. He could fix the plumbing in his house, repair the car, and even whip up a great liver pâté. When the roof of his new house started to leak, he decided to fix it himself rather than pay someone else to do it. This would all be well and good except that he already had more than enough projects on his plate. I suggested that he delegate the roof job to a professional to free up his time to do some programming he had been meaning to do for over a year. Nope. He was going to fix the roof and save the money (clients don't always take the coaching). On his way up the ladder, he fell off and broke his ankle in several places. While he missed the subtle message (Tip 69), he did get the hint at this point and hired a contractor to do the roof. With his foot elevated, he got a ton of valuable programming done. Unfortunately, he didn't have medical insurance (Tip 30), so now he not only has to pay for the roof, but also a couple thousand more in doctor bills.

Anytime you are doing something you hate to do, it is sapping your energy. I know one fellow who has hired a personal problem solver. Every time he has a problem that he doesn't want to deal with, he pays the problem solver to fix it. For example, if he gets double-charged on his credit card, he gives this to his assistant and it's handled. He argues that he can't afford *not* to do this because it costs so much of his energy. (If you are having a hard time with this, you probably skipped Part III on making money.) If you can't afford your own problem solver, try swapping chores with a friend who likes the very task you abhor. If you do my taxes I'll mow your lawn ten times. Do my laundry and I'll baby-sit your kids on Friday night. Of course, make sure both parties think the trade is fair and agreeable.

Look at your life and write down five things you have been doing that you would really rather not do. Then find out how much it would cost to hire an accountant, a housekeeper, a laundry service, a cook, a baby-sitter, an assistant, a computer tutor, or a plumber. It usually isn't as expensive as you think. In the long run, you may end up saving money. Congratulations on your first step toward mastery.

62. MASTER THE ART OF DELEGATING

"Next to doing a good job yourself the greatest joy is having someone else do a first-class job under your direction."

WILLIAM FEATHER,
THE BUSINESS OF LIFE

You don't have to be the boss to delegate. We all need this skill. As you start to attract the life you really want, you'll be delegating more of the things you don't enjoy doing and just doing what you love. So if you are the lone ranger type and haven't learned this skill, now is the time. Even parents delegate household chores and duties to children (if they have any sense, that is).

There are three secrets to delegating well. The first is to invest the time and energy required to fully train the person to whom you are delegating. The key word here is *fully*. If you don't fully train the other person to get it just right, to do the job exactly as you need it to be done, you cannot be upset, complain, or be surprised when it is not done just the way you want it. Most people think delegating is simply hiring someone and saying, "Here, you do it now." We are so eager to get rid of the task that we dump instead of delegate. Yes, sometimes you can in fact hire someone to do it for you. I hired a bookkeeper, and she set up all my accounts on an accounting program in a few hours. I had finally realized that I was never going to find the time to learn it with the manual (besides, I hate reading those nasty manuals). A big tip-off was that I hadn't even taken the software out of the box though I had purchased it over a year ago. Big red flag that I needed some help here. In a few hours, she not only set up the program but tailored it to the needs of my business, taught me how to reconcile my accounts, and printed a report for my accountant. Why didn't I do this ages ago? I wasted all sorts of time and energy trying to do it myself.

The second key ingredient to successful delegating is to delegate the whole job. Once the person is trained and knows what the end result should look like, let him or her figure out how to get there. Otherwise you rob the person of creativity. For example, suppose you delegate the job of cleaning your son's bedroom to your son. He in turn hires his little brother to do it and gives him some of his allowance. This is just fine, provided that he didn't bully him into doing it. The same end result is produced with a creative solution.

The third key is to establish a reporting or check-in system. Have the person you've hired report back to you in a manner and with a frequency that best supports you. For example, suppose you hire a housekeeper to clean the house while you are at work. You've taken the time to show him around the house and show him exactly how you like things to be cleaned. Before he arrives, make a list of special tasks, like "wipe off the shelves inside the medicine cabinet." Ask the housekeeper to make a list of things he accomplished or to check off your list, acknowledging what was done. Now that you have the secrets to successful delegating, go to it, and watch the fabulous results.

Michael had hired me to help him grow his business, which he was struggling to keep afloat with a big loan. He had a talented, full-time person working with him at $35,000 a year, but he really couldn't afford to pay her so I recommended that he let her go. He then had to do all of the work himself, from typing letters to balancing the books. This was fine at first, but as he started attracting more clients and his business grew, he needed to start delegating. I asked Michael to make an organizational chart of all the various functions in his business, including sales, marketing, administration, accounting, etc. Then he made a list of all the things he liked doing and a separate list of all the things he didn't like doing or wasn't particularly good at. We started with the bookkeeping. He hired an accountant for a small extra sum each month. This was a huge relief, as Michael was never fond of the financial details. Then he hired a bright college student as a part-time assistant for $8 an hour to come in and write press releases and other letters. As soon as he could afford to, Michael increased her wages to encourage her to stick around. This extra assistance enabled Michael to focus on working with the clients and on marketing the business—the parts he most enjoys. With a little coaching, Michael has successfully turned the business around and is attracting new clients as fast as he can handle them.

63. UNDER-PROMISE AND OVER-DELIVER

"One promises much, to avoid giving little."

LUC MARQUIS DE VAUVENARGUES

One of the easiest ways to quickly build a reserve of time is to under-promise and over-deliver. To under-promise is to give yourself twice the amount of time you think you'll need to get something done. To over-deliver means to complete the project ahead of the promised date and turn it in early. For example, the boss comes to you and says, "I want you to work on this important project. When can you get it to me?" Now your natural inclination is to over-promise. You think to yourself, "Hmm . . . it's Thursday afternoon, I could work today and tomorrow, come in a few hours Saturday, and have it ready by Monday morning." You tell your boss, trying to impress him with your dedication, "If I work hard and get right on it, I'll have it to you Monday morning." So you put aside your other work, you come in for more than a few hours on Saturday, and in spite of your efforts you still aren't ready because you're missing some information from another department. Monday arrives and you tell your boss, "I'm just about done. I'll have it ready this afternoon. I needed some information from George's department." She grumbles, and you've just blown everything you were trying to accomplish. Your boss is not impressed. You over-promised.

Now try this scenario: You think, "I could get this done by Monday." You tell your boss, "I will have this to you Wednesday afternoon." What did you just do? You just created an instant reserve of time—two days to be exact. You enjoy the weekend and go golfing. You are rested and more productive. You get the report done without the stress by Tuesday morning and run it by a colleague for proofreading. You turn it in on Tuesday afternoon. Congratulations—you just over-delivered. Your boss is impressed and thinks you're great; you are the one who always gets thing done *ahead* of schedule. This simple tip will dramatically reduce your stress level, and you will be less harried and more clear-headed—much more likely to attract success. Consistently under-promise and over-deliver and it will result in a bonus or raise.

What if your boss absolutely requires that it is done by Monday? While we often get specific deadlines, most of them can be negotiated. Request the extra two or three days. If you have been consistently under-promising, you will have a reserve of time in all your other projects, and you will actually have the time to crunch it out by Monday if you have to.

Under-promising works wonders in your personal life as well. When your wife asks when you'll get the garage organized, give yourself double the time you think you will really need. Then when you get it done in one month instead of two, she will be delighted. If you are cooking dinner, instead of bragging ahead of time that you are making a gourmet meal, say you are just cooking something simple and surprise your spouse with a fabulous meal. This also works with kids. Rather than promise trips to SeaWorld, the zoo, and the beach during your California vacation, just promise SeaWorld. Then if you do have time for the other things, it will be an unexpected bonus, and they will be thrilled. However, if you say up front, "If we have the time we'll also see the zoo and go bodysurfing in the ocean," you will definitely disappoint the kids if you run out of time. Keep expectations low and then surprise them. Otherwise you will spend your life apologizing.

64. TOSS YOUR TO-DO LIST

"One never notices what has been done, one can only see what remains to be done."

MARIE CURIE

"Too many people, too many demands, too much to do; competent, busy, hurrying people—it just isn't living at all."

ANNE SPENCER MORROW LINDBERGH

One way to more fully leverage the present moment and increase your productivity is to get rid of your to-do list. I know this sounds like heresy; I'm a lover of lists myself. Try keeping the list for work, but consider trashing your personal list. If throwing out your list sounds tough, try living without it for a week and see what happens. You will find that you naturally do what needs to be done. Max was ruled by his to-do list. He said, "You know, I almost get everything done, but there are always two or three things I don't get done." He would beat himself up about the two or three things he didn't do instead of congratulating himself for the ten things he did. If you just lived the day doing what needed to be done and didn't worry about the list, then you wouldn't feel bad about what didn't get done. Every little thing you stop doing that makes you feel inadequate or insufficient will take you one step closer to success. When was the last time you felt really good about *not* finishing a list of tasks? Yet we always seem to give ourselves more than we can do— a vicious circle.

Oftentimes we get so focused on the to-do list that we miss out on the really great opportunities all around us. A list can be a helpful tool, but it can also limit your vision. If you are a die-hard list maker, try just doing the "What Is Important About Today?" questions (Tip 35) as they will provide sufficient focus without burying you in details or overwhelming you with all there is to do. Toss your list and see how good you feel.

On the other hand, if you really love lists and feel great even if you only do one thing on the list, go right ahead, make your list. (I think you are getting the idea here—if it feels good, do it!) One client discovered a different technique for list-making that left her feeling empowered. Instead of crossing completed items off the list, she highlights them with bright yellow. She can't help but be drawn to the things she has already accomplished. She says to herself, "Ha! I did that, and that, and that too!" This spurs her on to do even more while making her feel great about what she has already done. She says she would never want to give up the pleasure of highlighting her accomplishments.

Now that you've tossed your to-do list, it is time to toss your goals. This may sound even worse than the previous recommendation. But really, if the goal is that important to you do you think you will forget it if you don't write it on a list? To really open up to your intuition and let it be your guide, you have to be willing to toss the goals list, which is usually generated from the head. It's what we think we *should* be going for in our lives. The big house, the nice car, the perfect relationship, the exquisite wardrobe, the trip to Europe, the flat stomach—how much of this is really your idea anyway? Sure this stuff would be nice, but most of it came from the media. In order to really tap into the goods of the world, you must be willing to let all this stuff go. Cross it off your goals and start with a clean slate.

I'm not saying you can't have goals. In my workshops I will even tell people to write down what they want because writing it down can help it become a reality. But for the meantime, give yourself a fresh start. Toss your old goals and see what comes to you naturally. You may be surprised. For example, I got the idea to make an audiotape. This wasn't even on my goal list a year ago, but when I tossed my goal to lose weight I felt free to work on something more interesting. Then I got the idea to write a book. But I had crossed these off my list: learn Portuguese and French, learn ballroom dancing, become a profitable potter, live in a foreign country, etc. Yes, I may end up doing these someday, but they aren't on my list anymore. I will allow my life to take its course naturally, and if I end up living in Paris, then I'll take a French class. It is impossible to go with the flow if you are run by your list of goals. The right goals will find you if you let them. And that is the whole point here: let things come to you naturally. Stop forcing, pushing, pressing, striving, working, and struggling to get what you want. Stop! You are much more likely to attract success if you stop chasing after it. Just relax and do want you feel like for a while, and see what happens.

Karen was reluctant to give up her goals. She was certain that, left to her own devices, she would do nothing but laze on a sunny beach, read brainless romance novels, drink margaritas, and get brown as a bean. Her life wouldn't amount to anything. So she pressed herself to work 80 to 100 hours a week in a job she enjoyed, but still, with that much time spent at work she didn't have a whole lot left for anything else. Finally, when she had gotten about as stressed as possible, she quit her job. She had talked things over with her husband, and he was happy to support her in doing whatever she wanted to do, even if that was sitting on the beach. She also had saved over a year's worth of living expenses, so she could afford to quit (Tip 27). Off she went to the beach, and after about two weeks of baking in the sun, she got bored. Yeah. She tried to waste her life away on the beach, but it didn't work. She started painting again—a hobby she had dabbled in before taking on the demanding job—and it turns out that she is very talented. Not only that, but she is more beautiful than ever because she is so relaxed and happy. The little furrow between her brows has completely disappeared, and she is now leading seminars and has plenty of free time to paint. There is a limit to how much leisure a person can take before the urge to do something will strike. You can trust yourself to throw away your goals and let the world provide you with the next opportunity.

Another client, Michael, an executive sales manager for a Fortune 500 company, has built his successful career on goals. He gives his sales team yearly goals, quarterly goals, weekly goals, daily goals. His whole life he has been driven to achieve by the idea of making the goal, exceeding the targeted number. Needless to say, Michael was not one bit pleased with the concept of tossing his goals. I allowed him to keep his work goals, but asked that he get rid of all his personal goals. He whined and complained and said he would feel lost, floating, aimless, but he agreed to try it for two weeks as an experiment. He tossed out the following list of personal goals: get a six-pack stomach, go whitewater rafting through the Grand Canyon, go on a safari in Africa, learn Spanish, learn karate, make new kitchen cabinets, and take his kids camping. I reminded Michael that crossing these items off didn't mean that he was giving up on them, or that he would never do them, but rather that he would allow things to occur naturally at the right time and place.

·The next week Michael called back amazed. Odd and incredible things were happening. For starters, all week the perfect parking space would open up just as he needed it. At work, Michael had been recruiting at a job fair, and his normal style would have been to buzz around with the other vendors and schmooze. He didn't have to. People were coming up to his booth saying so-and-so should talk to you. Three unsolicited referrals came to him. Some bizarre stuff was also happening at work. The company had recently bought out a competitor, and his new counterparts were messing around with his clients. Because there was no system for communicating with the new team, there was no way of controlling this behavior. All the players were shuffling at the top; nobody wanted to make a decision, and everything was being deferred to committees. Michael said that if this had happened six months ago he would have gone ballistic. Now he just supports his clients and is amazed at his cool sense of detachment in all the chaos. But the thing Michael was happiest about after one week of being goal-less? His golf score had inexplicably and dramatically improved. Toss your goals and allow things to come to you for a change.

65. Take a Power Nap

"Never be afraid to sit awhile and think."

Lorraine Hansberry

I am certainly not an expert on meditation and am not even sure that what I do is technically meditation. If you already meditate, good for you. For people like me, who feel that they don't have time to meditate and who are certain when they try to meditate that it isn't working, here's what I do. Call it beginning meditation for the super-stressed.

I lie down on the sofa with my head on a pillow, and a throw on my feet if it is chilly. I put a tiny malachite pyramid on my third eye—that's the part of your forehead above your nose. (My sister gave me this little stone and said it would bring me financial success so I figured I would try it. So far it has been working. Meditation for money would probably have the Buddhists turning over in their graves, but I figure you have to start somewhere.) Sometimes I'll put on relaxing music; the sound of waves crashing on the beach is very calming. I close my eyes, and I don't do anything. I usually don't fall asleep, but if you do, that is okay. Your body obviously needs the rest. I imagine opening my mind to receive any messages from the universe. Now all sorts of thoughts go popping into my head, most of them pretty mundane, like a comment my client made or what I should eat for dinner. Sometimes I keep a pad and pen handy to jot down the more interesting things that come into my head. This way I can forget about them because they are on paper. Whatever happens, I don't worry. I just lie there until I feel like getting up.

While I haven't received any messages from a deep, godlike voice, I do occasionally get a strong sense that I need to do something. I consider such messages my marching orders. I felt this way about making my audiotape, *Irresistible Attraction: A Way of Life*. Even though it didn't make good financial sense at the time, and despite rational protests from my loved ones, I went ahead and did it. Now these same loved ones are glad I did it. The point here is to take the time to meditate, nap, relax, and do nothing. Do it in any form that works for you, but do it. Who knows what messages you'll end up receiving?

My client Elaine has a different method of sitting and thinking. She is a production manager at a large oil company and is in charge of a team of twenty people. When she feels overwhelmed and stressed, she plays solitaire on the computer. Although an outside observer might say she is goldbricking, this mind-freeing and relaxing task enables her to tackle her work with fresh ideas and renewed energy. The fifteen or twenty minutes that she takes to play solitaire helps her relax and refocus instead of getting into a dither. In addition to being a calming influence, it frees her mind to come up with creative solutions to the problems she is facing at work. You may think this sounds silly, but the top consulting firms are now sending their employees into "think tanks" while they are on the job. These elaborate-sounding "think tanks" are nothing more than quiet, dark rooms with a place to lie down and take a power nap. If companies just gave their own employees a little latitude to come up with creative solutions, they would no doubt spare themselves paying thousands of dollars for outside consultants' bright ideas.

Find time to just sit and think. Work in a daily power nap and make some space for creative thought to flourish. It's okay to be creative as to how you do this—just don't get caught!

66. Do or Do Not

"If you think you can do a thing, or think you can't do a thing, you're right."

HENRY FORD

Trying is a ridiculous waste of time. As Yoda of the movie *Star Wars* said, "Do or do not. There is no try." He is right. If you don't believe this wise old character, here is an exercise that will prove it to you. Put a pencil on a table in front of you. Now try to pick it up. Do you have the pencil in your hand? Then you failed the exercise. I said *try* to pick it up. You successfully picked up the pencil. You did it. You didn't try. Trying, by definition, implies that it isn't done. Now this time, try to pick up the pencil. Your hand is on the pencil, you are grunting and groaning and moaning, but you do not lift the pencil off the table. Excellent. That is what it looks like to try. So stop trying and either do or do not.

Why is trying to make it or to prove something so unappealing? You've met people like this. They are striving and struggling and exerting all sorts of effort to be something they aren't. Just go out there and do it. It will either work or it won't. If it works, great, you've done it. Congratulations! If it doesn't work, what went wrong? What did you learn from the experience? Notice that I said do it, not try it. You do it and get the result you wanted, or you do it and don't get the result you wanted— or you don't do it and don't get any results. These are the only realities. Everything else is something you made up in your head. Trying is a waste of energy and goes against the natural flow of life.

Life wasn't meant to be a struggle. Yes, it may require a ton of work and commitment, but the struggling part is optional. You may not be able to avoid the work, but you can choose whether to struggle or not. You know the difference when work is a joy and when it's a drag. If something is a struggle, what could you do instead that would be fun and effortless?

How can you make it easier? Can you automate it or systematize it so that it becomes effortless? Could you delegate the part you don't like? If you want to have an awesome life, you'll have to give up struggling.

Susan, a business owner in her early forties, had a hard time with this concept. When I asked her to do a coaching assignment, she would always respond, "Well, I'll try." I wouldn't accept this and asked her to take the assignment, decline it, or counteroffer. She realized that the words "I'll try" were inherently disempowering and contained the seeds of defeat before she even began. She accepted the assignment and just went out and did it. It was much easier than trying to do it. There is no mental anguish in simply doing something. The anguish comes when you *try* to do something. Think about it. When I sit down to write, I just write. Sometimes it is good, and sometimes it is awful and needs reworking. The hard part is thinking and worrying about the writing I want to do. We have all fretted about doing something and, after actually doing it, found that it wasn't nearly as bad as we had anticipated.

67. Get Yourself Unstuck

"True life is lived when tiny changes occur."

LEO TOLSTOY

The key to making a big change is to make a little change. This has to do with inertia. We often get stuck in the idea of having to make some huge change in our lives, and it seems overwhelming so we don't do anything. We just wish, wait, and hope. Or we may just be stuck in a very comfortable routine. The trick is to realize that the force of inertia (the tendency of bodies at rest to stay at rest) will keep you exactly where you are unless you do something. That something doesn't even have to be related to what you want.

You've probably heard of taking a big goal and chunking it down into baby steps. This is a great idea, but sometimes we don't even know where to begin, what baby step to take. What you may not realize is that *any* change leads to more change. Just do *something* different. Wear red socks instead of navy socks. Take a different route to work. Eat at a different restaurant. Move the pictures and paintings in your house to different walls. Part your hair on the opposite side. Drink tea instead of coffee. Any change will do. This works because it gets you unstuck and into the change mode. The momentum will get you going on a roll, and before you know it, you'll be making bigger and bigger changes relatively effortlessly. This technique enables you to skip the hard part of mustering up enough motivation, willpower, or courage to tackle a big goal, project, or change.

Dave, a sixty-seven-year-old divorced and retired accountant, didn't know what to do with his life. There was nothing wrong with his life. He had a beautiful home, plenty of savings, and didn't have to work any more, but he found he wasn't satisfied just puttering around the house. He wanted to do something different, but he couldn't think of what to do and none of the suggestions people made seemed appealing. He was stuck in a rut, and the force of habit and routine kept him there. I suggested that he make some minor changes. Dave decided to eat at a different restaurant than the usual one. He took down all the paintings in his house and stored them in the attic; he thought he'd just leave the walls blank for a while and see what that was like. He donated almost every one of his business suits to charity because he realized he didn't wear them anymore. One change led to another, and Dave decided to go on a safari to Africa with his son, who was thrilled at the chance to take a break from his own hectic life. This was something Dave had always wanted to do, but he had never had the time or the money. Having gone on safari, Dave had the courage to take a two-week solo bike tour through the French countryside. Dave now travels whenever he wants and feels a sense of adventure he hasn't had in years.

Beth, a sales manager, was an attractive brunette but wasn't happy with the way she looked at 5'7" and 167 pounds. She wanted to lose twenty-five to thirty pounds, but didn't have time in her super-busy schedule to fit in a workout, and counting calories and other diets never seemed to work. Beth decided to make one little change at a time and keep on making adjustments until she reached her ideal weight. The first change she made was to have a simple breakfast of instant oatmeal, a banana, and green tea. She figured that she could eat this at her desk in the mornings instead of the donut and coffee. Then she started walking one hour to work each day. She realized that riding the bus or subway took forty minutes, and figured that for an extra twenty minutes a day she could gain an hour of exercise. With these two small changes, she lost five pounds in the first month. Then she was motivated to tackle her lunches. Instead of eating the usual fast-food combo—fried chicken, french fries, or a hamburger—she went to the salad bar and had as many vegetables as she wanted, a scoop of tuna or chicken salad, and three bagel chips. She lost another four pounds. Now she was on a roll and decided to jog around Central Park's reservoir on the weekends. Dinners came next. Beth didn't bother to cook at home, so instead of going out for Italian food, she opted for Asian food. She alternated a night of sushi and salad with a night of stir-fry beef, chicken, or shrimp with vegetables and brown rice. Slowly and steadily the weight melted right off. Six months later Beth was just five pounds away from her ideal. She decided to add the extra hour of walking each day and walk home from work too. This cost her an extra twenty minutes, but she felt that she was more relaxed and energized walking home than being jostled on crowded buses. She added five minutes of belly crunches in the morning. Within two months she had a flat tummy and was at her ideal. It was all thanks to making one little change after another.

68. MAKE A RADICAL CHANGE

"You were once wild here. Don't let them tame you!"

ISADORA DUNCAN

Sometimes my clients don't seem to be making any progress toward a particular goal and feel completely stuck. They come to me for advice on what to do. The first thing we look at is why they aren't making progress. Is there something preventing them from taking action other than pure procrastination? Maybe they don't have the knowledge or skill to do a particular task and need to delegate it to someone else (Tip 62). One of my clients was procrastinating about putting up a website for her speaking company. After a brief discussion, she realized that she was not interested in learning all that it takes to put up a website. She hired someone to do it and that was that—project completed.

Sometimes fear is stopping people. We take a look at the source of the fear (Tip 97) and alleviate that. Rob hired me because he wanted to quit his job and start his own business and was frustrated because he just couldn't make the leap. He thought he was acting cowardly or indecisively. Well, he had good reason to be afraid. He had over $8,000 in credit card debt and nothing saved to fund his new business. We set him up an aggressive debt repayment plan and a savings plan (Tip 24) and worked on ways he could start his new business in the evenings until its success made his old job unnecessary. It was a tough wake-up call for Rob, but in the end, he made the transition successfully. I've seen many people quit out of frustration before they have both the savings and the clients they need, and this is much more painful than making a well-planned transition.

Once we've removed any blocks and fears, if the client still can't progress it may be that the goal is wrong. I usually recommend that they ditch the goal and get a new one that they don't need motivation to tackle (Tip 4). Another reason clients don't reach goals is that they are doing one goal to get something else—the thing they *really* want. For example, you may be going to the gym to lose weight so that you can attract a man. Then you wonder why you have no motivation to go to the gym. Losing weight isn't your real goal—your real goal is to get a man. In this case, I'd recommend that the client go for what she wants directly and buy the book *How Not to Stay Single*, by Nita Tucker, and get busy. Go directly for what you want; don't waste time mucking around with other stuff. If you go directly for what you want and it doesn't work, *then* you might want to go back and try plan B—get in shape.

Now what if none of the above applies and the client is still stuck? It is time to make a radical change. Do something completely different, even go in the opposite direction, but whatever you do, don't do the same old thing because that has been getting you nowhere. It is crazy to do the same thing and expect a different result. If you want the same result, do the same thing; if you want a different result, try something different.

There is an exception to this, as with all things. Sometimes you will be taking actions and doing all the right things and staying on a plateau, getting nowhere—or so it seems. This doesn't mean you aren't progressing; it may just look like you aren't progressing. George Leonard describes this phenomenon in his book *Mastery*, and says that it is all part of the process of reaching excellence in any field. If you want to attain mastery of anything, you are bound to hit a plateau at some point. Most people give up, but the masters continue, and eventually, they break through to the next level. Leonard is a black belt martial artist and used his training experiences to illustrate his point. He would train and go through all the motions but not make it to the next level, and then one day he would be there. Some days you will even backslide. This is a normal part of the process and should be expected.

Joshua was frustrated because his business just didn't seem to be going to the next level. He had taken all the right actions, was speaking publicly to become known in the community, and had great relationships with the local papers, which would list his business events whenever he asked. He had an excellent track record. There didn't seem to be anything missing so I asked Joshua to continue taking all the actions. In two months, things started to kick in, and now his business is thriving. He just needed to stick with it.

What about radical change? If you aren't making progress, you may want to do the opposite of what you have been doing. One client was obese and wasn't happy about it. She had tried every diet known to man, and nothing seemed to work for her. I suggested that the only thing that seems to work in such extreme cases is something equally extreme. She needed to radically change her lifestyle if she really wanted to become fit—become an aerobics instructor or a lumberjack or something. This got her thinking, and she realized that small changes just weren't going to do it for her. She found someone to coach her through the process and evaluate every aspect of her exercise and eating until she could find a plan that worked for her. She has lost sixty-three pounds and has decided to join a runner's club and enter a marathon to burn off the rest.

Another client was working on a book and just couldn't get past the writer's block. We tried the opposite extreme. Instead of writing, he cleared out his house and hired a Feng Shui master to come and evaluate everything (Tip 20). He completely rearranged all the furniture in his home and office and got an incredible burst of energy. He cleaned out all his files and discovered he had articles filed away from 1974 that he meant to read someday. Once he cleared the space to think, the ideas poured forth, and he wrote effortlessly.

Let me give you another example. Marsha is one of the sweetest human beings around. It is nice to be nice, but for Marsha, being good all the time wasn't just an option—she felt she had to be good. As a result, if someone asked her to do something, she found it very difficult to say no. If someone said something unkind to her, she didn't know what to say in response. She always seemed to be at the butt end of jokes, and people teased her without mercy. Marsha just smiled and put up with it, but secretly she suffered. Everybody, even her own friends, seemed to be taking advantage of her. She went out of her way to help a friend after surgery, but when she was sick, her friend was nowhere in sight. She made plans to spend Thanksgiving with a fellow she had been seeing, and at the last minute he decided to go off with his friends instead. Marsha was a doormat and everybody was walking all over her.

I told Marsha that she would need to take radical action to break out of the mold. She was willing to try anything. I asked her to be bad for a whole week to break her of the need to be nice. She balked at this assignment. At first Marsha couldn't even think of something bad to do. I suggested she start with little things, like not answering the phone and letting the machine pick up the messages, or not returning a call if she didn't feel like it. The next week Marsha reported back with all the bad things she had done. She got out of some work she had volunteered to do. She just said, "It turns out I can't do this after all." She ate an entire angel food cake all by herself. She tore up a request for a donation with fiendish glee. She bought a totally impractical pair of sexy, high-heeled, black suede shoes with leopard spots on them   very bad! She showed up ten minutes late when she always on time.

Marsha discovered that she didn't always have to be good and that if she said "no" the world wouldn't end and people wouldn't hate her. The next week we worked on putting in place stronger boundaries (Tip 5). Marsha noticed an interesting thing: people weren't teasing her or taking advantage of her anymore. They respected her. Try being bad for twenty-four hours and see what happens. Then try it for a week. Don't worry, it won't kill you, and you can always go back to being good. Shake people up a bit.

Obviously, you must be prepared to live with the consequences of your actions. Of course, I'm not talking about breaking the law or endangering yourself or others. Most women have been raised to be nice. This is all very well and good, but our behavior is no longer our own—we end up *having* to be good. This stifles our creativity to the point that we don't know how to be any other way, limiting our growth and development. The point of this tip is to break out of your normal routine, break a pattern or an old way of being that you are stuck with, and see what happens. What radical action are you ready to take?

69. LEARN TO HEAR THOSE SUBTLE MESSAGES

"Life has this in common with prize fighting: If you've received a belly blow, it's likely to be followed by a right to the jaw."

AMANDA CROSS

Life is a marvelous instructor and usually a very kind one too. We get sent all sorts of subtle little messages that tell us to wake up, but more often than not, we fail to hear the cues. We are so busy we miss them altogether. Even if you do hear the message, "Hmm . . . the car is making a strange noise, I need to take it in for a tune-up," you may ignore it or postpone resolving it. When you ignore the message it gets a little louder and becomes a problem. When you continue to ignore the problem, it gets really loud and becomes a crisis. If you ignore the crisis, it may end up a disaster.

Take the example of my sister, who was training for the New York Marathon. She was going along just fine and then boom! She ends up in the hospital for two days with a kidney problem. She thought that the message was to drink more water, that she had gotten dehydrated. She kept on running and training and even did quite well in the marathon, her very first one. She continued to run, and a great deal of her time and energy was directed toward this training as she looked for different races to enter. Then she went skiing with her boyfriend and blew out her knee so badly that the doctor said it would need surgery. She hobbled around for a good two months hoping it would go away, but finally went in for a three-hour surgery to the tune of $60,000 (fortunately she had insurance, Tip 30). The doctor removed most of the cartilage from her knee and said that she should not run again. She can run, but it will wear the bones down. She was terribly depressed and sat around feeling sorry for herself for quite some time.

After about six months, when she was well into physical therapy, I asked her why she had this accident (since there are no accidents). After some thought, she realized that she had been going down a very demanding physical path and that her true path in life was meant to be more intellectual than physical. She would stay physically active, but not let her life revolve around it. She was literally stopped in her tracks from going down this path. Funny how the universe won't let you stray too far. If she had been more sensitive to the early subtle messages, she might have caught on sooner and realized at her first hospital visit that she was pushing her body too hard. That was a fully recoverable crisis, but the knee damage is permanent. What is the universe trying to tell you that you have been ignoring?

Listen to the subtle messages and take drastic and immediate measures to compensate. If you bounce a check, sign up for bounce protection, get automatic bill paying, and put more than you think you need in your checking account. If you lose a customer, take the client to lunch and find out why. Then survey all your customers to find out how to better meet their needs and make the changes to your business immediately. If you get the sniffles, take a megadose of vitamin C, get to bed early, and reevaluate your diet and exercise plan instead of pushing yourself harder and hoping it will go away.

Luke, the owner of an insurance company, really wanted to take some time off, but felt he couldn't afford to. He had big goals for the month of August. I usually take August off because it happens to be the lowest-energy month of the year. Most folks don't feel like ramping up their lives at this time of the year. Nobody really gets much done in August regardless of their great intentions. It is just too hot and humid to work, and it is the last month before school starts so a general lethargy seems to prevail. Rather than fight this general tendency, I prefer to surrender to it completely and just declare it a holiday month. Well, even though I encouraged Luke to listen to the subtle message and take a vacation break, he thought if he pushed hard while others were at the beach, he'd be ahead of the game. He wanted to hire and train a new person, go out and bring in some new clients, and find a bigger office space.

When Luke checked back in September, he was feeling more exhausted and discouraged than ever. He didn't find the new office space, he ended up hiring a recruiting firm to find the new employee, and he didn't go out and get any new clients. He pushed himself hard even though he really just wanted to take some time off. Worst of all, he ended up getting sick and had to stay home for two weeks (his body really needed the break whether or not Luke was willing to take it). Luke then mentioned that although he didn't do anything to bring them in, he did get some great referrals and got two new clients that met his sales goals for the summer. I pointed out that he had achieved two out of the three goals. Luke hesitated and then admitted this was true; he did meet his objectives even though he didn't meet them the way he had originally planned. Of course, he could have reached the same end result if he had just listened to the subtle message (take some time off) and spared himself the misery of being sick for two weeks.

It is far better to err on the side of over-responding than doing just enough to get by. Start seeing the little clue as a warning that something bigger is on its way, and responding to the little clue as if it were the big one. I'm not saying you should panic or make a big deal out of it; just handle it and handle it so well that you won't have to worry about it again. This is part of doing complete work (Tip 38). It is Murphy's Law that if you are prepared for it, it won't happen. And if it happens anyway, well, at least you are prepared for it. It is really hard to attract success when you are deluged with problems, so see if you can catch them early on— before things get ugly.

70. LEVERAGE THE TELEPHONE

"Life is too short for a long story."

LADY MARY WORTLEY MONTAGU

There are a number of ways that you can leverage the telephone to your advantage. First, put a ten-minute limit on phone calls. Long, drawn-out phone conversations become tiresome very quickly. Always try to end the phone conversation first and do so gracefully. For example, you can say, "It's been a real pleasure speaking with you." By keeping your phone calls short, friendly, and focused you will develop a reputation for being a professional whose time is valuable. This goes for personal calls too. If you end the call first, people will be left wanting more of you and will look forward to the next call.

Most folks have short attention spans, and if they know you have a tendency to talk a lot, they will tune you out. They may start doing something else while on the phone with you. If you keep your conversations laserlike, you'll get and keep their attention. As a bonus, you'll create extra time. You may want to make exceptions to the ten-minute rule for calls to Mom and Dad, significant others, and special friends. However, as much as you may enjoy them, all those phone calls will devour your time before you've realized it. Let your friends know the best time to call you. Pick a time when you aren't going to be focused on some other activity so that when they do call, you won't feel interrupted and can enjoy them.

Another way to leverage your telephone is to take advantage of the latest technology, such as voice mail, instead of letting the phone run your life. Deborah, a high-level real estate executive, works in an office with an open-door policy. She has a private office, but keeps the door open, so anyone can interrupt her at any time. She also believed that it made more sense to answer the phone when it rang and handle the call on the spot than it did to call back later and risk missing the person and playing phone tag. On a typical day she would get to work at 8:30 A.M. and leave at 7:00 or 7:30 P.M. Needless to say, she felt like a mashed potato when she finally got home from work. When I asked her when she got the most work done, she admitted that it was in the evenings. It hadn't occurred to her that this was when the phone had stopped ringing. All day long she got nothing accomplished because she was busy answering the phone (she even has a secretary, but didn't use her to screen calls). Now Deborah sets aside two hours a day, from 10:00 A.M. to 12 P.M., to get some serious work done. She unplugs her phone and uses voice mail. She shuts her office door, and the secretary tells would-be interrupters that she is working on a project and will be available at 12:00 P.M. Deborah is leveraging her secretary, her private office, and her voice mail to her advantage.

Don't be afraid to use your voice mail and answering machine to screen calls. Now Deborah gets out of work at 5:30 P.M. and feels like she has actually accomplished something for a change. With the extra time, she has started an exercise program with a personal trainer at the gym and has the energy to go out with friends in the evening. Thanks to her increased productivity, she got a bigger bonus than ever this year. She is also more relaxed in general and has attracted a man into her life. Use the phone as a tool to increase, not decrease, your effectiveness.

VIII.

....

COMMUNICATE
WITH POWER, GRACE,
AND STYLE

*"What good is it for a man to gain the whole world, and yet lose
or forfeit his very self?"*

JESUS OF NAZARETH, LUKE 9:25

"Make the most of yourself, for that is all there is of you."

RALPH WALDO EMERSON

YOU HAVE MADE it through seven parts of the coaching program and are
now easily attracting the good things you want in life. You put in place
a solid foundation for your life and increased your energy by getting rid
of the big energy drains and substituting positive energy sources. You created more than enough space and time for what you want in your life,
making it natural to attract more than enough money and love. With the
basics handled, it was easier to discover what you really wanted in life,
distinct from any media-instilled desires. Knowing what you wanted, you
started taking exceptionally good care of yourself and increased your willingness to have a great life. And now you are naturally and effortlessly
attracting what you have always wanted.

Part VIII is not about *doing* things, it is about a way of *being*, a way
of communicating with power, grace, and style. In one sense, this is the

most important part of all. It goes beyond eliminating what you are tolerating, beyond having a large cash reserve or a gorgeous house or body. We all know people who look successful, but are not *being* successful—they just have all the trappings in place, the nice car, wardrobe, and home. While having money makes it easier to be successful, it certainly doesn't guarantee it. It is difficult to maintain your success if you don't have the foundation in place. Parts I through VII make it easy for you to be your best all the time. Now that you have structured your life and environment to support you, it is almost impossible for you *not* to be your best, most successful self. You'd have to work pretty hard at being cranky with all the good things and people you have in your life. Now you are ready to learn to be successful—and to increase your success—by fine-tuning your communication skills.

71. STOP THE GOSSIP

"It is almost impossible to throw dirt on someone without getting a little on yourself."

ABIGAIL VAN BUREN

Can't resist passing on a juicy tidbit? Beware! As much as your friends and colleagues may love to hear the latest dirt on someone, secretly they can't help wondering what you are saying about them when they aren't around. No one really trusts a gossip. You will be missing out on the profound conversations that occur when someone trusts you implicitly. The rule here is to avoid talking about someone who isn't present. Every time you do this, it's gossip, plain and simple.

One of my standards (Tip 8) is not to gossip. Given my profession as a coach, this is imperative for my success in business. I also have a boundary that people don't gossip around me. One of my friends had a tendency to talk about the lives of people who weren't present; in other words, he liked to gossip. A graceful way to steer the conversation away from gossip and onto something else is to say, "I'd rather hear about you." This works most of the time and is very flattering. However, if this doesn't work, you may need to be more direct and say, "Do you realize that you are talking about someone who isn't present? It makes me feel uncomfortable." Or more simply, "I don't feel comfortable talking about someone who isn't present."

You may wonder what is the harm in a little friendly gossip. Well, it can be both harmful and destructive. A friend and colleague of mine told me about a new direction she was going with her business; she was writing a weekly column. This was exciting news. When I saw a mutual friend of ours and she asked about her, I told her the good news about the column. Word got back to my friend and she immediately called me up quite angry that I was spreading the word that she was giving up her old career for the new one. She was not giving up the old career, and my seemingly positive comment could have negatively hurt her business. I immediately apologized for my misunderstanding and called our mutual friend to apologize too. I was very embarrassed to say the least.

All this would have been prevented if the person were present. She would have ensured that the correct meaning was conveyed. A big benefit of giving up gossip is that your friends will start to trust you. If you already have a reputation as a gossip it will take a concerted effort to break the habit, and it may take time to reverse this reputation, but the rewards are well worth it. It is impossible to be attractive if you are a gossip or even participate in it at all. Gossip is seductive, not attractive. Take your pick.

72. Don't Spill Your Guts

"A closed mouth catches no flies."

Italian proverb

If you are discreet this doesn't apply to you, but if you feel compelled to tell all to your colleagues and new friends you might want to reconsider and hold your tongue. Most people really don't want to hear all the gory details of your past relationships or the problems you had growing up. Better to save these stories for your mother, therapist, coach, or longtime friends. Your mom will still love you, and your therapist or coach is getting paid to listen and respond. Another option is to go to a 12-step program and spill your guts there along with everyone else.

Matt worked in the fashion business and discovered that it was a chatty and social place. Everyone knew everything about what was going on in everyone's life. Gossip spread like wildfire, and the most popular people were the ones with the latest dirt. His colleagues thought nothing of asking him the most personal details of his life, who he was dating, how the date went, where did they eat, did they have sex, what did he wear—everything. Matt always felt a bit uncomfortable with this, but didn't want to seem standoffish and felt compelled to answer whatever question they asked.

It was natural for him to want to be liked and accepted by his colleagues. I pointed out that Matt was missing a boundary here: It is no longer okay for people to pry into my personal affairs. He would use the four-step model to enforce this boundary (Tip 6) from now on. The next day he went to work and when someone asked him something, he kept his answers short and simple without revealing all the details. If the person continued to press, Matt informed him or her, "That is a personal question," and left it at that. This worked and had an unexpected side effect. People at work started to respect and trust him more, and three months later he was promoted to the supervisor position. Don't spill your guts—it just isn't professional.

It is far better to bite your tongue, especially in the fragile early stages of any new relationship whether business or personal. It is tiresome to listen to most of this stuff. Why expose all so soon? As the relationship develops you may want to share important parts of your past, but don't divulge intimate details of your life too soon. Far better to err on the side of not telling everything. Be a little mysterious and focus your attention on listening to the person you are with.

Lois, an actor, was always eager to talk about herself and would prattle on without even bothering to see if you were interested in what she had to say. She was always reading the newspapers and magazines to look for interesting things to comment on. She felt like she had to be the entertainer. For one week I asked her to stop talking and listen first (Tip 73). She wasn't allowed to interrupt until the person she was with completed his or her story. Lois was amazed at the results. Since she didn't have to entertain anyone, she was more relaxed and simply focused her attention on the people she was with. Friends and colleagues she had known for years revealed personal sides of themselves she had never seen. She hadn't been giving them the chance. Lois felt closer to them than ever. Most people prefer to do the talking, so if you want to win friends and influence people, hold your stories until after the other person has shared. Be interested in the other person instead of trying to be so interesting.

73. Listen Profoundly

"It is not the voice that commands the story: it is the ear."

Italo Calvino

Now that you have stopped doing so much talking, you will have more time to listen. Most people like to think that they are good listeners. Very few people actually are. Think about the people you know. Of all your friends and family, how many really listen to you? Listening is an art and, like any life skill, takes practice. No one ever taught us how to listen; we were taught to speak. Stop worrying so much about what you are going to say. What really attracts people is not what you say, but how well you listen.

Listening and keeping your stories to yourself will lead to an unexpected result. The person who does the most talking ends up feeling he knows and trusts the listener. It seems like it should be the reverse, that the person listening should feel he knows the talker, but this isn't the case. A well-known reporter confirmed this. He said that the way to build trust is to listen and keep on listening and then keep on listening some more. It really doesn't matter what subject you start talking about, just let the other person do the talking, and eventually, he or she will start to tell you the really interesting stories.

As a rule of thumb, talk 20 percent of the time and listen 80 percent. Try this today and see what happens. You might be amazed at the things people tell you when you really listen. People will love you for listening. Here is a tip: if you are with someone and you aren't talking, but you are talking to yourself in your head, perhaps coming up with your response or judging and evaluating what he or she is saying, you aren't really listening. You are talking to yourself in your head. Yes, *that* little voice that just said, "What are you talking about? I don't talk to myself." You might just as well get up and stand in a corner and talk to yourself. Next time you are listening to someone notice how much you talk to yourself. Then shift your focus back to the other person. Hear everything he or she has to say before you even start to think of a response.

Listening profoundly is not easy; it takes practice. Experiment. This week try listening to your friends, colleagues, family, and boss for three minutes before you say your piece. Time yourself if you are talking with someone on the phone so you can start to get an idea of how long three minutes really is. It is okay to prompt the other person to say more by saying, "Uh-huh, tell me more, yes, go on." Just make sure that you are there listening to them, not thinking about what the solution is or what you want to say next (remember, that is talking to yourself in your head).

Phillip thought he was a pretty good listener. People often came to him to ask advice and to tell him their problems. When I gave him this exercise, he was astounded at how often that little voice in his head would go off. He realized that he wasn't listening as profoundly as he could be and made a concerted effort to relax and just soak in everything the other person said without judging, evaluating, or coming up with solutions in advance. An amazing thing happened. People started telling him things that he had never realized, revealing a deeper side of themselves to him. Phillip also noticed that if he listened long enough, they would often come up with the solution to the problem on their own, without his advice, yet they thanked him. The more profoundly you listen, the more people will enjoy being around you and the more opportunities you will attract.

74. TURN COMPLAINTS INTO REQUESTS

"Depend upon it, said he, that if a man talks of his misfortunes there is something in them that is not disagreeable to him . . ."

AS QUOTED IN JAMES BOSWELL'S BIOGRAPHY
THE LIFE OF SAMUEL JOHNSON, LL.D.

No one is attractive when complaining. No one—not even you, my dear. If you are serious about attracting success you are going to have to give up complaining. Let's face facts. Do you enjoy listening to someone complain? I didn't think so. So then what makes your complaints more interesting? Nothing. Next time someone is complaining, look at his face. Is he attractive? I think you get the point. While some mutual complaining can be satisfying in its own way, it is rarely productive and is generally a way to avoid the real issue.

The solution is simple. Turn your complaint into a request. Yes, it really is that simple, and it is easy too. Let's take a common complaint: "Oh, I hate my job, blah, blah, blah." What specifically do you hate about your job? "Well, I actually like what I do, but my boss is overbearing and always checking up on me." Okay. What request would you like to make of your boss? "I'd like to tell her to get the @#$! out of my face." Okay. Now how can you put that in a constructive form? "I don't know." How about, "I really do my best work when I'm not supervised closely. I'd like to report to you at the end of the week with the status and results. Would that be acceptable to you?"

With any request, there can be one of three responses. The person can accept your request—"Yes, that would be just fine." He can decline your request—"No." Or he can counteroffer—"Okay, but I'd prefer that you called me twice a week for the first month or two until I feel more comfortable." A counteroffer can then be countered by you and it becomes a negotiation. The next time you feel a complaint coming on, think of the request you'd really like to make. It helps to let your friends and family in on this one so that when they catch you complaining, they can softly say, "What's the request you'd really like to make?"

Edward managed a division of a large manufacturing company. He was suffering from burnout and frustration when he hired me. As the manager, he felt responsible for addressing and resolving all the problems that occurred in his department. At the end of the day he would come home exhausted because he had spent the whole day listening to his staff whine and complain about their problems. Again, this is just a case of a missing boundary: No one may complain to me. You really can set these kinds of boundaries with people. At the next meeting Ed announced the new procedure for complaints. He said he was still maintaining an open-door policy but all complaints needed to be presented in the form of a request. For example, the complaint "It's too hot in here" would become the request "Can we turn on the air conditioning?" It took a little coaching on Ed's part, but soon people got the idea and Ed's job was transformed. He no longer felt sapped of energy at the end of the day, and his staff felt empowered to think of the solutions themselves rather than dump everything on Ed. You may not be able to have a problem-free life, but you can have a complaint-free one.

Now, you may discover that some of your friends are chronic complainers. (You, of course, are not!) Once you become a little more sensitive you will realize how draining it is to be around these folks. You may not have to write them off as friends though if you retrain them. Remember, by allowing the behavior to persist, you have in effect trained people to complain around you, so you need to give them time to readjust to your new standards and boundaries. Be firm, neutral, and consistent and most people will catch on by the third time you mention it. I hadn't seen an old friend of mine, Mitchell, in five years, and when we met one afternoon for lunch I realized that he still had all the same complaints he had five years ago. He was still in debt, he was still short on cash, he was still suffering from bodily pains, and he was still not happy with his work. It dawned on me that I used to have many of the same host of complaints. Our relationship had been based on mutual gripe sessions. Now I didn't have any of those complaints and found his complaining intolerable. I casually informed him, "Mitch, do you realize that you have shared nothing but complaints with me today? I'd like to hear about the positive things that have happened in the last few years." This did the trick and we ended up having a good conversation.

75. BITE YOUR TONGUE

"Civility costs nothing, and buys everything."

LADY MARY WORTLEY MONTAGU

Our natural tendency is to think that everyone wants to hear the wonderful advice we have to offer. In fact, people may or may not want to hear what you have to say. They may not even be ready to hear your words of wisdom. A simple way to save your breath (and your friendships) is to ask permission first. Let's see this in action. You are having dinner with your friend, and he is talking about a problem with his boss. You've been listening (Tip 73) and have a clear picture of the problem. The best thing is to wait until your friend says all and then asks for your input. However, if your friend isn't asking and has finished talking, you could say, "Hmm . . . I have a suggestion that might work. Would you be interested in hearing it?" Don't assume that just because you have an idea he or she wants to hear it. Your friend may respond by saying, "Actually, I think in talking to you, I've cleared this up." Great! Your wisdom wasn't needed, just your listening. Other options for asking permission might sound like this: "Would you like to hear how I handled a similar situation?" Or, "Could I give you some advice?" Always ask before giving advice; it is the gracious and effective thing to do. With a little practice, it will become an effortless habit.

Jeanne, a forty-nine-year-old successful portfolio manager, was also the eldest of five siblings. She couldn't help but give unsolicited advice at every opportunity to friends, family, colleagues, and even the fellows she was dating. A vivacious and loving woman, Jeanne had not been able to attract a marriageable man. I suggested that she was too critical and ended up mothering the men in her life. Jeanne admitted this was true—she couldn't help it. After all, being the big sister came naturally to her. I gave Jeanne the following pebble exercise to increase her awareness of how much she criticized both herself and others. Every time Jeanne was aware of being critical she took a pebble from a little bowl full of pebbles and put it into an empty bowl. At the end of the day she could see how many pebbles she had collected and then record the number in her calendar. The next day she started fresh. The idea was to see just how often Jeanne was being critical. (Other clients have used a handheld number clicker with equal success.) I wasn't surprised to see that Jeanne was pretty hard on herself—she got thirty-four stones in one day. And when one date started calling her for advice instead of asking her out to dinner, she realized she was giving advice all the time.

This was sufficient motivation for her to change. I told her that she could only give advice or criticism if requested to do so. Jeanne bit her tongue again and again. Her sisters were the first to notice the change, and they welcomed it. For the first time she wasn't "the oldest," but a friend they could confide in. Then Jeanne's dates became a little more romantic, and now she is dating a charming businessman who is interested in marrying and settling down.

76. SAY IT LIKE IT IS, BUT GENTLY

*"True kindness presupposes the faculty of imagining as one's own
the suffering and joys of others."*

ANDRÉ GIDE

Prepare people for what you have to say. When you get in the habit of
stepping over nothing (Tip 7) you may find that you have some difficult,
awkward, perhaps even painful or embarrassing things to say. While there
is no easy way to say or hear these things, you can make it easier by conditioning it first. This is very simple. Just say it like it is. For example,
suppose you need to have a discussion with your employee about poor
performance. "Susan, what I want to talk about isn't easy for me to say,
and may be difficult for you to hear. (Pause.) Your performance has been
below standard for the past two weeks. What is going on?" The point is
not to sugarcoat what you say, but to enable you to say exactly what you
need to say in a way that the other person can hear it and understand it.
It doesn't do much good to say something that just upsets the other person and doesn't change the behavior.

   Veronica was concerned about her husband. He was a talented electrical
engineer, yet he always seemed to take jobs for much less money than he deserved. She was a computer programmer and wanted to work part-time in
order to spend more time at home with their two toddlers, but she couldn't
because she was the primary breadwinner. Veronica had brought up the subject in the past, and her husband always seemed to get angry and defensive.
At this point, she was afraid to say anything, as he was going through the interview process for a new job. A company had made him an offer that she
knew was below market, and she was afraid that he would accept it without
even negotiating. In the past he had gotten great performance evaluations
and was frequently rewarded with honors. She couldn't understand why he
accepted such low pay. Veronica called me desperate for advice.

   First of all, I asked if he had signed the contract. No, he hadn't signed
anything yet. Good! There was still time to negotiate because a verbal
acceptance didn't hold him to anything. Second, I asked Veronica to tell
me exactly how she had told her husband that he was worth more than
he was getting. She said something to the effect of, "Honey, you really
should be making more money. You are so qualified and talented. They
don't pay you enough. How am I ever going to be able to stay home with

the kids if you don't get a high enough income?" It was pretty obvious that Veronica's comments were disempowering. After a conversation like this he would feel inadequate, and this would only exacerbate his low self-esteem at work. I told Veronica that she had to be constructive in everything she said to her husband. Pretend that he can do no wrong. Give him all your love and support. Tell him how wonderful he is and remind him of all his past successes and all the awards he has won. Boost him up big-time.

Veronica called me back the next day. She had done exactly what I recommended and had spent the night before her husband's final interview reminding him how valuable he was, that he had been awarded for his creative and innovative work at his last job. He was certainly worth more than the average engineer who made $60,000. Veronica never once criticized him. She made him feel terrific and powerful. The next morning when they woke up, he thanked her for all her support and said that he was going to ask for more money and hint that he had other offers pending. Veronica hadn't even suggested this. He came back and had accepted an offer for $15,000 more plus added benefits. Veronica was amazed, and her husband was proud to be the primary breadwinner. They went to a financial planner and figured out that with his new higher salary, they could afford to live on his income alone. Her dream had come true—she could stay home and raise the children. This is the power of being unconditionally constructive and positive in everything you say.

77. CONVERT COMPLIMENTS INTO ACKNOWLEDGMENTS

"The words that enlighten the soul are more precious than jewels."

HAZRAT INAYAT KHAN

One simple and highly effective way to attract success is to convert your compliments into acknowledgments. People get compliments fairly often: "Oh, what a lovely sweater." "You sure look handsome today!" Don't get me wrong, compliments are great, but acknowledgments are even better. An acknowledgment is about *who* the person is, while a compliment is usually about *what* the person has or does. For example, "Robert, I really appreciate the support you've shown by coming all the way out from New Jersey to attend this workshop. Your presence lights up the whole room." That's an acknowledgment; it is very personal and leaves Robert feeling great about himself. There's nothing wrong with a compliment, but you'll be more attractive if you convert your compliments into acknowledgments.

Think of some way you can acknowledge someone for who they are, and be as specific as possible. Don't just say, "You're terrific." Say, "You're a skillful speaker. I admire how gracefully you handled that rude comment." Or, "You are a generous and loving person. You know just the right thing to say to make a person feel good." Instead of saying to the cook, "What a delicious dinner!" you could say, "This is a superb meal. Your attention to detail is incredible. Not only is this delicious, but it is artistically and beautifully presented." People will want to be around you if you are in the habit of giving acknowledgments. You will be energized because it feels really good to give acknowledgments. Change this one little thing and you'll immediately attract people to you.

At a workshop I was demonstrating the difference between giving a compliment and an acknowledgment. I told one gentleman that he had a very handsome tie. He said thanks. Then I picked a woman and looked her right in the eye and said, "Thank you for being here. You light up the room with your presence and your comments have forwarded the discussion for the whole group." This was true, but I was demonstrating a point. It didn't matter. The acknowledgment was so powerful that she was moved to tears. After the workshop, she came up to me and thanked me. Then she invited me out to dinner with a group of her friends and gave me a personal tour of her city. We are in contact to this day thanks to the power of a single acknowledgment.

78. ACCEPT GRACIOUSLY

"Let us open up our natures, throw wide the doors of our hearts and let in the sunshine of good will and kindness."

O. S. MARDEN

Most people don't have any problem giving gifts or compliments, but for some reason, we find it difficult to accept them. Graciously accepting is one secret to attracting more of what you want. It is not only impolite but also unattractive to reject a gift or compliment by saying things like, "You shouldn't have," "It was really nothing," "Oh, this old thing?" or, "I just bought it on sale." There is no need for you to do anything or make any explanation. Simply say, "Thank you!" and smile. Any other comment is a subtle way of telling the person that he doesn't know what he's talking about; it is insulting to both you and the giver. The art of graciously accepting a compliment may take some practice but is well worth learning.

Think about it in reverse. Imagine that you went out and bought a gift for a friend. You give it to her and how do you feel? You feel really good, right? In fact, it probably feels even better to give a gift than to receive one. You feel all warm and wonderful inside, and then the recipient says, "Oh, no. You shouldn't have." This actually diminishes the pleasure of giving. When you say "Thank you" you grant the giver full satisfaction.

The same goes for compliments. Anything you say to counter or diminish the compliment is just like giving the gift back. How rude. Stop doing that. Just say, "Thank you." Let the giver enjoy the experience. Accept the gift, the compliment, the acknowledgment, or the thanks graciously. After some practice, this will come naturally to you. Look for opportunities to acknowlege people. As an experiment, during the next week give three genuine compliments a day to different people and notice how they respond. Then notice how you feel about the response. You will discover that you want to give more to those who accept graciously because they make *you* feel great. Open up your heart and start receiving graciously.

In addition to accepting graciously, it is also a good idea to *be* gracious. Sharon and Steve have a houseboat and invited everyone who worked for them in the office to stay on the boat with the condition that each night a different person had to bring the food and cook. Fair enough deal. While everyone else in the office made the typical burgers and hotdogs on their night to cook, Patty, the office manager, knocked herself out and made a really exquisite Indian chicken dish. This dish happened to include tumeric, a bright yellow-orange spice that gives the chicken an exotic flavor. In the process of cooking, Patty got a little tumeric on the hot pads and on the kitchen floor mat. The spice stains, so she couldn't get these tiny orange spots out and informed her hostess. Well, Sharon, who never cooks and rarely sets foot in the kitchen, saw these little spots, got upset, and told Patty not to do that again. Patty felt just terrible and went out and bought a whole set of new hot pads and a new kitchen mat. Now this is an example of an ungracious hostess. You want to make your guests feel at home, and if you invite them to cook in your kitchen you should expect a few spots as part of the process. Any chef will tell you that things are bound to get a little spotted (that's why they wear those aprons). Patty, on the other hand, was a perfectly gracious guest in replacing the damaged goods. If you always put people ahead of things, you will end up being gracious, and that is a very attractive quality.

79. STOP TRYING TO CHANGE PEOPLE

"It says nothing against the ripeness of a spirit that it has a few worms."

FRIEDRICH NIETZSCHE

It is a waste of energy to try to change people. The only thing you can do is be a model for them and if they don't pick up on it, move on. Life is too short. You could easily spend a lifetime trying to change someone to no avail.

The people in our lives are often mirrors of ourselves. If there is something about someone else that you don't like, it is probably a mirror for the same trait you don't like in yourself. Perhaps he or she is reflecting the opposite of one of your traits to show you that you need to balance out. If you are obsessed with neatness and attract a carefree slob into your life, that person may be there to help you relax and loosen up a bit. Or it may just be a sign to move on and meet someone else.

Laura was having difficulty communicating with her husband. She said that he had to be right all the time, and it was driving her crazy. She would say, "Turn left here," and he would say, "I know." Everything she did to try to be helpful he rebuffed. He always said, "I know." Lately they had been fighting about the stupidest little things. She felt that she wasn't being heard. We had identified that Laura needed to feel accepted, and every time her husband said, "I know," she felt worthless and unappreciated. I asked Laura to tell her husband about this need to feel accepted and let him know that she felt he didn't accept or value her. She had a conversation with him and discovered an interesting thing about her honey: he valued her quite a bit and definitely listened to and appreciated her input. In fact, when he said, "I know," what he really meant was, "You're right."

This was a revelation to Laura. On the next coaching call she said, "Well, why can't he just say what he means then?" I asked her to give up trying to change him, and instead pretend he was from Mars and translate for him in her head. Every time he said, "I know," she translated it to, "You're right." It probably saved their marriage. She feels loved and appreciated by her husband, and he isn't walking on eggshells afraid that he will say the wrong thing and set her off on a tirade. Learn what you can from other people, but forget changing them. It is a tremendous waste of energy that would be better put to work on your own life. You want people to love you just the way you are, so be a sport and love other people just the way they are. In fact, see if you can't find their faults adorable.

80. SPEAK AND BE HEARD

"Be sparing of speech, and things will come right of themselves."

LAO-TZU

The number one reason why people don't listen is that they haven't finished speaking. If you interrupt or try to compete with someone who is speaking, he will be thinking about what he was trying to say or wanting to say and won't really be listening to you. Thus, the first secret to speaking so that people really hear you is to make sure that they have finished speaking first. How do you do this? You simply ask, "Is there anything else?" Ninety percent of the time, even when they have stopped speaking, they haven't finished their thoughts. If you give people the time and space to do so, they will usually find that there is something else they wanted to say. If they really are done speaking, they'll let you know. Stop wasting your breath. Make sure the other person is ready to listen and you are much more likely to be fully heard.

The second reason why people don't listen is that you aren't speaking in an effective or appealing manner. Is your voice easy on the ear? If you speak with a high-pitched or nasal voice, or have a difficult or heavy accent, people may just tune you out because it is too much work to listen to you. Fortunately, we all have control over our voice. Listen to yourself on tape and ask for feedback from honest friends. If you have an unattractive, grating voice or accent, work with a voice teacher and learn how to change your voice. Everyone can learn simple techniques for lowering the voice and eliminating unpleasant accents or harsh tones. Actors have been doing this for years.

The third reason people don't listen to you is because you aren't speaking powerfully and concisely. Learn to say what you want to say with a minimum of words. In business, short and to the point is always going to be more powerful than long-winded explanations that leave people snoozing. Make your statement and shut up.

Here are a few communication tools that will dramatically improve the way you are heard. Delete the word "I" from your vocabulary. For example, you are in a meeting and you don't understand something. You raise your hand and say, "I didn't understand your point about XYZ project, could you please clarify?" Instead say, "Would you please clarify your point about XYZ project?" You don't need to emphasize that you didn't understand. The same goes if you want to share your thoughts or an opinion. Instead of saying, "I think this project is going to exceed budget," delete "I think" and deliver your opinion as a statement: "This project is going to exceed budget." That will catch people's attention. Instead of, "I don't think this project will be successful because . . ." say, "This project is headed toward failure unless the XYZ problem is resolved." Instead of prefacing your questions with, "I have a question," ask your question directly: "What is the deadline for this project?" This one simple change will make a huge difference in how you are perceived even though you are asking the same question.

The same applies to giving compliments and acknowledgments. Most people would much rather hear, "You are terrific," than, "I think you are terrific." The first sounds like a universal truth, while the second sounds like an opinion. Practice deleting "I" from your vocabulary this week and see how people respond. You will immediately come across as powerful and direct.

Another simple communication tool is to convert your questions into statements. In general, women are perfectly comfortable with questions.

In fact, women feel it is more polite to ask a question than it is to give an instruction. Thus, women tend to make the mistake of asking men questions too. The problem with this is that most men prefer instructions or statements to questions. For instance, instead of asking a male boss, "How can I improve my performance?" say, "Tell me what I could do to improve my performance." You are more likely to get a response this way. This works at home too. If your husband comes home from work and you ask, "How was your day, honey?" you might get a one-word response: "Fine." Instead, try, "Tell me about your day, honey," and you may get a full account—just make sure you are ready to listen.

Convert your questions to statements or instructions this week and see what happens. Notice how men talk to other men. They don't usually ask a lot of questions. Also, delete the word "I" from your vocabulary this week and notice the results. You will find that people are taking notice when you speak.

IX.

....

TAKING CARE OF
YOUR BEST ASSET

"So much is a man worth as he esteems himself."

FRANÇOIS RABELAIS,
GARGANTUA AND PANTAGRUEL

YOU HAVE FIGURED out what you really love to do in life and have set up your life to do that (Part VI). You've handled the money, so that isn't a problem (Part III). Now comes the really good stuff. It is time to start taking care of your best asset: you! You are ready to have everything in your life be just the way you want it—your job, home, family, relationships, health, and body. This is not about showing off; it is about taking extremely good care of yourself. The areas in your life that are not just the way you want them deplete your energy, and the areas that are perfect give you energy. By perfect, I mean that they are perfect for you and reflect your personal taste and style. The more energy you have, the more successful you will be and the more you will be able to give to others. Now that you have more than enough time and money, it is easy and natural to improve the quality of your life.

I used to think only the rich could afford to indulge in exceptional self-care on a regular basis, and the rest of us folks would just have to be content with an occasional splurge. But now I see that it works in reverse: *you attract wealth and opportunities simply by taking exceptionally good care of yourself.* My first breakthrough in self-care was to get my front tooth fixed (Tip 83). I figured this was a highly irresponsible thing to do given my credit card debts. Shortly thereafter I got a raise that more than covered this extra expense—no money problems so far, in fact more money. Then I hired a personal trainer (Tip 85) and a few months later got a bonus at work. Do I detect a pattern emerging? I treated myself to a weekend at a day spa in town. Then a fellow I was dating took me to vacation in Mexico for a whole week. As I started to take better care of myself, so did the people around me. While I was regularly saving 10 percent of my earnings, paying off my debts, and doing things to perfect the present, more money started coming in from unexpected places: Out of the blue, my bank offered all the employees stock options. My sales team exceeded goal and we all got bonuses. My accountant did my taxes and found I was due a refund. I received another nice bonus, so I could start my business without money worries. A colleague let me use his retreat house for two months at absolutely no cost. I was surprised myself at all the abundance that was coming into my life. In three years I went from being in debt to having over a year's living expenses in savings, and I didn't suffer in the process. I'd never imagined that I'd have a housekeeper, a personal trainer, a weekly massage, regular manicures and pedicures, an apartment decorated by an interior designer, and access to a beach house.

I realize that this may sound magical to you, but once again, it is all about energy. As Donald J. Walters explains in *Money Magnetism*, "Whenever we will something to happen, or to be drawn to us, a ray of energy goes out, projected by the power of our thought, or will. The energy, in its turn, generates a magnetic force field. It is this magnetic force that attracts to us the object of our expectations." In other words, when you take better care of yourself, you start believing that you are worth more. You are sending out the message to the universe that you deserve more, and thus it isn't surprising that you attract more. You only have what you think you deserve to have. Napoleon Hill had this figured out years ago in his classic book *Think and Grow Rich* when he said, "No one is *ready* for a thing until he *believes* he can acquire it. The state of mind must be *belief,* not mere hope or wish." Hill's point is that you must know with certainty that you can have it. If you are hoping and wishing, then the message you are sending out is one of lack. The most effective way I've seen to increase your own readiness and willingness to have what you want is to start perfecting the present and doing the things you don't think you deserve.

Sometimes people think Part IX is about spending lots of money. There is a reason why it comes well after handling the money one—it is easier to do if you've handled the money—but it isn't necessary to wait. Many of these tips can be accomplished with little or no money, and you can always be creative about finding ways to do the others. Barter, swap services with a friend, and be willing to let the universe help you out in any number of ways. Focus on what you want, not on the money that it would take to go out and buy it. You can do these tips even if you have credit card debt, just be prudent.

Don't wait to win the lottery, start taking extremely good care of yourself today. Be responsible about it (don't go into debt), and make sure you aren't wasting your money on things you don't really enjoy and value (Tip 52). What is one thing you can afford to do right now that seems like an incredible luxury? Do that! No matter how little or how much money you have, there is something you can do to spoil yourself today. No excuses. Read on for simple tips on taking care of your best asset.

81. Dress the Part

"I'm tired of all this nonsense about beauty being only skin deep. That's deep enough. What do you want—an adorable pancreas?"

Jean Kerr

My grandmother always says, "If it isn't 100 percent, don't buy it." How many times have you bought something, a new suit, a sweater, that wasn't quite right, but it was a good price? You take it home and maybe wear it once or twice, and then it sits in your closet, taking up space, making you feel guilty because it is too new to give away. If you have to ask, "Do I look good in this?" it probably isn't right. We've all had an experience of putting something on and feeling great in it, loving the color, cut, and feel of the fabric and design. It is either flattering to your figure or not. The next time you are out shopping, don't buy it if it isn't 100 percent.

This goes for damaged goods too. How many times have you bought something that was on sale because it was missing a button or the zipper was broken, and you thought you could get a new button or replace the zipper, and then you never got around to it? Perhaps you love the color, but hardly wear it because the fabric is too scratchy. Imagine how wonderful it would be to open your closet door and know that everything you have makes you look great. It is much easier to attract success if you feel great—whether you are just hanging around the house in your cozy black velvet leggings or out on the town in a fabulous tuxedo. Why not feel like a million bucks all the time?

Edith Wharton commented, "It is almost as stupid to let your clothes betray that you know you are ugly as to have them proclaim that you think you are beautiful." You may want to enlist a trusted friend who has an excellent sense of style and fashion or hire a professional image consultant to help you weed out the unflattering pieces and design a wardrobe that really makes you feel and look your best. The initial investment in professional help will save you a small fortune down the line because you'll know which colors, fabrics, and styles look great on you and which do not. A professional can help you find the most flattering shapes, styles, and colors, and then you can stick with them for the rest of your life. Our image is a key element in our sense of self and is a visual representation of our inner self. As Carolyn Gustafson, a terrific image consultant in New York, aptly puts it, "In order to feel good about how we look, we must feel that we look like who we are."

Marilyn, an administrative assistant at an investment company, hired me because she was frustrated with her work. She had been working for the same company for twenty-one years and felt unappreciated by her boss. She felt she was getting nowhere and was bored with her job. Marilyn started the coaching program, and one of her first assignments was to clean out her closet. I referred her to a fabulous image consultant, who gave her wardrobe a complete overhaul. First she worked with Marilyn to determine which were her most flattering colors. Marilyn was thrilled with the final selection and realized that for the rest of her life shopping would be a breeze—no more wondering if this was the best color or not. Then she went to Marilyn's house and went through her closet, weeding items out one by one. If it was the wrong color, out it went. Stained? Out! Too tight or too big? Out or to the tailor. Out-of-date? Out! Soon Marilyn had a huge pile of clothes on the floor and about three suits left in her closet. They did the same for Marilyn's scarves, bags, shoes, jewelry, and makeup. Then they went shopping to fill in the gaps, and Marilyn came home with a few perfect suits and a whole new image. She was no longer stiff and conservative, but elegant, classy, and soft. Marilyn not only felt terrific with her new look, but she had a powerful sense of confidence knowing that she looked as good as she possibly could.

This inner confidence paid off at work. After four months of coaching, Marilyn had a new job in the same company and had been promoted to Client Relationship Manager with a salary increase too. She loves the department she is working in and the people she is working with. She has blasted through her old image of being the downtrodden assistant, has started asking for what she wants and getting it (Tip 44). Marilyn feels more attractive inside and out and more confident than ever.

Gordon, a polished and successful sales executive, had recently received a promotion and was now golfing and dining with senators, senior executives, and other high-level professionals. He was a laid-back, funny fellow who made people comfortable and always had a joke to share. However, with the new responsibilities of his job he was suddenly self-conscious, and his usual sense of humor disappeared overnight. Although he was already well dressed and professional looking, I referred him to my image consultant, Carolyn, to take his image up to the next level. She recommended some subtle changes that brought his wardrobe up to the appropriate level, and helped him pick out a stylish new pair of eyeglasses and a different haircut. The combination of these subtle changes made a big difference in his overall appearance. Knowing that he looks the part, Gordon has lost his self-consciousness and is now back to cracking jokes—with senators.

A key part of looking your best is giving your body the best and most nutritious foods. For clear skin, bright eyes, and healthy hair and nails, your body needs the right fuel. Everybody is unique, and what works well for one person may add pounds to another. The recent book by Dr. Peter J. D'Adamo, *Eat Right for Your Type*, is one of the first diet books I've ever read that takes into account different body chemistry and blood types. My client Michael was frustrated because he had been on a high protein, low carbohydrate diet and didn't lose a pound. It turns out his blood type was A and he was really better off being a vegetarian. He went out and bought soy milk, tofu, and other foods he had never tried in his life, and after one week, he felt better and had lost two pounds. If you have blood type O, however, D'Adamo suggests you will lose weight quickly and feel more energetic on a high protein, low carbohydrate, wheat-free diet. When my client Jennie was frustrated at not losing the ten pounds she had gained after giving birth, she cut the wheat and pasta out completely and started eating meat, and the weight came off in two weeks. If you have an eating disorder or are seriously overweight, seek qualified professionals to help you out. Life is too short to spend all our time obsessing about food and weight. One busy client didn't have the time or energy to prepare nutritious home-cooked meals so he hired a cook to do it for him. He thought it would cost him more, but figured it was worth the investment. At the end of the month, he realized he was actually saving money because he was spending so much less dining out and getting food and snacks on the run. Whatever you do, get the support you need and get on with the more interesting things in life.

82. REJUVENATE AND REVITALIZE

"I can't stand a naked light bulb, any more than I can a rude remark or vulgar action."

TENNESSEE WILLIAMS

"If you want a golden rule that will fit everything, this is it: Have nothing in your houses that you do not know to be useful or believe to be beautiful."

WILLIAM MORRIS

Your environment has tremendous impact on your psyche. In fact, your environment is a reflection of your mental state. Take a look around you. What does your office environment say about you? How would a friend describe your home? Is it warm, cozy, and organized? Is it cool, aloof, upbeat, or modern? Most important, how do you feel in your own home? Relaxed, peaceful? Is it easy to unwind in your home? Do you feel special, surrounded by things that you thoroughly enjoy? I have a set of bright floral chintz pillows that I absolutely love; just looking at them makes me happy. Surround yourself with beautiful items. Make sure you love every single painting or piece of artwork that you have displayed. If any objects that you don't love are too good to throw out, put them in a cardboard box in your closet, or better yet, give them to friends or charity. (Sometimes it is easier to get rid of stuff if you first store it and later realize that you didn't miss it.)

The objective is to make your home and office not only clean and organized, but also a reflection of who you are. There may be limits to what you can do at the office, but at a minimum, see if you can bring in a plant or fresh flowers and a beautiful print for the wall. At home, however, you have more control so take full advantage of it. You want your home to rejuvenate you so you have the energy to go to work again the next day. The first place to start is your bedroom. Make this room a haven, a place to retreat and relax. If you have a TV in the bedroom, move it out to another room; you'll sleep better. June had always had the TV in the bedroom and would often fall asleep watching the eleven o'clock news. She couldn't understand why she was frequently depressed and unmotivated. I suggested that she stop watching the late-night news. The very last thing you should do before going to bed is fill your head with visions of murder and mayhem. Ideally, you want to fall asleep thinking positive, happy thoughts—yes, those sugarplum fairies. The next week, June was remarkably positive. She felt rested and had more energy than she'd had in years. These little things can make a big difference.

Bob, a forty-seven-year-old systems engineer, was worried that he wouldn't ever find the woman of his dreams. He wanted to get married in the worst way. I put him to work fixing up his house, and he tackled the project with gusto. He had always admired his sister's house because it felt good just hanging around there. I told him there was no reason why he couldn't create the same peaceful feeling in his own home. He started by getting rid of all the furniture he had never liked—a wobbly table, a worn sofa, a set of bookshelves. Then he repainted the house in colors he loved—a deep blue in the living room and a soft pink in the bedroom. Bob installed a new bathroom cabinet, replaced the old radiators, and put in new blinds. About halfway through this project, Bob met a dynamic and successful woman who just couldn't keep her hands off him. He was amazed. He kept working until he had the house just the way he wanted it. Now Bob's complaint is that he has more women to date than he has time for. It is well worth the investment to set up your home so that it gives you energy. Take the time to make your home a sanctuary and it will restore and revitalize you in return.

83. ZAP THOSE PESKY IMPERFECTIONS

"Perfection is a trifle dull. It is not the least of life's ironies that this, which we all aim at, is better not quite achieved."

W. SOMERSET MAUGHAM

Now what about having a perfect body? If you are busy perfecting the present situation, it makes sense that you take a look at your body. A perfect body is not only healthy and fit, but reflects who you are. Our bodies are inextricably linked to our minds, so if there is something about your body that bothers you, some pesky imperfection, take care of it. Those imperfections prevent you from being your best and can drain your energy. If you feel great in your own skin, it will show. This does not mean that everybody needs to achieve some supermodel image of perfection. Supermodels aren't perfect, and the photos in the magazines are airbrushed into impossible perfection. Even Cindy Crawford, who is about as close to perfect as a body can be, had her belly airbrushed in a swimsuit spread. No one would have known except that they airbrushed her belly button out and forgot to put it back in. If Cindy had to get her stomach airbrushed, I can't imagine what they'd do to mine!

Your body is a reflection of your self. If you're worried about some part of your body, that worry will prevent you from fully being with other people. My front tooth is dead. It was knocked back in high school and turned brown. When giving presentations I was always worried that people would be looking at my tooth and thinking, "Hmm . . . her front tooth is brown." Of course no one noticed, but I thought that all people could see was this tooth. It was preventing me from being fully relaxed with other people. The tooth is a perfect example of an annoying imperfection—it was draining my energy and preventing me from being my best in front of an audience. I was even self-conscious about smiling and would try to smile without showing my teeth. I went to the best cosmetic dentist I could find, and she fixed it up beautifully. Now I don't even think about it. All my energy is available to give to the people in my seminars.

If there is something that is bothering you about your body, get it fixed. Get a mole removed if it bugs you. It's worth it because it is preventing you from relaxing and being your best. If you're fine with the way things are, don't fix them. If you are fifty pounds overweight and it doesn't bother you, then it's not a problem. As Marlon Brando said, "I don't mind that I'm fat. You still get the same money." We don't mind that he's fat because he doesn't mind. It's only a problem if it's getting in the way of you being with other people. Now I am not suggesting that you go out and get breast implants or get your nose fixed to become more attractive. Notice that Barbra Streisand certainly has a nose, and she is clearly attractive. Don't let a little weight problem stop you from doing what you want to do. Oprah Winfrey didn't wait to lose the pounds before becoming a TV star; she did it on the show twice and entertained millions of people in the process. Oprah is attractive with or without the weight. Forget the perfect body and instead just zap all the pesky imperfections you can. Invest in attractive eyeglasses, get contacts, get that hair removed. Fix your teeth. Anything you do that makes you feel better about yourself will make you that much more attractive to the world and to success.

84. Massage the Machine

"The more high technology around us, the more the need for human touch."

John Naisbitt, *Megatrends*

"Only the person who is relaxed can create, and to that mind ideas flow like lightning."

Cicero

Most folks have overly busy, stressful lives. A massage is a truly fine and wonderful thing, and it may be the only time you give yourself a chance to totally relax and unwind. There are all sorts of different types of massage—sports, therapeutic, Reiki healing, shiatsu, acupressure, foot reflexology. I used to enjoy the superintense, beat and pound the muscles into submission kind of massage. Then I discovered Reiki massage. Reiki deeply relaxes the muscles without causing them to tense up and resist back. Now I don't get the beat 'em up massages because I've noticed the difference. Find a massage therapist who is sufficiently skilled to apply just the right amount of pressure to relax your muscles.

Massage is a superb way to combat the stresses of hectic modern living. Aside from the immediate and obvious benefits of being more relaxed, I have noticed other changes in myself. It is now easier for me to meditate on my own (I was too busy to meditate before, and when I tried it, I couldn't relax enough to meditate—a sorry case). As another curious side benefit, my intuition is getting much stronger. Perhaps it is more accurate to say that my intuition was always there, but I wasn't relaxed enough to listen to it. Now I often get flash insights that are right on target. We all have intuition, but may not be relaxed enough to hear it (Tip 57). My personal trainer is amazed that I rarely get sore, stiff muscles even after a very intense weight workout. This is thanks to the weekly massages that keep my muscles flexible. If I skip my massage, I notice the soreness in the muscles. Russians athletes have long known and practiced the competitive advantage of sports massage. Davis Phinney, U.S. Olympic cyclist, says, "At our level of competition, there is such a subtle difference between winning and losing that you need every advantage possible. Massage is one of them." It is also a competitive advantage in your business life. If you are serious about being happier and more successful, get a regular massage, at least once a month if not weekly.

Try different massage therapists until you find the one who works for you. You should feel completely comfortable and at ease with your massage therapist. A skillful therapist works differently with different people, adapting her touch to your unique needs. During a massage you may even release pent up emotions that you've been holding back in tense muscles. It is perfectly normal to have a good cry on the massage table, and many massage therapists provide a safe and protective space for these natural emotional releases to occur. You will feel transported away from your worries and concerns, and afterward you will feel both physically and emotionally nurtured and rejuvenated.

A regional marketing director hired me to help her make it through a challenging career transition. She was training a replacement to run her old department, training for her new and bigger job, and moving a family with two teenage daughters, a dog, and a bird to another state. I said that she was going through three of the major life stressors at once and would need to take extreme measures to keep her health and vitality intact. She mentioned, rather wistfully, that she had heard Bob Hope had a massage every single day, and that must be heaven. I gave her that as homework. Coach's orders: get a massage every single day. She was a bit shocked at this unusual assignment. Raised a Catholic, she wasn't sure if she could take all the guilt of doing something so purely selfish. I encouraged her to give it a try for one week. The next week she came back and said that the massages were a godsend. It was the only time during the day that she had completely to herself. She would let her mind wander, and difficult problems would sort themselves out. I gave her the same assignment the next week and the next week after that. After three weeks of daily massages, she reported that she never thought she'd be saying this, but she was beginning to feel that she'd had enough massages. Now she feels satiated with a weekly massage.

Another client, Edward, had been without a girlfriend for over a year. I recommended that he get a massage because he was not getting enough touching in his life (and I don't mean sex—a licensed therapist should never cross that line). Part of being human is having a physical need to be touched. Anyone who doesn't have regular, close physical contact with another person is not getting enough touching and is missing a critical element of health and well-being. Edward started treating himself to a weekly massage, and a few months later he met a woman. They have been dating ever since. If you don't need it, you are more likely to attract it (Tip 43).

85. GET OFF YOUR BUTT

"The girl who can't dance says the band can't play."

YIDDISH PROVERB

How many years have you had "lose weight" or "get in shape" as your New Year's resolution? If you've had this goal for a number of years then you have two options. First, toss this goal out (Tip 4). Why waste any more energy not doing it for another year and then feeling bad about it? If you really can't do the first option, then go for the second option: delegate it and hire a personal trainer to whip you into shape. Take Oprah Winfrey, for example. The key to her diet success the second time around was giving up the idea that she could do it herself and hiring someone to do it for her. She put her physical fitness in the hands of someone much more qualified. If you wait until the moment of inspiration hits you, you could be waiting a good long time. The problem with moments of inspiration is just that—they last about one moment.

You are probably saying, "I can't afford a personal trainer every day like Oprah." Well, how about once a week? If you can't afford that, how about once a month to keep you on track throughout the year? Or perhaps you can hire a trainer once or twice to show you an effective workout routine, and then you'll be confident enough to do it on your own. Or sign up for a dance class, a yoga class, or anything that will inspire you to get yourself moving. (Again, if you are having trouble coming up with the money for taking extremely good care of yourself, go back and work on handling the money and on getting your needs met.) All you really need is a superstrong structure for support. That could be a jogging partner who will knock on your door and make sure you are up at 6:00 A.M. for a run. If you aren't moving, you just don't have the proper support system in place.

The key thing is to get some help getting over the initial inertia. The technical definition of inertia is "a property of matter by which it remains at rest or in uniform motion in the same straight line unless acted upon by some external force." In other words, inertia is the tendency of bodies at rest to remain at rest, and it is a very powerful force indeed. Momentum is the tendency for bodies in motion to remain in motion. This explains why it is so hard to get up off the sofa (inertia is keeping you there!) and get to the gym, but once you are at the gym, you find it is pretty easy to do an extra ten minutes on the treadmill (momentum). So the key to success is to find some "external force" to provide the necessary boost to get you moving. Any external force will do as long as it works. Willpower isn't terribly effective because it is an internal force and isn't very reliable, so I highly recommend that you choose some other force.

My client Yvette was becoming quite the couch potato. She was working full time and starting a business, so she really didn't have much free time. She started to notice that her once firm thighs were getting rather bumpy looking. This was mildly disturbing. I suggested that she stop beating herself up for not exercising and hire a personal trainer to come to her home every Friday night to work her out. For a while, this was the only exercise she did. Then Yvette started walking to work one hour in the mornings. A few months later she joined a gym and did an additional session of aerobics without her trainer. Now Yvette exercises three to five times a week on her own. Yvette still wouldn't describe herself as "motivated" in the fitness department, but she feels better and has actually noticed some muscles developing in her arms—triceps to be exact. This is progress! Her personal trainer, a gorgeous, muscular man, has tons of energy and compassion. He more than makes up for any motivation Yvette may be lacking. He knows just how hard to push her and ensures that her heart gets into the appropriate training range. Left to her own devices, she wouldn't work up nearly as much sweat. Just looking at him inspires her to work harder. He encourages her to go beyond where she would normally stop on her own; that, she hates to admit, would be the sofa. For my male clients, I recommend that they find an attractive female trainer so that they will work hard to impress her. The point here is to find *someone else* to motivate and inspire you. Don't waste any more energy trying to motivate yourself.

My client Howard, an entrepreneur, discovered that he hated going to the gym and working out. After joining a gym, he went the first few weeks, got bored, and stopped going. He felt guilty wasting all that money but couldn't seem to find the motivation to go. I pointed out that in all areas of his life, he thrives on variety. Howard needs the constant change and challenge of different activities to keep his interest. Don't feel you have to go to the gym to get a great workout. Howard now makes a tennis date one day, goes roller-blading another day, golfs or sails on the weekend, goes for a morning jog when he feels like it, and takes yoga once a week to relax and keep limber. Don't feel that you need to do one activity all the time. In fact, Howard is using many different muscles in his body in different ways and as a result is now extremely strong, lithe, and flexible. Above all, make sure you are having fun. If you get sick of doing aerobics at the gym, take up ballroom dancing instead, and before you know it you'll be dancing for three to five hours straight because it's so . much fun.

There is nothing attractive about a couch potato. Don't try to work up the motivation by yourself. Call your friends and find a workout partner, sign up for a class, or get the name of a great trainer and make your first appointment today.

86. SURROUND YOURSELF WITH BEAUTY AND LUXURY

"Beauty is an ecstasy; it is as simple as hunger. There is really nothing to be said about it. It is like the perfume of a rose: you can smell it and that is all."

W. SOMERSET MAUGHAM

The most mundane activities become luxuries if you do one or two small things to transform them into special occasions. A bowl of cereal served in a beautiful bowl with a handful of fresh raspberries sprinkled on top becomes a special treat. An ordinary cup of tea becomes a rich treat with a spoonful of real cream. How much time does it take to light a candle at your dinner table? Two seconds lends instant ambience. Drink your water out of a lovely wineglass. A bathtub of water becomes a spa retreat with a few handfuls of Epsom salts, lavender-scented bath oil, and a scrubby brush. Light a candle, turn on music, and relax. Splurge and get yourself one set of plush and elegant bath towels or start with the hand towels. Instead of twenty cheap pens that jam your desk drawer, buy one exquisite pen that you love to write with.

What is luxurious to you? An ergonomic chair for your office? Maybe it's a goose-down feather bed to pounce into at night. Or if not the whole bed, spring for one goose-down pillow for yourself. Use cloth instead of paper napkins at every meal. If you usually dine alone or with one other person, instead of spending $100 for eight place settings, buy just two place settings and pick the most exquisite china. If you have extra company, use pretty paper plates and napkins, and you won't have to wash all those dishes afterward. A single fresh flower in a vase by your bed is beautiful. Take those nasty wire hangers back to the dry cleaner for recycling and use real cedar hangers for all your clothes. You will not only discourage moths, but uniform hangers will also prevent your clothes from getting jammed together and wrinkled. Make sure your doorbell, phone, and alarm clock all have a pleasant-sounding ring or chime. These subtle things will make a tremendous difference in your quality of life. Being unavailable is a luxury so don't hesitate to use your answering machine or even unplug the phone when you are meditating, relaxing, or winding down for bed. Schedule your next business appointment for a late afternoon tea at a lovely hotel. Men, try using a silver-tip badger shaving brush from Caswell-Massey for your morning shave. Invest in a real piece of artwork that you absolutely love for your home or office—a sculpture or painting. Stack beautiful books of art or inspiring photographs on your coffee table and leaf through them on occasion. Make sure everyday items like teapots and frying pans are not only functional, but also beautiful to look at. Use a high-quality knife in the kitchen for slicing vegetables. Drink your morning tea or coffee from a lovely cup or special mug. Grow fresh herbs on a windowsill or planter and incorporate them into your meals. Rub fresh rosemary over a chicken and bake it, and you will have a simple and delicious meal. Add fresh basil leaves to your salad. Chop fresh parsley and chives for your scrambled eggs or omelets. Start surrounding yourself with luxury, and you will begin to attract even more luxury.

One way to add instant luxury to even the dullest office is to bring in some fresh flowers. As May Sarton, the Belgian/American novelist, poet, and playwright aptly puts it, "Flowers and plants are silent presences, they nourish every sense except the ear." If you flip through any magazine like *Better Homes and Gardens*, you will notice that practically every single room in the photographs has a lovely bouquet of fresh flowers in a beautiful vase or a bowl of fresh fruit. Take the flowers or fruit away and, no matter how lovely the architecture or the furniture arrangement, it looks like an ordinary room. The quickest and least expensive way to add elegance to any room is to buy some fresh flowers and put them in a beautiful vase. Men, this goes for you too.

Treat yourself to this little luxury. You will be amazed at how special and attractive you will feel. Even carrying the flowers down the street will make you feel special. If you think they are too expensive, buy some potted flowers and transfer them from the ugly plastic container into a ceramic or clay flowerpot. They will last a little longer than cut flowers. However, just about anyone can afford daisies or carnations at $3 or $4 a bouquet, and with a little flower food in the vase, they will last for two weeks. Or plant and grow your own bouquets in a backyard or windowsill garden.

Douglas Koch, an award-winning New York florist, offers the following helpful advice to increase the life of your cut flowers:

- Cut all flower stems on the diagonal before you put them into water. If you cut them straight across the flower can't get as much water up the stem, and it is water that keeps them fresh.
- Put a little flower food or Floralife® in the water to extend their life.
- Make sure you cut off all the greens and leaves that would be immersed in the water, as they will rot in the water, creating bacteria.
- Change the water every two days.
- If the head of a rose hangs limp, recut the base of the stem on the diagonal and place the entire rose in a sink of hot water for a few minutes to perk the rose up again. (Roses get limp when an air bubble gets trapped in the stem, preventing water from getting to the head. The hot water usually causes the air bubble to disperse.)

Indulge yourself. Flowers nourish our sense of beauty and spirit. After living in New York City for eight years I found myself buying floral pillows, sheets, prints, and paintings. I collected a mishmash of floral designs in the apartment before realizing that I was craving greenery and plants because I wasn't getting enough of them in the concrete jungle. We *need* to be surrounded by plant life to be our best. What are some ways you can surround yourself with beauty and luxury today?

87. PUT YOURSELF FIRST

"You have no idea how promising the world begins to look once you have decided to have it all for yourself. And how much healthier your decisions are once they become entirely selfish."

ANITA BROOKNER

We have been raised to think that being selfish is bad; it is, if you hurt others in the process. In general, being selfish is a good thing—in the sense of honoring your highest self. In fact, if you want to attract success, you will have to put yourself first. You can't take care of anyone else until you take care of yourself. That is why the airlines tell parents to put the oxygen mask on first and then to put it on the child. It takes a willingness to be selfish to set up a sacred evening (Tip 40). It takes selfishness to say "no" when you are asked to help organize the PTA's fundraiser and really don't want to but feel that you should. When I organized "Neat Street" (Tip 56) my motives were purely selfish. I didn't want my block to look trashy, and I felt uncomfortable every time I passed a homeless person on the street. Now when a homeless person asks for money I offer him or her a job sweeping streets—there is no shortage of dirty streets in Manhattan. If everyone were truly selfish and took some small action to eliminate what bothers them, we wouldn't have car alarms, pollution, homelessness, and hunger because nobody really likes this stuff. I realize this may sound like idealistic hogwash, but think about it. If you took an action to ensure that you and your family had clean air and water, it might mean getting the neighbors together to ban diesel buses or to carpool to work. Every little action is like a pebble tossed in the pond; it sets off a ripple effect. You'll be amazed at how far those ripples go. Just take care of yourself and the world will be taken care of in the process.

What can you do to be really selfish? If you were totally selfish what changes would you make in your own life right now? One client, Carlotta, was so busy taking care of her ten- and twelve-year-old daughters and working full time that she didn't have a spare moment to herself. She had a gym membership but spent so much time driving the girls to their extracurricular activities that she never had time for her own. I asked Carlotta to start putting herself first for a change. The first thing she realized was that she would have to find some other way to get the kids to their activities. She felt it was important that they participate in sports and school activities, but was no longer willing to do so at her own expense. Carlotta sat down and told the girls that she wanted time for herself and told them what she needed. The girls asked around and found friends who were willing to drive them home after volleyball practice. In the course of the conversation, the girls realized that they too were overly involved and stressed-out by doing so many things. They each decided to drop one extracurricular activity so that they would have time for more family meals. What Carlotta thought was going to make the girls upset ended up making everyone happier in the end.

Mitch was recently married, and although he was thrilled with his new wife and eager to please her, he soon began to miss his weekly nights out playing basketball with the guys. For Mitch, being selfish meant reinstating his night out. He was worried that Kate wouldn't be terribly happy about it, but he told her what he wanted and, to his surprise, she didn't mind at all. She was just as glad to have a night to herself to go out with her old girlfriends, whom she hadn't seen in ages. Time and time again, I have found that when you truly take care of yourself, it works best for all parties concerned. One of my colleagues felt a bit under the weather one day and decided to cancel all of his coaching calls so he could take it easy. He was being purely selfish, but when he made the calls to cancel, every one of his clients said that it actually worked out better for them to reschedule for one reason or another. He was being a great role model for his clients too. By taking such excellent care of himself, he gave them permission to do the same.

Curiously enough, when you take care of yourself first, others will like you more and will be attracted to you. Try it and see. Don't get me wrong; selfishness is not the same as stinginess. There is all the difference in the world. If you are stingy and don't give up your seat to the handicapped or elderly, who really ends up feeling bad? You do! If you give up your seat, you will feel amazingly great. By the way, giving gifts and compliments is ultimately selfish—*you* get pleasure from the giving (Tip 49). So go right ahead and put yourself first.

88. INVEST IN YOURSELF

"In a time of drastic change it is the learners who inherit the future. The learned usually find themselves equipped to live in a world that no longer exists."

ERIC HOFFER

Let's face it, what is your best asset? *You.* I am always amazed at people who are reluctant to invest in themselves. You not only deserve, but also *require* ongoing training and development to be your best. As a rule of thumb, it is a good idea to invest 5 to 10 percent of your income in further training. Statistics have proven that those with higher and more specialized training make more money. But money aside, you owe it to your-self to be the best you can be. Every three months 25 percent of what we know about computers is already obsolete because technology is chang-ing that fast. This means that in one year, if you aren't keeping up-to-date, your knowledge base is obsolete and someone else is already doing it faster and better. Scary thought, but not if you make the commitment to continually grow and develop.

Curiosity is irresistible. Curious people are fresh and eager to learn regardless of their age. They are constantly interested in learning new things and improving themselves and their skills. If you aren't learning and growing, you might as well be dead. The only proof of life is growth. Now that just about anybody can easily access a wealth of information on the Internet, you don't have to know everything. You just have to know how to find it. The emphasis for the future will not be the knowledge you have, but your ability to quickly and continually learn and adapt. The quick and the curious will rule the day. The rest will be out-of-date in a hurry.

So how do you become curious? The place to start is to realize that you don't know everything. In fact, knowing everything would make you pretty dull. Curious people understand that the more they know about a subject, the more there is to know. This keeps them humble and open-minded, which makes them infinitely more attractive than those folks who think they know it all. Once you realize that you don't know it all and can't know it all, it is easier to walk around with an open mind willing to learn and absorb new things. Ever notice how the know-it-alls don't have room to hear new information? They are spending all their energy on being right about what they do know rather than relaxing and seeing what else there is to learn.

Curiosity comes from an internal desire to constantly grow and develop as a human being. I personally believe that this is our purpose in life, or at least one purpose. It is only natural that I would want to seek ways to grow and develop for the rest of my life. I'll never arrive because it is an ongoing process. You can only get better. All of my coaching clients are curious; they want to improve themselves and their lives, and they are will-ing to try new ideas and new ways of doing things. If you don't have the success you desire, and you are doing everything you know to do, you must be missing something. It takes a fairly extraordinary person to recognize this and then get the advice and support he or she needs to make whatever changes are necessary to be successful. For some peculiar reason, there are people who aren't interested in being the absolute best they can be. Many people aren't coachable because they think they already know.

Let me give you Rob as an example. He was a devastatingly handsome, arrogant know-it-all. When you talked to Rob you somehow got the impression that he was looking down his nose at you. He was working in a prestigious investment bank on Wall Street and couldn't seem to understand why his boss wasn't giving him the recognition he was due. He felt that she was an idiot. He complained that he spent one whole weekend working like crazy to produce a report for her, and then on Monday she marked it up with all sorts of changes (completely unnecessary in his mind) and asked him to do it again. He made some rude remark under his breath and huffed out of her office, the report clutched in his hand. Every morning he showed up late for the staff meeting—they never discussed anything worth hearing anyway, and besides, he worked late all the time. Well, I wasn't surprised that he got fired, but Rob was. He couldn't believe it. This was the second Wall Street firm that had fired him after a year. It was a huge blow to his ego. He finally admitted that if he was going to succeed, he needed to find out what he was doing wrong. In that moment, Rob made the critical shift from thinking he had all the answers to realizing that he didn't and that he needed to get some help. After listening to his story, I referred Rob to a coach who served on several boards of different companies and had been in the business world for over thirty years. Rob was a difficult client, but to his credit, he was willing to listen to the coaching and changed his style. After a few months, he found a new job at another firm and got a fresh start. This time he approached the job with a willingness to learn as much as he could from his boss and his colleagues, even if he didn't think they were always right. A year later he is still employed, and his prospects at the company look very good. Rob is not as frustrated, and he is a whole lot more fun to be around.

Another way to open your mind and become humble is to study something that you know absolutely nothing about. Take poetry or physics or study the tango. It doesn't matter what—pick anything of interest to you. Become a student again and start from the very beginning. Surround yourself with people who are much smarter than you are. Keep your mind constantly growing and stretching.

Training, once considered a luxury, is a matter of survival today. Still haven't figured out how to use your home computer? Stop struggling with the manual and invest in a class or even a private tutor. Want to work in the international division at work? Ask your company to pay for language classes at night. Almost all companies have a fund for training and development. If they don't, ask anyway. Take advantage of every company-sponsored training program you can, and if you want to take a course that isn't in the standard offerings, ask your boss. I've encouraged my clients to take thousands of dollars worth of classes all on the company, including everything from private tutoring for business Spanish to public relations and financial accounting at the local colleges. All they needed to do was make a case for how the course would improve and develop them as managers/employees. Since most big companies require that managers oversee the training and development of their employees, make it easy for your manager and bring a course schedule to him or her with a convincing argument. If you are working on your own, you may need even more classes, as you will probably find yourself doing a little bit of everything from bookkeeping to sales. Lack management skills? Need to brush up on computer skills? Take a class. Don't be left behind. There is nothing successful about incompetence. Take the time to master your field and then keep on learning.

89. BANISH ADRENALINE BURNOUT

"I have had a good many more uplifting thoughts, creative and expansive visions while soaking in comfortable baths in well-equipped American bathrooms than I have ever had in any cathedral."

EDMUND WILSON

"Sabbath. A weekly festival having its origin in the fact that God made the world in six days and was arrested on the seventh."

AMBROSE BIERCE

You will burn out if you aren't taking at least one day a week completely off. Somewhere, somehow this got lost. We schedule our weekends away. Our bodies, our souls need a day of rest. According to the Bible, even God took a day of rest. What better role model could there be? You need a day to do whatever you want with no plans, no list of things to do, no scheduled brunches, no lunches—a day to be totally free and spontaneous, to rest, to play, to honor your spiritual self. This doesn't mean that you have to spend the day alone (although that might be refreshing if you usually don't), but rather that you leave the day open so if you wake up and feel like lounging in your bathrobe until noon, you are free to do so without upsetting any brunch plans. Those who observe the Sabbath hold it as a sacred time set aside from the business of the workweek, a time to focus on matters of the spirit. For different people, focusing on the matters of the spirit may take different forms. Some people do it in synagogues or churches. Others may feel closer to the spirit by spending time in nature or meditating.

On the other hand, you may wake up and feel like calling your buddies to go to brunch or go fly-fishing. The point is not to schedule anything. Let yourself do whatever you feel like. This is what it is to be in the flow of life. Let your natural inclinations lead you, not your head. You may be thinking that you'll never clean the house or do the laundry—not true. On some days, I feel a natural urge to get rid of clutter and toss out old clothes, and I start a veritable cleaning frenzy. Since these frenzies are few and far between, I like to take full advantage of them when the mood strikes. Whatever it takes, give yourself a day of rest at least one day of the week. You not only deserve it, but it is a must for you to be your best.

Mona, a thirty-four-year-old writer, was vaguely discontent and couldn't understand why. She had a wonderful man in her life, she had a good job, she was starting an interesting sideline business that intrigued her, but she just wasn't happy. After a little examination, it became clear that Mona didn't have a pure day of rest. Her weekends got booked with social engagements, and it was the only time she had to really play and enjoy her husband. And she wanted to socialize on weekends because she worked at home during the week and didn't have much opportunity to see people. So taking a day of rest on the weekend didn't appeal to her. I suggested that she take Fridays off for herself. This would be her day of rest. Mona didn't think she could do it. I told her it wasn't optional. If she wanted to be her best, she absolutely required some time for herself. This apparently did the trick. She started taking Friday afternoons off, and when she discovered how wonderful it was to have completely free time, she rearranged all her work so that she could take the whole day off. Taking one day off changed her entire outlook. Mona realized that she had to take care of herself before she would be able to enjoy her husband, her work, and her friends. Although she now holds this day as sacred, she said she never would have done it if I hadn't said it wasn't optional. Whatever you do, take a day of rest. It is the only way to be your best.

Another simple, inexpensive way to banish adrenaline burnout is to take a bath. Ours is a shower culture, so much so that you can easily go a year or two without taking a bath. You could even forget how wonderful a nice hot bath is. A bath has a number of advantages over a shower: It is more relaxing to give your body a real soak. A bath becomes a luxurious occasion if you add bubbles or use scented bath oils or soaps. You can finally shave those hard-to-reach spots without risking a nick. You can read a book or a magazine. You can drink a glass of champagne or fruit juice, or just lie back with one of those little blow-up pillows and meditate with lit candles and incense. Pipe in your favorite music. Throw in a few handfuls of Epsom salts for a spa bath retreat. A bath is a wonderful thing. If you find you are so busy that you don't have time for yourself, use the bath as an excuse to get away. When you shut the door, shut the world out and enter your private sanctuary. You deserve it. And when you step out, you will feel completely relaxed.

At a spa in Colorado recently, I treated myself to a salt rubdown and a massage. While the therapist vigorously rubbed me down with a mixture of salt, cornmeal, and coconut oil, she explained that salt has the property of removing the negative energy of others. When Eric, a client of mine, was frustrated with tenants who weren't paying the rent, I suggested he delegate the unpleasant task to an attorney and give himself a salt rubdown or bath to remove their negative energy. He did both and felt much better immediately.

My father wrote most of his novel while sitting in the tub. It can be a great place to come up with ideas and creative thoughts. Following his example, I wrote a good part of this book while luxuriating in the bathtub. Ideas just popped into my head. When my mom lived in the Arizona desert she was always very conscious of saving water. She enjoys a long, hot shower, but felt guilty for using all that water. A bath enables her to sit back, relax, and enjoy guilt-free. This is one readily available, inexpensive way anyone can pamper themselves. Indulge and relax. What do you do to relax? Incorporate regular relaxation into your week and you will be more productive, more effective, and happier.

90. SPOIL YOURSELF SILLY ON A SHOESTRING

"Do not take life too seriously. You will never get out of it alive."

ELBERT HUBBARD

Sometimes my clients are feeling strapped financially and think that the only way to have any fun is to spend money. This is just a pure lack of creativity. To get you thinking, here is a list of fun things to do that won't break the bank. Feel free to add whatever you think would feel good that won't ruin your spending plan.

1. Sit by a river, pond, or lake for at least twenty minutes.
2. Take a chair or blanket to your backyard or the local park and have a picnic. Bring a good book.
3. Go to a museum and get inspired by some great art.
4. Go to a flower shop and smell all the flowers.
5. Check out books, CDs, and videos from your local library.
6. Take fun classes like painting, drawing, or dancing from the local parks and recreation department.
7. Sit on the beach and sip lemonade.
8. Take a weekend retreat to a monastery where they don't charge you much to stay.
9. Sit in a beautiful cathedral or church and pray or meditate.
10. Go to the botanical gardens.
11. Find secret places in your city.
12. Have afternoon tea at an elegant old hotel.
13. Plant a flower, herb, or vegetable garden, or a window box.
14. Go to a pet store or animal shelter and pet the puppies.

15. Stargaze.
16. Watch the sunset with a friend and share a split of wine or champagne.
17. Dine out at a fancy restaurant for lunch or the early bird special instead of dinner.
18. Have a hot-fudge sundae with the works.
19. Rent a video and make popcorn instead of going to the movies.
20. Volunteer as an usher at plays, concerts, and symphonies and see the show for free.

X.

....

EFFORTLESS SUCCESS

*"Dignity consists not in possessing honors, but in the conscious-
ness that we deserve them."*

ARISTOTLE

AT THIS STAGE in the coaching process you will have already attracted any
number of wonderful things, opportunities, and people into your life. You
have gotten rid of the things you have been tolerating; you have plenty of
energy, time, space, money, and love. You have figured out what you want
and are doing what you most love to do. And you have been taking exceptional care of yourself. Your life should look pretty amazing. Now you are
ready to attract a specific thing that you want into your life. This is pretty
advanced. Perhaps you want to attract a great job, the perfect business partner, the love of your life, or the ideal home. The first step is to realize
that you can have anything that you are willing to allow yourself to have.
Part IX, Taking Care of Your Best Asset, is a prerequisite because it helps
you expand you willingness to have things be really great. Most people
sabotage themselves at some point because they aren't willing to have life
so good. By dramatically increasing your self-care, you stretch and
strengthen your "willingness-to-have" muscle. It is nearly impossible to
attract something if you don't think you deserve it. So don't skip Part IX
if you have any tendency whatsoever to sabotage your success. Those of
you already taking extremely good care of yourself are ready to proceed.
Here are some tips on how to attract whatever you want.

91. ATTRACT WHAT YOU WANT WITHOUT REALLY TRYING

"Ah, but a man's reach should exceed his grasp.
Or what's a heaven for?"

ROBERT BROWNING

Before you can have whatever you want, you have to be willing to allow yourself to have it. Think of something you really wanted, perhaps a particular job, an award, a material possession, or a sum of money. You might have had the thought, "I want this and I can't have this." The reality then became based on the underlying belief, "I can't have it," and of course you didn't get it. When you make the shift to thinking, "I can have it," "How can I have it?" or even, "I do have it," then you will receive it. Your thoughts are extremely powerful and manifest in your reality. If you want to see what people think about themselves, just look at their lives. You attract what you think you deserve.

When my client Josephine wanted to leave her career in insurance to start her own consulting business full time, she thought it would be nice to leave with a severance package from her company, which had recently merged. Josephine asked her supervisor and was informed that there was no chance of that happening. She would have to work on a team for eighteen months before she would be eligible for the severance package. Josephine's supervisor was very pessimistic about her chances of receiving any severance, and as a result, so was she. Then she heard through the grapevine that another good employee had quietly left the bank for "personal reasons" and was given a severance package. Suddenly her thinking changed. If that employee could do it, so could she. From then on severance was a definite possibility. Josephine made the shift from *wanting* it to *having* it. With this newfound belief, her actions changed. She told her boss's manager that she would like to get severance, and two months later, after he realized that he couldn't persuade her to stay, he gave her severance along with a whole host of other benefits. If she had not changed her belief, she would not have been so persistent. Josephine certainly wouldn't have gone over her boss's head.

Your reality is simply a reflection of your thoughts. The more you are willing to allow yourself to have, the more you will have. Usually, you have to believe you *can* have it before it will become a reality. Peter, a struggling actor in New York, was frustrated because he was living in a dingy apartment far from the center of town and hated it. All of his friends were living in a more chic and expensive area. He very much wanted an apartment in a better location, but was convinced that he would never be able to find anything for under $500 a month, which was all he could afford. I told him that if he believed that was true, then he certainly wouldn't find anything. His assignment was to describe his ideal apartment, in writing, in as much detail as possible, including the amount that he would pay. He wanted a studio apartment in the West Village with a garden in the back, no roommate, quiet neighbors, lots of sunlight, and close to the gym for $500 or less. Now the going rate for such an apartment was at least $750, and the market was tight so it would have been reasonable to expect nothing. I told Peter to keep his ideal in mind and see himself living in and enjoying the apartment. Within three weeks he had found the impossible. A friend of a friend had a sublet for $400 a month—a garden studio in the West Village in walking distance from the gym. It even had an exposed brick wall and was charming and sunny. Peter was thrilled. He loves his new apartment, and his friends can't believe his luck.

Your thoughts determine your actions, which determine your results. Easy to say, but now you are probably wondering how on earth you change your thoughts. Read on, my friend.

92. Write It Down Fifteen Times a Day

"The words 'I am . . .' are potent words; be careful what you hitch them to. The thing you're claiming has a way of reaching back and claiming you."

A. L. Kitselman

To shift your thinking from wanting to having, write down what you want fifteen times a day. I know this sounds ridiculously simple, but if it worked for Scott Adams, the number-one cartoonist in the world, why can't it work for you? Adams is the inventor of "Dilbert." Adams himself was initially skeptical of this method, but tried it anyway. He started out with small goals—impressing a certain woman and picking a winning stock—and when he got those wishes, he decided he needed more empirical evidence. He was about to take the GMAT test to get into business school and asked for the precise score of 94. When the results came in, he had received a 94. He was now convinced of the power of writing his goal down fifteen times a day and started to write, "I will be the best cartoonist on the planet." Now at the time that Adams was writing this it seemed pretty impossible. Ahead of him in the rankings were Gary Larson ("The Far Side") and Bill Watterson ("Calvin and Hobbes"). An astounding thing happened: both of these cartoonists retired, leaving Adams in the number-one slot. It should be noted that Adams was also taking action to this goal; he was writing cartoons and a book.

Although Adams wrote his goal in the future tense, it is even more powerful if you write it down in the present tense and start your sentence with "I am . . ." Instead of, "I will be a millionaire," write, "I am a millionaire." If you are not getting what you want, it may be that it isn't in your best interest or in the best interest of all concerned. For example, it would not be wise to wish your competitors or boss dead, leaving you number one. Keep your thoughts completely positive. Negative thoughts boomerang back to you with negative results. Who would you like to be? Write down your biggest "I am" statement fifteen times a day and the genie of the universe will go to work.

If you have been paying any attention, you should be wondering why this isn't in conflict with tossing your goal list. You are quite right, it is. But by this time you have tossed your old goals and figured out what you *really* want so it is okay to add a specific goal. Of course, if you prefer to remain goal-less, by all means go right ahead. For those of you who do have a specific goal, give this technique a shot, especially if you have some doubts about your ability to reach it.

Matthew, an editor at a major publishing house, was in the process of interviewing for another company. He knew they were going to make an offer and would probably ask him how much he wanted. After some discussion with his wife, he came up with the figure he wanted. He then wrote down fifteen times, "I am earning X thousand and have four weeks of vacation a year." This number was a significant leap from his current salary, and it was pretty rare in his industry to get this much vacation.

The next day he was offered the job, and sure enough, they asked him how much he wanted. Matt rattled off the figure without missing a beat. And he got it! He got the four weeks of vacation too. He called me up to thank me. He said if he hadn't written it down until he actually believed it, his voice would have wavered, he would have been awkward or embarrassed, and he would have blown his opportunity. The only thing Matt wishes now is that he had asked for even more money.

The point of writing your wish down fifteen times a day is to beat it into your brain until you actually start believing it is true. The first time you write down what you want, all those little voices in your head will start screaming, "Who do you think you are? You'll never get this. Who are you kidding? Come on, get real, you can't do this." Let them scream and keep writing. Eventually you will get to the point where the little voices are saying, "Hey, you can do this. Piece of cake. What's the big deal?" Then you know you've made the necessary mental shift from wanting to having. So get out your pen and get busy.

93. NEVER CONSIDER THE NEGATIVE

"The mind is its own place, and in itself can make heav'n of hell, a hell of heav'n."

MILTON, *PARADISE LOST*

There is a principle in martial arts that you never consider the negative. In other words, as you are about to engage in battle with your opponent, decide what you are going to do and do that. Do *not* visualize yourself getting hit, or being pulverized into a little mashed potato, or that is very likely what will happen. Focus on moving forward. I recently discovered that this principle is also useful in mountain biking. I was visiting my sister in Colorado and thought it might be fun to try mountain biking. Martin, her fiancé, took me to the top of a small mountain, showed me how the gears worked, strapped my head into a helmet, and off we went. I was having a tough time getting in the right gear at the right time. I always seemed to be in the downhill gear when I needed to go uphill and vice versa. To complicate matters, we were zipping along the edge of a cliff, bouncing over large rocks on the path. I couldn't help but look down and imagine the worst—my body hurtling down the side of the mountain. Needless to say, I was scared to death, but fortunately, no mishaps ensued aside from some minor bruises. At the end of the trip, I confessed my terror and ineptitude and Martin said, "It really helps if you look where you *want* to go ahead of you, not where you don't want to go [over the edge of the cliff]." Keep your eyes on the path ahead and your body will usually follow. Now that is sound coaching advice for life. Remember the principle that whatever you focus on expands. If you focus on the negative, you are more likely to bring that into your life. Like attracts like.

Banishing those negative thoughts is easier said than done, especially when one is hurtling through space on a mountain bike on the edge of a cliff. So what do you do with those self-defeating negative thoughts that keep popping into your head at the most inopportune times? Try talking to them: "Oh, hi, it's you again. What are you doing here? Get lost." Then focus on what you want: "I am a natural athlete and going up this hill is a piece of cake." You can just as easily psyche yourself into something as out of something with a few thoughts.

One of my clients, Birgit, a forty-one-year-old graphic designer, was talking about an upcoming vacation she had scheduled with her boyfriend. She was worried that it wouldn't be any fun and imagined them getting into terrible fights because she liked to bum around on the beach and read novels, and he liked to be constantly active, playing golf, hiking, and seeing the local sights. I pointed out to her that if she thought she was going to have a bad vacation, she would probably succeed in doing just that. She was mentally planning and preparing to have a rotten trip, and that was ridiculous. She laughed and realized what she had been doing. Instead she started to picture them both having a great time and not feeling obligated to spend every single second of their vacation time together. He could do his thing and she could do hers. Two weeks later Birgit called to report that they had a marvelous time and only one tiny fight, which they quickly resolved. They felt closer than ever before. Life brings the best to you, if you let it.

Let's take a deeper look at negative thoughts. A thought or observation may be negative, but your response doesn't have to be. For example, "That person was certainly inconsiderate." This is an observation. Now you have a number of options. You can expand on that thought—"I can't believe she had the nerve to step right in front of that handicapped person!"—and go home and tell everyone all about it. Or you can say something, right then and there. "Did you realize you just cut in line ahead of this person?" The moment you address things on the spot, you can completely forget about them. This is much more effective than feeding them with more and more negative energy. I was talking to a client, Michael, the other day, and he realized he had completely forgotten an incident that normally would have offended him for weeks because he had addressed it on the spot (Tip 7).

You might notice some other negative fact such as, "Hmm . . . I can't seem to get my pants zipped up." You can choose all sorts of different responses. Negative: "I must be gaining weight again. I have no willpower. I'm a terrible person. Nobody will like me if I get fat." Head in the sand: "My pants must have shrunk in the dryer." Or positive: "This is a sure sign that I'm not taking proper care of myself. I'm going to start a program for extreme self-care today!" Notice that focusing on the positive does not mean denying the facts of the situation. It is acknowledging what is the case and taking a positive course of action. Oftentimes something negative is a message that is prompting us to take an appropriate course of action (Tip 69). If you aren't willing to do something about the negative thought, then you might as well accept it. If you can't accept it, then do something.

Here are some other helpful tips to banish persistent negative thoughts:

- Use pennies or tick marks to record how many negative thoughts you have in a day. Often just noticing how many times you are negative is enough to change your behavior. One of my clients was extremely hard on herself. I asked her to make a log of all the negative things she said to herself. Her number-one negative thought was, "I'm so stupid." When she realized she was saying that about fifty-seven times a day, she decided to stop and say, "Actually, I'm pretty clever."
- Write down all your negative thoughts on a piece of paper and then burn them.
- Read the book *You Can't Afford the Luxury of a Negative Thought*, by Peter McWilliams.

94. KEEP AN ACE UP YOUR SLEEVE

"Those who want the fewest things are nearest to the gods."

SOCRATES

The secret to attracting everything you want in life is to not want any-thing. I know, it is another big catch-22. Why is it that when we don't want something it is so easy to get it? Have you ever noticed that the guy or gal whom you aren't the least bit interested in keeps calling? I've read plenty of books that tell you to detach yourself from the outcome, but how in the world can you when you want something so badly you can taste it? And there are just as many books that say the opposite, that you should pursue the object of your desire with single-minded passion. The problem is that you have to do both. To attract what you want you need to want it with all of your heart, and at the same time not need it or have to have it. This is no small task. The easiest way to detach from the out-come is to have something in reserve, an ace up your sleeve so to speak. It also helps to focus on getting your needs met first. This reduces your neediness and automatically increases your ability to attract what you want (Tip 43). The next step is to keep your options open and to have a lot of options (Tip 95). If you really want one particular job, it helps to have offers at a number of other places too so that you increase your bargain-ing power. If you rely on one person or organization to meet your needs, you'll soon be in trouble because you will depend too much on them and end up repelling them (Tip 44). If you are totally wild about a particu-lar man or woman, you can balance this by going out with other friends and dates. Notice that you can still be passionate about the person or job, but you don't *need* them so much anymore. The less you need them, the more likely they will want you around. I know it stinks that life is this way, but it is, so you might as well get used to it.

Take writing this book for instance. I am passionate about coaching and about helping people achieve happy and successful lives. I very much want the book to be wildly successful, and I am willing to do whatever it takes to help that process along, but I am not relying on this book to pay the rent. I have a successful coaching company and that is paying the bills. The book is a bonus. If I depended on this book for income, I would have been desperate to find an agent and a publisher and probably would have scared them off. People can sniff out desperation a mile away. As it was, I was able to relax and enjoy the publishing process. I had an intention to attract a terrific agent, and I found one of the best in the business with very little effort. And she did the hard work of finding the right publisher. I also kept the option of self-publishing in the event that no publisher was interested. On the other hand, if I were totally blasé about writing the book, I never would have been able to go through with the process because it is an incredible amount of work. My passion is what kept me writing on a sunny weekend when everyone else was off to the Hamptons to laze around on the beach. I didn't see this as a sacrifice because I thoroughly enjoyed the process with all of its ups and downs and challenges.

Maxine was in sales, and she was struggling. She found it almost impossible to make cold calls and dreaded people hanging up on her with the comment, "I hear from about twenty people like you a day—leave off, will you!" which unfortunately was par for the course in her line of work. I wasn't surprised to hear that Maxine wasn't happy. She was attached to the result of getting an appointment with every single call and felt like a failure if she didn't get one. We changed her focus. Maxine's new goal was to make the twenty-five calls a day and just develop relationships with people. She didn't have to sell them anything. She didn't have to convince them or persuade them to set up an appointment. Her new focus was on getting to know people, and her attitude was one of "How can I help?" Maxine is a very sociable and likeable person with tons of friends so this new goal sounded like a lot more fun. Once she took the pressure off, she could relax and be herself. Immediately her results improved. She started getting to know the clients and finding out what their needs were instead of trying to pitch her service. Once she detached from the result and stopped trying to force the outcome, the numbers she wanted came effortlessly.

Another key to detaching from the outcome is to enjoy the process so much that the result doesn't matter. Only a handful of people, when asked what they would change about their lives if they were to win a million dollars, would say, "Not a thing. I would keep on doing the same thing I do today because I love doing it." Now *that* is a life worth living. I read a story in *Forbes* about the lives of the wealthiest people on the planet, and one multibillionaire lived in a modest, perfectly ordinary home and wore perfectly ordinary clothes. His passion in life was his work, and he didn't care a whit about stuff. Ask yourself the hard questions: Would you still love if you didn't receive love in return? If you loved to write but never sold your story or book, would you still write? Would you stop working if you didn't get recognition, achieve a certain status? Think for a moment about why you do the things you do. Is it for the end result, or is it for the pure pleasure of doing it? Start structuring your entire life so that you do only the things you enjoy—that is the ultimate success. You can begin in one small area and let the momentum carry you to all areas of your life.

Where in your life are you trying to force a certain outcome? What do you *have* to have in your life to be happy? Look to see what other options you can create and find other ways to get your needs met, and you will be twice as likely to attract the thing you want because you don't *have* to have it anymore. Keep an ace up your sleeve and it will give you the added confidence that draws success to you.

95. CAST PLENTY OF PEBBLES

"An ounce of action is worth a ton of theory."

FRIEDRICH ENGELS

"Let your hook always be cast. In the pool where you least expect it, will be a fish."

OVID

If you want to attract success you need to relax and allow people and things to come to you. Pushing, pressing, arm-bending, seducing, convincing, and persuading may work, but they are not, I repeat, *not* attractive. It is easy to waste an awful lot of time and energy trying to guide the ripples when you'd be better off casting more pebbles and seeing which ripples find their way back to you. If you aren't exactly sure what direction you want to head in your career or if you are looking for a great relationship, it is easier and more fun to try a lot of different things. Go on informational interviews in places you've always thought would be interesting even if you don't have the right training or background. Experiment with many different ideas and options and don't worry about it. Your job is to cast plenty of pebbles.

Frank wanted to get some clients for an accounting program he had designed. He was sending out thick, expensive packets to the top accounting firms in the country and not getting much response. We decided to try sending a concise one-page letter to a thousand firms and see which ones expressed an interest. Then he would send those folks the detailed package. This not only cut down on his printing expenses, but he wasn't wasting time with people who weren't interested.

The same applies to relationships. Looking for someone special? Great! Go out with a lot of different people, don't get wrapped up with just one man or woman who seems pretty good. We are all looking for that one in a million person, but how many people have you actually gone out with? Thirty? I've got news for you: that's a long way from a million. You don't have to go out with a million people, but it would certainly improve your odds if you saw a few more people. Nita Tucker's lighthearted and terrific book on dating, *How Not to Stay Single*, suggests smiling at every single person you see. Cast plenty of smiles and see if you get one back.

If you are trying to "win over" a particular person, let him or her go. It probably isn't worth it. Move on to the next and don't waste your time. Either it is fun and effortless to create a new relationship, or it's probably not worth it. If you are working that hard to seduce someone, it probably won't work out in the end anyway so you might as well cut your losses and look elsewhere. You just can't force someone to like you. This is not to say that if you already have a good relationship, it doesn't take work to maintain it. But if you are struggling to make things work at the very start of a relationship, you can bet that the maintaining won't be a cakewalk.

96. LET LOOSE THE BERRIES

"You can't build a reputation on what you're going to do."

HENRY FORD

If you add extra value to every interaction, you will be successful. Let's start with a business. The fastest way to grow a business is to make raving fans of your customers. You want people raving about the service or product to all their friends and family. This is the most powerful and effective advertising you could have. It is well worth the investment of time to figure out how to enhance your service or product. You must provide more than your clients expect to receive—anticipate what would please and delight them before they even figure it out for themselves. This will be different for every business. Think about the last time you got unexpected value from a company. Enhancing the value of your services doesn't even have to cost more. For example, a clothing store can add value by letting you take as many outfits into the dressing room as you want instead of limiting you to some fixed number. A grocery store found out that customers wanted to pick their strawberries individually instead of buying them preboxed. Once it let loose the berries, sales went up because people ended up buying more strawberries than they would have if they had just picked up a single box. Some department stores offer free gift-wrapping for all purchases. Many stores have excellent return policies that enable people to shop freely, knowing if there is a problem they can always return it.

Enhancing value may be linked to your purpose or vision in life. The Greyston Bakery in New York hires and trains homeless people to work in its bakery. It is committed to training and developing people in the community and to creating scrumptious baked goods made with all-natural ingredients. The added value of this bakery that distinguishes it from others is its social mission. When you buy a cake there, you are also supporting an impoverished community. This added value appealed to Ben & Jerry's, which is on the lookout for suppliers that support their local communities. The company hired the Greyston Bakery to make the fudge brownies for its ice cream.

Okay, but what about you, personally? How can you enhance or add value to every situation? Maybe you smile at the bus driver. You acknowledge people for who they are (Tip 77). You forgive in advance (Tip 42). You do a favor and don't tell anyone you did it. You call someone just to say, "I love you." You listen profoundly (Tip 73). You let someone ahead of you in line. Get the idea? Just think about how you can enhance every interaction. This is fun! If it's not fun you are doing it because you think you "should"—beware the "shoulds!" You are better off not doing it if it becomes a "should" (Tip 4). What ways can you let loose the berries in your life? Give the unexpected and you will naturally attract success.

97. BEFRIEND YOUR FEAR

"Life shrinks or expands in proportion to one's courage."

ANAÏS NIN

On occasion my clients give me the excuse that they can't do something because they are afraid. They hate to admit this because they think that fear is a bad thing or that they shouldn't be afraid. I usually stop right there and ask them about the source of their fear. What are they really afraid of? You see, fear isn't the bad guy, fear is our friend. We usually are afraid for some pretty darn good reasons. And quite often the best solution is to address the fear and then take the action.

Ron had been working in the same company for twelve years although he wasn't particularly happy in his work. What he really wanted to do was quit his job and start his own consulting business. Our conversation went like this: So, why don't you? Well, I'm afraid; what if I fail? Well, that is a possibility; what is the source of the fear? I'm afraid that I won't have enough money and that I'll lose my shirt and be out on the streets. That sounds like a reasonable fear to me, but the fear isn't so much about starting your own business as it is about not having enough money. Yep, that's it. Well, how many month's living expenses do you have saved up as a cushion for leaving your job? Three months. Well, no wonder you are afraid—that isn't enough. If you had nine months to a year of living expenses tucked away, would that reduce the fear? Sure. Let's create a plan to increase your savings so that you can make the transition to your own business without worrying about paying the mortgage. Great!

So you see fear can be a very useful ally. Take a good look at *why* you are afraid of something and see if you can't do something to alleviate the fear at its source. Then it will be much easier to take the action required.

Sometimes you shouldn't try to eliminate your fears because they could come in handy. A friend of mine went to an excellent hypnotherapist to stop smoking. It worked so well, he thought he might as well get rid of a few other things that were troubling him. He told the therapist that he had a morbid fear of sharks and would really have a lot more fun boating and swimming around in the oceans if he didn't have this dread of a shark biting him in the butt. The hypnotherapist took one look at him and said, "Absolutely not. It is *good* to be afraid of sharks!"

Fear can be created from all sorts of different sources. It is worth examining the source of your fears to see where they came from and to determine whether they are unfounded. Many times you will discover that your fear is completely unfounded. Fears can be instilled by our parents in an effort to protect us. "Don't talk to strangers" is perfectly fine advice for a five-year-old, but at some point you will have to talk to strangers to survive in this world. Fears can come from cultural or religious prohibitions. And one of the most pervasive fear breeders is the news. My grandmother saw a news story about a woman traveling alone who was raped and murdered. Naturally, the program scared her, and she didn't want anyone in the family to travel alone. How can I live my life, have adventures, and give seminars around the country if I don't travel alone? Fear is a good thing sometimes, but we forget that the news is all the bad stuff and is not an accurate reflection of what's happening in the world. They don't show the stories about the other 500,000 women who traveled alone happily and successfully. It just isn't news.

Although I always knew intellectually that TV news was exaggerated, I didn't realize just how bad it was until after the bombing of the World Trade Center in downtown Manhattan. I was walking into Grand Central Station in midtown on my way to work the next day and was stopped by a news reporter, microphone in hand, asking, "Aren't you afraid to go into this public building after the bombing of the World Trade Center?" I replied, "No, one can't go around living in fear. That is precisely what the terrorists want." This was not the answer he was looking for so he asked the next person on the street, who also said he wasn't afraid, as did the next. I overheard the reporter mutter under his breath, "Isn't anyone in this city afraid? We haven't gotten one good clip yet." I smiled to myself, thinking, "Hooray for New Yorkers!" We aren't about to be put into a panic by a bunch of lousy terrorists.

That night on the news I saw the same reporter and was expecting to see all those calm and unruffled New Yorkers. Instead they featured a number of hysterical, screaming misfits wailing about how terrible it was and how they couldn't go into any major buildings. They must have looked high and low to find this bunch of nuts. This opened my eyes to what news really is: it is not an accurate report of the facts; it is all about drama. I stopped watching the news on television, realizing it was a waste of my time. If you are going to live your dreams, you will have to take some risks—don't let the media or anyone else stop you.

Another way to deal with fear is to start taking more risks in life. (I'm not suggesting that you do anything to put yourself in physical danger.) Take some little or even big risks. Why? Because taking a risk, doing something that might even scare you, will make you feel fully alive and vibrating. The fear will get your heart pumping and toes tingling. Plus, you'll become a stronger, more powerful human being. Here are some suggestions for strengthening your risk muscle:

1. Ask your boss for a raise. Most people are underpaid for what they do, so ask!
2. Call someone up you've been meaning to call and, for whatever reason, haven't.
3. Ask someone to meet one of your needs (Tip 44).
4. Apologize to somebody for something you did that hurt him or her, even if they don't know you did it.
5. Return something that you stole or "borrowed" with the appropriate apologies.
6. Volunteer to give a presentation or speech.
7. Take a trip by yourself.
8. Take the opposing side of an argument (stand up for what you think).
9. Go to dinner by yourself at a nice restaurant.
10. Take a scuba diving class.

How is this related to attracting the success you want? People who never take risks are rather dry and stale. They may be stuck in a comfortable groove that even they find boring by this time. A risk or two will freshen you up and shake loose any cobwebs that might have been gathering around you. What are you afraid to do? Do it this week. Make a dare with your friends if you need to. Keep challenging yourself to do something new and scary, and you'll attract wonderful opportunities.

98. PLAY MORE

"It is the child in man that is the source of his uniqueness and creativeness, and the playground is the optimal milieu for the unfolding of his capacities and talents."

G. K. CHESTERTON

It is easy to get too busy for the things we really enjoy—those activities that nurture you, that give you energy. But at some point, you have to stop and ask yourself, "What is the point of doing all this work if I don't have time to enjoy myself?" When I begin coaching new clients, I ask them to start doing more of the things they really enjoy. The sad fact is that, more often that not, they can't even think of anything. Playing rejuvenates and energizes you so you can go back to your work with enthusiasm and joy. Any job, no matter how fulfilling, becomes drudgery if it is not balanced with sufficient play. You need play to be your best, most successful self.

One of the ways to figure out your "flow" activities (Tip 55) is to think back to what you did for fun when you were a little kid. When you were young, you weren't weighed down by adult responsibilities and instinctively did things that increased your energy. If you can't remember, ask your mom or dad what you did for fun when you were little.

When I was a little girl, my mom would frequently find me sitting in the middle of a mud puddle playing away, having the time of my life, covered head to toe in mud. I guess I have a natural affinity for mud. The adult version of this activity is pottery. It's really just an excuse to get my hands in a whole lot of mud, and I love it. Then I got really busy working full time and starting a coaching practice in the evenings. My boyfriend was complaining that he didn't get to see me much anymore so I stopped doing pottery. My family started to ask when I was going to do pottery again; they missed getting the pretty bowls and plates. I signed up for one month at the studio, figuring that for one month my boyfriend wouldn't mind. A surprising thing happened. After the first morning spent making pots, I met my boyfriend for a late brunch. I was so relaxed, happy, and fun to be with that he said, "You really should do pottery more often." And here I was cutting out this nurturing activity so I'd have more time for him.

Make time in your life to play. The success of the activity depends on being totally present in the moment. It could be reading, hiking, painting, dancing, basketball, soccer, cooking—do whatever it is for you. My client Anton was a superb soccer player, but he had given it up because he just didn't have time for it anymore. I advised him to cut something else out and put soccer back in, because when he was playing soccer he was totally turned on about life and full of vitality. This flow activity gave him the energy he needed for the rest of his life. He started playing soccer again and reduced a sideline business instead. Much to his surprise, his primary business results started to skyrocket almost overnight. He was flooded with new clients. He didn't need to *work* harder to make money, he needed to *play* harder. You'll be more successful if you play because flow activities not only give you energy, but also deep personal satisfaction.

99. REALIZE THAT HAVING IT ALL IS ONLY THE BEGINNING

"Many are called, but few get up."

OLIVER HERFORD

At this point in the program you really have it all. You have love, money, opportunities, and time, and your health should be intact because you didn't have to stress yourself out getting it all. What's next? You are leagues ahead of most people, who devote the greater part of their lives to getting even a portion of what they want. But in doing this program— especially in identifying your needs and getting them met, and in orienting your life around what you truly love to do—you've discovered that you don't want all the stuff you wanted in the beginning. In fact, by now you have realized that most of the stuff you thought you wanted wasn't even that interesting and certainly wasn't fulfilling. This makes life a whole lot easier. Why waste your precious energy going after things you aren't going to want when you get them? Exactly! When I promised that you would attract everything you've always wanted, I meant it. But now you don't want it. Ha! Tricked you! Just kidding. The really neat thing about this is that now you are no longer a slave to your wants and desires. You are free to live your life the way you choose. And that is how it was supposed to be all along. Most of us just got sidetracked or hoodwinked into thinking we wanted to do something other than that.

When I first realized that I could actually achieve financial independence in my lifetime, and that it was possible to accomplish all the steps in this program within a few years, I was astounded. This was what I had been prepared to spend the rest of my life achieving. I figured once I had done it, well, that was enough and I could die. I hadn't even considered what would be next. Financial independence and a life doing what I loved to do appeared to be the ultimate objective. Now, however, I realize that it is only the beginning. It is the foundation upon which to create an incredible and inspiring life.

The ten parts in this program are the keys to success, and real success is living your life the way *you* want to. Now the world is your oyster; you can do whatever your heart desires. What is the legacy you'd like to leave behind? How would you like the world to remember you? What would you like to contribute? At this point, you will be ready for the next level, the next challenge in life—that is the only way to stay in the flow and be fulfilled. You serve only because it gives you great joy and pleasure. And the way you choose to serve is completely up to you.

100. CELEBRATE YOUR SUCCESS

"We may allow ourselves a brief period of rejoicing."

WINSTON CHURCHILL, ON THE
DAY WORLD WAR II ENDED

Now is the time to rejoice and celebrate your new life. You have accomplished a tremendous amount, and you won't realize just how much until you take stock and write it all down. List all the shifts and changes you have made, the new people and friends you have attracted, the new things you are doing, the beauty of your home. Take time to bask in the love you feel for yourself. You can pat yourself on the back and give yourself some acknowledgment for all that you have done. The more you appreciate the success you have already achieved, the more success you will attract. Tough life, isn't it?

Most people don't take any time at all to rest on their laurels. It all goes back to the puritan work ethic; we feel guilty stopping for a moment and celebrating our successes. We also have this hang-up that if we love ourselves, we will become vain, egotistical, snotty, and all manner of horrible things. This is ridiculous. People who are vain, egotistical, and self-centered are all those things precisely because they *don't* love themselves profoundly enough. It is just a front for deep-seated insecurity and a lot of unmet needs. It is impossible to love yourself too much. In fact, the more you love yourself, the more love you have to give to others. That is how it works. So celebrate your success. Throw a big party and invite all your friends over or, better yet, have a friend throw a party for you.

I had one client who did just that. When Simon started coaching he was two months away from bankruptcy and financial ruin and didn't realize it. He was unemployed and struggling to get his own business going. He was separated from his wife, but she didn't want to get divorced, even though she had been unfaithful. And he had lost his faith. After seven months of coaching, Simon had turned his life around. He was legally divorced. He had a full-time job and was making an excellent income. He had cut his expenses in half. His sideline business was doing well. He had time to volunteer and coach children to live their dreams and time to play tennis. And he had reconnected to his faith and joined the choir in his local church. The theme for his party was freedom. Have a party. Go forth and celebrate your new life!

101. BE BRILLIANT, GORGEOUS, TALENTED, AND FABULOUS

"Our deepest fear is not that we are inadequate.
Our deepest fear is that we are powerful beyond measure.
It is our light, not our darkness that most frightens us.
We ask ourselves, Who am I to be brilliant, gorgeous,
*   talented, fabulous?*
Actually, who are you not to be?

You are a child of God.
Your playing small doesn't serve the world.
There's nothing enlightened about shrinking so that other
*   people won't feel insecure around you.*
We are all meant to shine, as children do.
We were born to make manifest the glory of God that is
*   within us.*
It's not just in some of us; it's in everyone.
And as we let our own light shine, we unconsciously give
*   other people permission to do the same.*
As we're liberated from our own fear, our presence
*   automatically liberates others."*

MARIANNE WILLIAMSON,
A RETURN TO LOVE

For years writers such as Napoleon Hill, author of *Think and Grow Rich*, have been insisting that the key to success is harnessing the power of thought. But, for the most part, we have remained skeptics, viewing thoughts as intangible and unimportant. However, recent scientific evidence demonstrates that thoughts are very powerful indeed.

The April 5, 1999, *Newsweek* article, "Thinking Will Make It So" by Sharon Begley describes how thoughts are electrical signals that can be picked up by an electroencephalograph (EEG) to control mechanical equipment. Neurobiologist Niels Birbaumer of Germany's University of Tübingen has six patients with sound minds trapped in completely paralyzed bodies. Living with the aid of machines, these patients are wired to a "thought translation device" which amplifies their brain waves and enables them to select letters of the alphabet from a computer video screen and compose sentences. Here's how they did it: Tübingen's team placed electrodes behind the patient's ear and on the scalp. The electrodes are designed to detect brain waves and carry them to an EEG, which picks out a single type of wave from the many waves, much like you'd tune in a radio to pick up a favorite station. After hundreds of hours of practice the patients learned to control their brain waves, by focusing on an audio tone. Once they master this they can spell out words on a video screen using only their thoughts. The researchers' next project is to go wireless by creating electronics sensitive enough to "grab" brain waves out of the air. This groundbreaking science proves that thoughts are not only real, but interact with the environment.

Once again, it all comes back to energy. Thoughts are electrical signals—just another form of energy as real as a solid mahogany desk or the book in your hands. Science is catching up to what many radical or New Age thinkers have been saying all along—that our thoughts create our reality. Only there is nothing mystical or magical about it—it is simply the power of thought.

While the results of this coaching program may seem magical, there is nothing magical about this either. Acting on these coaching tips makes your thoughts much more powerful, clear, and vibrant by reducing or eliminating static and other energy drains while adding things that give you energy. The more energy you have, the clearer and stronger your thoughts will be. Most people send out weak, often conflicting thoughts. It's not surprising that their lives reflect this. For example, you may have the thought, "I'd like to be president of this company." And in the next second you think, "That's impossible. Who do I think I am? I'm not good enough." Now that you know thoughts are real, you can see that negative thoughts are much more dangerous than you may have realized. With thoughts like these, who needs enemies! How about thinking that you are brilliant, gorgeous, and talented for a change? Our thoughts *are* our reality. Everyone is constantly sending out signals to the universe. What signals are you sending?

Now that you've completed this coaching program, you have structured your life so that it is rare to have a bad day or a negative thought. Think about it: when you are on cloud nine and feeling on top of the world, loving your work and your friends, negative thoughts just don't stick. On the other hand, it does no good for someone to tell you to think positively when you are moping around because you are unhappy with your job or fighting with your family. First you have to eliminate the source of all those negative thoughts. And that is where these concrete and practical tips come into play. This explains why writing what you want fifteen times a day really works. You are sending out a consistent, positive message of what you want every day until you get it. People who get to be president of the company are those who *think* they can be president.

I've given you all the coaching tips required to help you be brilliant, gorgeous, talented, and fabulous. The rest is up to you. Go forth and shine!

I would love to hear the steps you are taking to attract success. Please write to me at Talane Coaching Company, P.O. Box 1080, New York, NY 10156 (and include a stamped, self-addressed #10 envelope) or send me an E-mail at talane@talane.com. I'm looking forward to hearing your comments and success stories. Thank you!

Appendix A:

HOW COACHABLE
ARE YOU?

1. I have the time to invest in myself.

   Yes ❑ No ❑

2. I keep my word and promises to myself and others without struggling.

   Yes ❑ No ❑

3. There is a big gap between where I am now and where I want to be.

   Yes ❑ No ❑

4. I am willing and able to do the work required.

   Yes ❑ No ❑

5. I am willing to give up self-sabotaging behaviors that limit my success.

   Yes ❑ No ❑

6. I am willing to try new concepts even if I'm not sure they will work.

   Yes ❑ No ❑

7. I have the support I need to make big changes in my life.

   Yes ❑ No ❑

8. Coaching is the appropriate discipline for the changes I want to make (as opposed to therapy, medical treatment, or 12-step programs).

   Yes ❏ No ❏

9. I am fully responsible for my own life and the decisions I make.

   Yes ❏ No ❏

If you answered no to two or more of these questions, coaching will probably not be effective. Once you have addressed these issues, you will be ready to begin. (Some clients pursue therapy and coaching at the same time. I recommend you discuss this with your therapist if you have any concerns.)

Appendix B:

HOW TO FIND A COACH

"It is the commonest of mistakes to consider that the limit of our power of perception is also the limit of all there is to perceive."

C. W. LEADBEATER

HERE WE ARE at the end of the book, and you probably see a few areas that need some work. It doesn't take forever to attract the success and the life you want. The rewards are well worth the work and start to kick in immediately, so don't wait, start today. If you want to make it easy on yourself, hire a coach to help you through this process and keep you on track. Left to our own devices, we don't progress as quickly. We all have blind spots, and it is helpful to have an outsider point them out. Anyone who has hired a personal trainer knows it is much more fun to go to the gym or do ten pushups with someone egging you on and keeping an eye on your posture. The same goes for a life coach. When you are discouraged and ready to quit, you can count on your coach to be there to keep you going through the tough spots. You can count on your coach to tell you the truth. Your friends and family can't always tell you the truth because they don't want to risk the relationship or because they have their own agendas in mind. Here are some pointers on finding an excellent coach.

Hire a professional, someone who has been through a specialized coach training program, so you know he or she has some basic skills. Plenty of people are suddenly calling themselves coaches when in fact they are therapists, counselors, or consultants and have never completed a real coach training program. When you interview the coach, you should feel that you can tell this person the whole truth. Is this a person you can confide in? A person whom you trust and respect? Do you feel listened to and understood? As a general rule, do not hire a close friend or a family member, for the reasons mentioned. You don't want the coaching to affect your relationship. You can always fire your coach, but you can't fire your cousin or uncle. Does this coach have the experience, skills, and qualifications you are looking for? Don't be afraid to ask to speak to some of the coach's clients for a recommendation, especially those who had success in the area you want to develop. Ask about the coach's style, philosophy, and whether he or she has any specialties. Some coaches specialize in relationships, some in working with creative clients, some with entrepreneurs, people with head injuries, you name it. Whatever your particular need, I guarantee that there is a coach out there who specializes in it.

Don't worry about where the coach lives. Most coaches work by telephone, as it is more effective and efficient than in-person meetings. My clients are all over the map, and most of them I've never met in person. It makes no difference in the results they achieve.

In the first few sessions of coaching you will typically assess your current situation and talk about where you'd like to be. In a corporate setting, you may discuss how the company goals work in relation to your own. You can expect your coach to provide ongoing positive support and encouragement, to ask you to go beyond where you'd normally stop, to try new skills, to provide follow-up discussion on the goals you are working on, and to give you life-work assignments every week. If you aren't having fun and seeing results with your coach, tell your coach what you need from him or her, and if that doesn't work ask for a referral to a different coach. It is perfectly okay to tell your coach how you are best coached. I usually ask my clients this anyway. Also, let your coach know when you are likely to "cheat" or pull a sly one so that your coach will catch you when you are trying to weasel out of something.

Whenever you find yourself getting bogged down or overwhelmed with a project, it is a good idea to find some help, whether that is a tutor to help you decipher a new computer program or a coach to help you live your dreams and attract everything you've always wanted. You can do this!

The International Coach Federation
2123 FM 1960 West, Suite 219
Houston, TX 77090
(888) 423-3131
www.coachfederation.org

The ICF is an organization of professional coaches and hosts an annual coaching conference in addition to providing an extensive referral list of coaches and a Web-based referral service to help you find the right coach. It also offers two coaching certifications, PCC (Professional Coach Certification) and the more advanced MCC (Master Coach Certification).

Coach University Coach Referral Service
(800) 48-COACH
www.coachu.com

All coaches listed on this referral service are either graduates of or in training at Coach University.

Professional Coaches and Mentors Association
3020 Old Ranch Parkway, Suite 300
Seal Beach, CA 90740
(714) 220-9431

Professional and Personal Coaches Association
P.O. Box 2838
San Francisco, CA 94126
(415) 522-8789

Tampa Bay Professional Coaching Association
21629 Teal Court
Lutz, FL 33549
(813) 949-0718

International Coaching Society
4750 Vista Street
San Diego, CA 92116
(619) 282-5760

Bay Area Professional Coaches Alliance
P.O. Box 26606
San Francisco, CA 96126
(415) 435-7532

Appendix C:

HOW TO BECOME A COACH

Coach University
(800) 48-COACH
www.coachu.com
www.coachreferral.com

Take the free four-week 123 Coach TeleClass at Coach University and find out if this is the right training program for you. Training is conducted via highly effective interactive teleclasses, which allows for international participation. This is where I got my training. The course is both challenging and fun and takes approximately two years for most people to complete. New coaches are encouraged to find an experienced mentor coach, which is a very good idea and makes the learning process much easier.

The Coaches Training Institute
1879 Second Street
San Rafael, CA 94901
(415) 274-7551
coachtraining@aol.com
www.thecoaches.com

See the International Coach Federation website at www.coachfedera tion.org for a complete listing of coach training schools and institutions. Programs vary widely in quality and content.

Appendix D:

RESOURCE CENTER

THIS APPENDIX LISTS helpful books, tapes, people, and organizations for each part of the coaching process. Books can be ordered directly on-line at www.lifecoach.com.

I. Increase Your Natural Power

The Seven Spiritual Laws of Success: A Practical Guide to the Fulfillment of Your Dreams, by Deepak Chopra. San Rafael, California: Amber-Allen Publishing and New World Library, 1994.

You Can't Afford the Luxury of a Negative Thought: A Book for People with Any Life-Threatening Illness—Including Life, by Peter McWilliams. Los Angeles, California: Prelude Press, 1988. This is a terrific book for anyone with any negative thoughts. Don't wait until you have a life-threatening disease before you buy this one.

At a Journal Workshop: Writing to Access the Power of the Unconscious and Evoke Creative Ability, by Ira Progoff, Ph.D. New York: G. P. Putnam's Sons, 1975. The Intensive Journal Process combines one of the oldest methods of self-exploration and expression—keeping a journal—with a structured format that enables you to get to know the inner core of your life on ever-deeper levels and gain a fuller perspective on where you are. Use this comprehensive workbook to learn about yourself. Helpful if you really want to get into writing your life story.

The Red Horse Healing Institute
P.O. Box 825
Pearce, AZ, 85625
(520) 826-3737

Overcome hidden blocks to success and well-being through a variety of techniques, including Spiritual Response Therapy; Results; Body Alignment; Brain Repatterning; Hypnosis; NLP (Neuro Linguistic Programming); and Reiki. Offers classes to empower students to heal themselves and others.

II. Clean Up Your Act

Clutter Control: Putting Your Home on a Diet, by Jeff Campbell. New York: Dell Trade Paperback, 1992. This is one of the best books on getting organized and getting rid of clutter. Its simple and practical approach works on even die-hard pack rats like me.

Simplify Your Life: 100 Ways to Slow Down and Enjoy the Things That Really Matter, by Elaine St. James. New York: Hyperion, 1994. This inspiring little book is chock-full of easy things anyone can do to simplify.

When I Say No, I Feel Guilty, by Manuel J. Smith. New York: Bantam Books, 1975. If you say yes more often than you should, read this classic for some straightforward guidelines to ending the doormat syndrome once and for all.

Creating Sacred Space with Feng Shui: Learn the Art of Space Clearing and Bring New Energy into Your Life, by Karen Kingston. New York: Broadway Books, 1997. Feng shui is the ancient oriental art of enhancing and harmonizing the flow of energy in your surroundings. This easy-to-follow guide shows you how to apply the principles of feng shui to enhance the energy in your home or workplace and increase happiness and prosperity.

The Feng Shui Guild
(303) 444-1548
www.fengshuiguild.com
info@fengshuiguild.com
Contact this organization for a referral to a feng shui practitioner in your community or obtain information on how you can use the principles of feng shui to create a nurturing environment.

National Association of Professional Organizers

www.napo.net/

(512) 206-0151

If you are having difficulty getting organized, call this association for a referral to a professional organizer in your area. It offers an E-mail referral service too.

Zero Junk Mail

www.zerojunkmail.com

Contact this organization to eliminate telemarketing calls and junk mail (E-mail and regular), and create some extra space in your life.

Salvation Army

www.salvationarmy.org

(800) 95-TRUCK

Goodwill

www.goodwill.org

(301) 530-6500

Call for a pickup of your unwanted furniture, clothing, etc., or find out where the nearest donation site is located.

EBay

www.ebay.com

The world's largest and most popular on-line auction site adds more than 80,000 new items daily. It sells more than half of everything offered for sale. Antiques, books, collectibles, memorabilia, stamps, and trading cards.

Excite Classifieds & Auctions

www.classifieds2000.com

This is an on-line service where you can place a free ad for things you'd like to clear out of your house.

Onsale

www.onsale.com/atauction.htm

Computer hardware and software, home fitness products, vacation packages and other travel services, and home office equipment.

Ubid.com

www.ubid.com

Brand-name, new and used computer equipment.

Yahoo! Auctions

auctions.yahoo.com

Toys, sports equipment, memorabilia, electronics, cameras, bestselling video games.

Merry Maids

www.merrymaids.com

(800) WE-SERVE

Tired of cleaning? Contact Merry Maids, a national cleaning service, to find a housekeeper in your area.

Healthy Meal Express and Body Magic

(888) 344-DIET

No time to cook? Call for a distributor near you if you would like a week's worth of nutritious meals delivered to your home.

III. Making Money Work for You

The Richest Man in Babylon, by George S. Clason. New York: Penguin Books, 1955. If you are having trouble saving 20 percent of your income, this short parable will be the inspiration you need.

Your Money or Your Life: Transforming Your Relationship with Money and Achieving Financial Independence, by Joe Dominguez and Vicki Robin. New York: Penguin Books, 1993. This is a super book for helping you realize just how much you are spending and how much the stuff you buy is *really* costing you. The authors factor in not just your hourly salary, but also the time spent preparing for and commuting to work—an eye-opening exercise. They show you how you can retire early and still live the American dream on a shoestring.

The Instant Millionaire: A Tale of Wisdom and Wealth, by Mark Fisher. San Rafael, California: New World Library, 1990. If you are having trouble believing that you'll ever reach financial independence, this book will help you shift your thinking. Short and easy to read, but don't let its simplicity deceive you. Its message is a good one: financial prosperity and a life well lived are goals we can all achieve if we understand and practice the principles of success.

How to Be Rich, by Getty, J. Paul. New York: Jove Books, 1965. It isn't enough to have money; you also need to learn how to be rich—how to responsibly manage and maintain large sums of money. Getty talks about who you need to be first.

Think and Grow Rich, by Napoleon Hill. New York: Fawcett Crest, 1960. A timeless classic on the power of thinking your way to success. Hill plainly makes the case that man can create nothing that he does not first conceive as a thought. Your thoughts are incredibly powerful.

A Random Walk Down Wall Street, by Burton G. Malkiel. New York: W.W. Norton & Company, 1996. An incredibly thorough guide for personal money management that will help you create a long-range investment strategy tailored to your financial objectives and your particular income at any age. Malkiel also explains the difference between various insurance options and provides a life-cycle guide to investing.

How to Get Out of Debt, Stay Out of Debt and Live Prosperously, by Jerrold Mundis. New York: Bantam Books, 1990. A straightforward, inspiring, easy-to-read book for anyone with credit card debt. This book will give you the practical step-by-step process for getting out of debt permanently, and show you how to design a spending plan. The more closely you follow the plan, the sooner you'll be out of debt. It worked for me.

Creating Money: Keys to Abundance, by Sanaya Roman and Duane Packer. Tiburon, California: HJ Kramer, 1988. If you like New Age/spiritual books, this one will be right up your alley. Full of great affirmations, exercises, and meditations for attracting wealth into your life.

Money Magnetism: How to Attract What You Need When You Need It, by Donald J. Walters. California: Crystal Clarity Publishers, 1992. I like what Walters says about the mechanics of attraction, but some might be put off by his references to Jesus and God.

Attracting Infinite Riches, by Alphasonics International and Dr. Mark Victor Hansen. Cuesta Road, Santa Fe, NM 87505; (505) 466-7773 or (800) 937-2574. A subliminal audiotape which suggests such ideas as, "I create prosperity; earning money makes me feel good; multiplying money is fun;

I am happy about my wealth; rivers of riches are flowing to me." All you will hear is a babbling brook. Contact Alphasonics for more information on how subliminal tapes work and for information on all the other subliminal tapes that they carry.

Debt Counselors of America
(800) 680-3328
www.dca.org
This is an IRS-approved, nonprofit organization that helps individuals and families consolidate their debts and provides answers to financial questions and problems. This is a great service with many free publications.

Genus Credit Management
(800) 210-4455
www.genus.org
A nonprofit organization that provides free debt management and educational programs to help financially distressed families and individuals effectively manage their personal finances.

Credit Counseling Centers of America
(800) 493-2222
www.cccamerica.org/
A nonprofit organization that offers free credit counseling to individuals and families who are having trouble making payments to credit cards, banks, and other financial institutions.

CreditComm Services LLC
10400 Eaton Place, Suite 400
Fairfax, VA 22030
(800) 789-9952
This company will provide you with an easy-to-understand report of your personal credit history from all three major credit bureaus in the United States. This typically costs about $30. For an additional fee, they will help you correct inaccurate information and will monitor your credit files from all three bureaus throughout the year.

Institute of Certified Financial Planners (ICFP)
(303) 759-4900 or (800) 282-PLAN
www.icfp.org
A professional association of more than twelve thousand CFP licensees nationwide. Call or search on-line for a CFP near you.

American Institute of Certified Public Accountants
www.aicpa.org
To receive a referral to a CPA in your area.

IV. Make Time When There Isn't Any

Speed Cleaning, by Jeff Campbell and the Clean Team Staff. New York: Dell Trade Paperback, 1987. A simple and easy system for cleaning your home in record time. Even has tips on how to supervise a housekeeper.

How to Get Control of Your Time and Your Life, by Alan Lakein. New York: Penguin Books, 1973. Practical tips on how to handle paper only once, cope with information overload, create time for yourself, and much more.

Assist U
(410) 666-5900
www.assistu.com
For a referral to a well-trained virtual assistant who will handle administrative, accounting, and other tasks, contact Assist U. This company also trains people to become virtual assistants.

Russell & Associates
New York
Contact: Virginia Russell
(212) 288-0344
Don't even have the time to train your executive assistant or secretary? Russell & Associates specializes in training administrative assistants and support staff to do the job efficiently and well. They work in person, one-on-one with your assistant, and provide group training classes.

V. Build Powerful Relationships

Tuesdays with Morrie, by Mitch Albom. New York: Doubleday, 1997. A marvelous gem of a story that puts things in perspective and reminds us what is really important in life. I laughed and cried my way through it.

Power Networking: 55 Secrets for Personal & Professional Success, by Donna Fisher and Sandy Vilas. Austin: Mountain Harbour Publications, 1991. An excellent guide to building lasting and powerful business alliances.

The Art of Loving, by Erich Fromm. New York: HarperCollins, 1956. Learning to love, like any other art, demands practice and concentration, insight and understanding. The psychoanalyst discusses all aspects of love from romantic to brotherly, self-love to spiritual love.

How Not to Stay Single: 10 Steps to a Great Relationship, by Nita Tucker with Randi Moret. New York: Crown Trade Paperbacks, 1996. If you are serious about finding the right partner I'd highly recommend this excellent program. I have coached several clients through the ten steps outlined, and it works.

Big Brothers Big Sisters of America

www.bbbsa.org

(215) 567-7000

Big Brothers Big Sisters of America has been providing one-on-one mentoring between adult volunteers and children at risk since 1904. If you feel like you don't have enough love in your life and you like children, this might be just the place for you.

Future Possibilities Inc.

Contact: Lorraine White

www.futurepossibilities.org

A grassroots organization, Future Possibilities coaches inner-city children ages six to ten one-on-one and in groups. Trained volunteer coaches provide children with the tools to enhance their self-esteem and motivation and to develop life skills to help them achieve their goals and dreams.

VI. Do Work You Love

Flow: The Psychology of Optimal Experience, by Mihaly Csikszentmihalyi. New York: Harper Perennial, 1990. A fascinating study on the state of consciousness called "flow"—a state of concentration so focused that it amounts to absolute absorption in an activity.

Instructions to the Cook: A Zen Master's Lessons in Living a Life That Matters, by Bernard Glassman and Rick Fields. New York: Bell Tower, 1997. If you lack the motivation to start work on your own special project, this little book will inspire you. You will learn to use what you have and recognize your faults as your best ingredients.

The Path: Creating Your Mission Statement for Work and for Life, by Laurie Beth Jones. New York: Hyperion, 1996. Step-by-step process for creating a mission statement for your life that can be used to initiate, evaluate, and refine all of life's activities. Excellent questions to answer to create your own life plan.

Sanctuaries: The Complete United States: A Guide to Lodgings in Monasteries, Abbeys, and Retreats, by Jack and Marcia Kelly. New York: Bell Tower, 1996. Take a real retreat to get away and find yourself in the process. This guide includes affordable places for people of all denominations.

Molecules of Emotion: Why You Feel the Way You Feel, by Candace B. Pert, Ph.D. New York: Scribner, 1997. A fascinating account by the neuroscientist who made the groundbreaking discovery that emotions and health are linked at a molecular level.

VII. Work Smarter, Not Harder

Take Yourself to the Top: The Secrets of America's #1 Career Coach, by Laura Berman Fortgang. New York: Warner Books, 1998. One of my coaching colleagues, Berman Fortgang does a great job of describing the most common career problems and coaching you out of them—including how to leap out of career rut and what today's entrepreneurs must do to make a profit.

Creative Visualization, by Shakti Gawain. New York: Bantam Books, 1978. Shakti's classic book shows you how to attract what you want by visualization, meditation, and affirmation. A great technique for increasing your intuition. There is an updated edition called *Creative Visualization: Use the Power of Your Imagination to Create What You Want in Your Life*, published in May 1995.

Do What You Are: Discover the Perfect Career for You Through the Secrets of Personality Type, by Paul D. Tieger and Barbara Barron-Tieger. Boston: Little Brown and Company, 1992. Uses the Myers-Briggs Type Indicator

(MBTI®) to help you identify your personality type and natural strengths and then suggests possible careers that match. This will help you strengthen your strengths and give up struggling.

A Whack on the Side of the Head: How You Can Be More Creative, by Roger Von Oech. California: Creative Think, 1983, 1992. This book comes with the Creative Whack Pack®—a deck of cards with different creative strategies. Stuck on a problem? Draw a card at random and it will get you thinking outside the box.

VIII. Communicate with Power, Grace, and Style

You Can Negotiate Anything, by Herb Cohen. New York: Bantam Books, 1980. A timeless and inspiring classic that teaches you how to negotiate and leaves you knowing that *everything* is negotiable. Cohen's collaborative, win-win philosophy is appealing and effective.

IX. Taking Care of Your Best Asset

A Natural History of the Senses, by Diane Ackerman. New York: Vintage Books, 1991. If you feel you have lost touch with the sensual delights of this world, this book will reawaken and delight you. Diane covers smell, taste, touch, hearing, and vision in this richly thorough and fascinating book.

Eat Right for Your Type: The Individualized Diet Solution to Staying Healthy, Living Longer & Achieving Your Ideal Weight, by Dr. Peter J. D'Adamo. New York: G.P. Putnam's Sons, 1996. The first sensible diet book I've seen. Takes into consideration your blood type and then suggests the foods that work best for your body.

Shelter for the Spirit: Create Your Own Haven in a Hectic World, by Victoria Moran. New York: HarperCollins, 1997. Everything you need to know to make your home a nurturing and restorative foundation for the rest of your life. With useful tips on home birthing, homeschooling, and home business.

Take Time for Your Life: A Personal Coach's Seven-Step Program for Creating the Life You Want, by Cheryl Richardson. New York: Broadway Books, 1998. Richardson is another one of my coaching colleagues, and she outlines an excellent program for extreme self-care.

Living a Beautiful Life: 500 Ways to Add Elegance, Order, Beauty, and Joy to Every Day of Your Life, by Alexandra Stoddard. New York: Avon Books, 1986. If you need some help surrounding yourself with beauty and luxury, this book is full of ways to make your home a lovely oasis of tranquillity. Ideas run the gamut from storing candles so that they burn longer to arranging mirrors. Includes many inexpensive ways to increase the quality of your daily life.

1-800-Flowers.com
www.1800flowers.com
Send flowers to someone or order them for yourself.

Two fabulous, award-winning flower designers in New York:

Douglas Koch Visual, Inc.
23 East 7th Street
New York, NY 10003
(212) 387-8674
Douglas Koch Visual designs lovely floral arrangements (fresh or dried) for special events, weddings, and gifts.

Calabria—The Art of the Special Occasion
216 West 18th Street
New York, NY 10011
(212) 675-2688
Fax: (212) 675-3393
www.calabrianyc.com
Calabria designs incredibly beautiful flower arrangements for events, gifts, gift baskets, and weddings. They do the floral arrangements for NBC's *Today Show*.

American Massage Therapy Association (AMTA)
820 Davis Street, Suite 100
Evanston, IL 60201-4444
(847) 864-0123
www.amtamassage.org
Call for a referral to a licensed massage therapist in your area.

Associated Bodywork and Masssage Professionals (ABMP)
28677 Buffalo Park Road
Evergreen, CO 80439-7347
(800) 458-2267
www.abmp.com
Call for referrals to massage therapists and other types of bodywork professionals.

Association of Image Consultants International
(800) 383-8831
Call this number for referrals to professional image consultants in your area. I recommend that you interview a few consultants before making your final choice.

New York area:
Image Strategy for Men and Women
(212) 755-4456
Carolyn Gustafson, AICI
Carolyn is my image consultant and one of the best in New York.

X. Effortless Success

Thinking Body, Dancing Mind: Tao Sports for Extraordinary Performance in Athletics, Business and Life, by Chungliang Al Huang and Jerry Lynch. New York: Bantam Books, 1992. T'ai chi expert Chungliang Al Huang and Olympic sports psychologist Jerry Lynch teach you the time-honored principles of successful performance. This book will help you let go of your obsession to win so that you can be effortlessly successful.

The Book of Life: Daily Meditations with Krishnamurti, by J. Krishnamurti. California: HarperSanFrancisco, 1995. Contains 365 inspiring daily meditations from the wise sage and spiritual teacher J. Krishnamurti. Well worth reading, as it will give you a fresh perspective on life.

Mastery: The Keys to Success and Long-term Fulfillment, by George Leonard. New York: Plume, 1992. This book outlines the five keys to mastery in any field or endeavor: instruction, practice, surrender, intentionality, and "the edge." The key thing I learned from this book is that plateaus do not mean that you aren't making progress. You are, but it just doesn't look that way, so keep on practicing and doing what you are doing and you will break through to the next level.

The Portable Coach: 28 Surefire Strategies for Business and Personal Success, by Thomas J. Leonard. New York: Scribner, 1998. Leonard, the founder of Coach University, has packed most of the coaching curriculum into this book. It contains excellent checklists—the same ones that coaches use with their clients. A very good resource book for anyone interested in coaching.

INDEX

ABOUT THE AUTHOR

ONE OF THE most widely recognized life coaches in the world, Talane Miedaner has earned international prominence by guiding hundreds of clients to wealth, success, and happiness. Talane's work has been featured in numerous magazines, from *Newsweek* to *Men's Fitness*, and she has appeared on national and international television and radio programs, including CBS *News Saturday Morning*. As owner and founder of Talane Coaching Company, Talane helps people structure their lives so that they can easily attract the opportunities they want in life. Her cutting-edge company works with executives, public officials, entrepreneurs, and business owners around the world in person, by phone, and on-line. Talane leads seminars nationally and internationally, and teaches at Coach University, where she received her coach certification. She is a member of the International Coach Federation and a Master Certified Coach. She published the audiocassette program *Irresistible Attraction: A Way of Life* as well as a workbook for coaching.

Talane holds a degree in International Affairs from the School of Foreign Service and a master's in English from Georgetown University. Prior to becoming a coach, Talane held a corporate position as second vice president at Chase Manhattan Bank.

Talane Coaching Company

Talane Coaching Company provides you with the latest in coaching technology and the most highly trained coaches in the world. Your coach will help you design the life you have always wanted. The company offers the following services:

- Individual Coaching
- Group Coaching
- Corporate Coaching and Consulting
- Corporate Keynotes and Workshops
- Retreats and Seminars designed to meet the needs of your organization or group
- Monthly TeleClass series via internationally accessible teleconferencing

For a free E-mail subscription to "Talane's Coaching Tip of the Week," send an E-mail to subscribe@talane.com or sign up directly at the website: www.talane.com. For a free one-hour TeleClass, "Coach Yourself to Success," please sign up directly at the website. For a free on-line brochure, please send an E-mail to brochure@talane.com.

For support in implementing these 101 coaching tips, join the *Coach Yourself to Success* monthly TeleClass program led by one of Talane's master coaches. To register, simply call (212) 683-2595, send an E-mail to coachyourselftosuccess@tulane.com, or sign up on-line.

For more information on any of these services, please call, write, or E-mail:

Talane Coaching Company
P.O. Box 1080
New York, NY 10156
(212) 683-2595 or (888) 4-TALANE
talane@talane.com